What people are saying about *Infinite Wealth* . . .

"The game has changed! Using historical perspective and powerful analyses, Barry Carter beautifully teaches the new rules and the new paradigms which everyone must both understand and embrace to 'make it today.'"
—**Dr. Stephen R. Covey**, Author, *The 7 Habits of Highly Effective People*

"The powerful idea behind this important book—that everyone now has immediate access to unlimited knowledge, opportunity, and income potential—constitutes the ultimate liberation from poverty and ignorance, two of the greatest curses of men and women for centuries. Imagine: a world with no more victims! We are free at last, free at last. And Barry instructs us how to make responsible and wise use of our precious wealth and freedom."
—**Ken Shelton**, Editor of *Executive Excellence* magazine,
and Author, *Beyond Counterfeit Leadership* and *Real Success*

"A courageous, brilliant, and convincing model for an all-win future for humankind. A must read for all who would make the world a better place. With courage and vision and commitment we can create this future. Brave Barry Carter."
—**Don Carew**, Co-author, *The One-Minute Manager Builds
High Performing Teams*, and Professor Emeritus, Organization
Development, University of Massachusetts

"Barry Carter has a vision of a far better world, a liberating economy that harnesses the creative power of ordinary power of ordinary people to produce unheard of possibilities. *Infinite Wealth* is a wildly optimistic manifesto—that is exactly right. It will leave you inspired with fresh ideas and boundless hope."
—**William E. Halal**, George Washington University,
Author, *The Infinite Resource* (Jossey-Bass)

"The new millennium requires a whole new way of thinking about work, wealth creation, customer satisfaction, and the future of competitive enterprises. This book is a powerful synthesis of practical ideas that anyone can use to build a more creative and effective enterprise."   —**Brian Tracy**, Brian Tracy International

"Barry Carter is a futurist of the first rank. His vision of mass privatization will enrich every life in the 21st century. Those who wish to prosper in the Information Age should read *Infinite Wealth*."
—**Richard Poe**, Author, *Wave 3* and *Wave 4: Network Marketing in the 21st Century*

"As one who operated as a home-based virtual networker/entrepreneur for 25 years, I can attest to the growing reality of Barry's win/win world. We are indeed transiting from the Industrial Age to the cooperative, knowledge-sharing societies of the Age of Light and true enlightenment. Barry Carter is a shining personal example of this transformative human journey beyond the economics of fear and scarcity."
—**Hazel Henderson**, Author, *Building a Win-Win World*
and *Creating Alternative Futures*

"*Infinite Wealth* is a provocative vision and a pragmatic blueprint for every leader wishing to be successful in the new millennium."   —**Chip R. Bell**, Author, *Customers As Partners*

"Carter uses many examples of new-paradigm organizations to demonstrate how society is moving from a belief in scarcity and limitation to the possibility of widespread abundance. *Infinite Wealth* not only provides a vision of material abundance for all of humankind, it also enables us to catch a glimpse of a new, more emotionally and spiritually fulfilling way of structuring work. This book integrates current knowledge-based economic concepts with cutting-edge scientific theories and state-of-the-art technology. It gives us a vivid image of a win/win world of infinite abundance."

—**Charlotte Shelton**, Author, *Quantum Leaps: 7 Skills for Workplace ReCreation*

"Carter provides an indispensable roadmap for the next century, in the way Toffler provided a roadmap for the Information Age. *Infinite Wealth* is packed with imaginative ideas, suggestions, and explanations that only the foolhardy would ignore. In a world that doesn't make sense, Carter does! Carter represents a new breed of author that will 'rock your world.'"

—**Jim McDermid**, Director, Medtronic

"All wealth comes through people. Barry Carter has written a terrific treatise on how we can access and share *Infinite Wealth* with one another."

—**Laurie Beth Jones**, President, Jesus CEO Foundation, a nonprofit corporation,
Author, *Jesus, CEO, The Path* and *The Power of Positive Prophecy*

"We view leadership as authentic self-expression that creates value. In *Infinite Wealth*, Barry Carter gets to the heart of creating sustainable value, that is, connecting the infinite potential of human beings to create infinite value in relationships. A powerful, transformational reading experience!"

—**Kevin Cashman**, CEO of LeaderSource, Author, *Leadeship from the Inside Out*

"My every encounter with Barry Carter resulted in the equivalent of intellectual fission, a virtual nuclear reaction of ideas and possibilities. Barry's optimistic brilliance was overpowering, and *Infinite Wealth* is the result, clearly illuminating what the twenty-first century *can* be." —**Dr. Paul Browning**, Principal of Socastee High School in Myrtle Beach, SC,
and Executive Director of "Touching the Lives of Children,"
formerly, Superintendent of Greene County Schools and
Professor of Educational Leadership at East Carolina University

"With vivid perceptions—peppered with solid case examples—Barry Carter's *Infinite Wealth* makes sense out of the current management paralysis. He traces the roots, intertwined trends and a compelling rationale for mass privatization."

—**Debra Amidon**, Author, *Innovation Strategy for the Knowledge Economy: The Ken Awakening*, Founder and Chief Strategist, Entovation International Ltd.

"In *Infinite Wealth*, Barry Carter has outlined and pinpointed the elements of a win/win world. As a whole, he has defined a grand, uplifting vision around which the people of the world can unite. Upon reading I experienced a surge of synthesis and integration that propelled me forward in the development of The Uni-v.e.r.s.e. (a mass privatization community) I highly recommend *Infinite Wealth* for anyone in business or not, who wishes to grasp the future and succeed in the present." —**James North**, www.uni-verse.net

"Barry Carter clearly has his finger on the pulse of the future."

—**Jessica Lipnack** and **Jeffrey Stamps**, Co-authors,
Virtual Teams, and CEOs of NetAge, Inc.

Infinite Wealth

Infinite Wealth

A New World of Collaboration and Abundance in the Knowledge Era

Barry C. Carter

Boston   Oxford   Auckland   Johannesburg   Melbourne   New Delhi

Butterworth–Heinemann supports the efforts of American Forests and the Global ReLeaf program in its campaign for the betterment of trees, forests, and our environment.

Library of Congress Cataloging-in-Publication Data

Carter, Barry C.
    Infinite wealth : a new world of collaboration and abundance in
    the knowledge era / Barry C. Carter.
        p.   cm.
    Includes bibliographical references and index.
    ISBN 0-7506-7184-X (alk. paper)
    1. Knowledge management. 2. Information technology.
    3. Privatization. 4. Diversity in the workplace. 5. Wealth.
    6. Social change. I. Title.
    HD30.2.C374 1999
    338.9—dc21   99-18730
                                                                        CIP

British Library Cataloguing-in-Publication Data
A catalogue record for this book is available from the British Library.

The publisher offers special discounts on bulk orders of this book.
For information, please contact:

Manager of Special Sales
Butterworth–Heinemann
225 Wildwood Avenue
Woburn, MA 01801–2041
Tel: 781-904-2500
Fax: 781-904-2620

For information on all Butterworth–Heinemann publications available, contact our World Wide Web home page at: http://www.bh.com

10 9 8 7 6 5 4 3 2 1

Printed in the United States of America

This book is dedicated to my parents, Charles and Eleanor Carter, who allowed me the freedom to learn and grow in my own way. It is also dedicated to Travis for time borrowed.

Contents

Acknowledgments

First I must thank my wife, Linda Keres Carter, who has been a partner in the writing of this book. Linda is the real "writer" in the family and has helped structure, edit, and write this book in a way that people could understand it. She helped turn a mammoth 800-page manuscript into a leaner and cleaner book and has served as sounding board, collaborator, and igniter of many of the ideas. She has spent the last 12 years putting up with my Information Age obsession.

This book likely would not have been written if it were not for Alvin and Heidi Toffler. In 1986 they gave me a fresh and thought-provoking vision of what was occurring in society with their books *The Third Wave* and *PowerShift*—it was a foundation on which to build. The Tofflers are two of the foremost thinkers of our time. They must be credited with the creation of tremendous wealth and the saving of perhaps thousands or millions of lives by providing a beacon to steer us into an Information Age. I am forever indebted to Alvin and Heidi Toffler for their contribution to my awakening.

I am deeply beholden to Sandy Hardy, Jan Nickerson, and Vicky Bryant, partners who believed in the book and provided continued encouragement and feedback regarding versions of the book.

I owe a great deal of gratitude to the following people: Don Carew, Jim McDermid, Phil Taylor, Paul Browning, Marc Allen, and Steven Persanti, who read versions of the book and provided helpful feedback. Trent Price of Executive Excellence, my partner and agent, stuck with and helped guide a first-time author through the perils of the publishing world and provided direction and insight regarding the concepts in the book. I am obliged to Betty Storz for providing a tremendous editorial effort and Ken Shelton of Executive Excellence for believing in the book. Ted Diab of Applied Computer helped me learn what real win/win partnering could be like, and George Morrow of IBM showed me what empowerment and freedom in work are all about. I owe a great deal of appreciation to Karen Speerstra, my publisher at Butterworth–Heinemann, for believing in the book and Rita Lombard and Jodie Allen of Butterworth–Heinemann for their tremendous support. I am also grateful to James North, Flemming Funch, and many other pioneers who are creating mass privatization communities and leading the greatest peaceful revolution in history.

A special thanks is owed my oldest son, Travis, who paid a large price for this book in lost playtime with his dad. Then there are the newcomers to the clan, Jeremy, Chelsea, and Chastidy, who are teaching me all about teamwork and collaboration. I am eternally grateful to my mother and father, Charles and Eleanor Carter, for providing me with the freedom to develop, learn, and think in my own way.

Customized Reading Guide

Chapters of this book can be supplemented with additional material on the WinWinWorld.net website at **http://www.winwinworld.net**

Brief Overview: Chapter 1. This gives you only an overview and does not get to the bottom line of the book.

Summary Overview: Chapters 1, 4, 5, 10, and 12. If you wish to get to the bottom line quickly without reading the entire book, try this reading. If you are not already a believer in mass privatization, then this reading alone likely will not convince you.

The Incoming Win/Win World of Work and Business: Chapters 1, 2, 3, 4, 5, 6, 7, 11, and 13 and referenced website material.

"How-to" Information for Shifting to Win/Win Business and Work and a Win/Win World: Chapters 4, 5, 7, and 13 and referenced website material. If you already believe in mass privatization and only desire practical "how-to" information, try this selection.

The End of Racial, Sexual, and Human Divisions and the Shift to Thriving on Diversity: Chapters 4, 5, 8, and 12 and referenced website material.

The End of Poverty and Oppression and the Shift to Affluence for All: Chapters 1, 2, 3, 4, 5, 7, 8, 10, 11, and 12 and referenced website material.

The End of Violence, Crime, and Terrorism and the Rise of a Win/ Win World: Chapters 1, 2, 3, 4, 5, 7, 8, 10, 11, and 12 and referenced website material.

The Shift to True Democracy: Chapters 1, 4, 5, 6, 8, and 10 and referenced website material.

The Urgency and Extreme Danger of Not Shifting to Win/Win Wealth Creation: Chapters 8 and 9 and referenced website material.

The Shift to a Family-Centered World: Chapter 6 and referenced website material.

The End of Taxes from Mass Privatization: Chapter 6 and referenced website material.

PART I

The Third Millennium
A Time for Optimism

We are at that very point in time when a 400-year-old age is dying and another is struggling to be born—a shifting of culture, science, society, and institutions enormously greater than the world has ever experienced. Ahead, the possibility of the regeneration of individuality, liberty, community, and ethics such as the world has never known, and a harmony with nature, with one another, and with the divine intelligence such as the world has never dreamed.

—Dee Ward Hock, Visa founder

1

The Rise of a New Win/Win Civilization

The Maturing of Humanity Driven by Wealth Creation

A new civilization is emerging in our lives, and blind men everywhere are trying to suppress it.
—Alvin Toffler, *The Third Wave*

Imagine working in an organization in which you love your work as much as your favorite hobby. Work is fun, exhilarating, and challenging. Imagine being eager to wake up each morning to get to work. Your work makes you feel that you are making a difference in the world. It connects you with a deeper meaning in life.

Within your organization you work in a small team—a collaborative partnership in which you are connected with partners on a personal level. Your team is interconnected with and interdependent upon other small teams. It forms business units and a massive global networked organization, all through the information superhighway. *All* members of your team and organization are as passionate and devoted to their work as you are to yours.

Imagine a customer-focused system in which the more one genuinely cares for others the more financial success one has. Teams and individuals excel financially by understanding and being tightly focused on meeting the needs of other people—customers and partners. It is an environment in which you directly receive a percentage of

3

income based on the value you add for customers and partners. The more value you add, the more income you receive. In addition, the more value your small team and other small teams add, the more income you receive. It is a system based on *alignment* (Naisbitt and Aburdene 1985, p. 41). The better you are at meeting customer needs and helping others win, the more income you *directly* make for yourself. People, therefore, do the "right thing" because they work in aligned organizing structures in which helping others—partners, potential partners, suppliers, and customers—is in their direct best interest.

Imagine a society made up of thousands of these organizations or communities all interconnected through the information super-highway with the shared purpose of helping other people. The communities are overlapped and chaotically interconnected and intertwined to form a seamless, ordered, and interdependent global society. Individuals act locally while thinking globally. Every individual on the planet is directly or indirectly interconnected electronically, financially, socially, and spiritually to every other individual.

Imagine a world of six billion liberated, interconnected individuals who are extremely creative, challenged, and productive. Teams routinely tap near-genius levels of creative potential. These ideas are readily passed on to thousands of other partners, because it helps the individual, partners, customers, and the organization—all win. Organizations, therefore, are structured to liberate and propagate knowledge and wealth flow as opposed to controlling or monopolizing those things.

Imagine a knowledge era in which the premier power and creator of wealth in society is knowledge—an infinite resource, one that can be used by many people at the same time with everyone winning. It is a civilization devoid of oppression because the means of production is widely dispersed and controlled by the masses of individuals in society. This is because individuals own the brains that produce the knowledge.

Imagine a customer-driven world in which each product or service is tailor-made to fit each customer's exact, unique needs. It is, therefore, a world in which tremendous empathy toward other diverse individuals is the key to meeting customers' needs and thus thriving financially. In this new world, racial division has all but disappeared because people thrive economically when they understand, empathize, and work with diverse people. The more diversity there is, the more wealth there is.

Imagine that on a daily basis your work puts you in contact with many diverse people from around the world—partners, potential partners, suppliers, and customers. Potential partners routinely approach you about various ventures. Likewise, organizations and teams continually seek new partners and ventures because this is how they grow and produce more income for themselves. One works by connecting with others on the information superhighway and finding niches where one can add value for customers and partners by adding to what an existing community is already doing. This is done with minimal risk for all.

Because everyone has immediate access to unlimited opportunity and income potential, we live in a world in which poverty and scarcity have all but disappeared. In fact, we live in a world in which the vast majority of the world's population is wealthy, both materially and nonmaterially.

As astonishing as it sounds, directly before our eyes we are shifting to this new world as we enter "the third millennium." What we are seeing is a shift at the very foundation of our civilization—wealth creation and work. For all of human history the powerful forces of wealth creation (the meeting of our daily practical needs) have driven people apart—to compete for scarce resources, to control the wealth-creation process, to only see from our own narrow perspectives and therefore to remain immature. Today, however, the powerful forces of wealth creation are driving people toward helping one another, meeting others' needs, interconnecting, and becoming interdependent. We are moving toward a deeper understanding of who we are and toward a higher level of maturation.

Wealth creation and work are changing so fundamentally as to reorder civilization and replace tens of thousands of years of human social norms. Infinite wealth is replacing finite wealth. Win/lose social norms are giving way to win/win norms. A paradigm of abundance is abolishing the illusion of scarcity. Collaboration is beating out competition. Human interconnectedness is revealing the illusion of human separation. Empowered masses are overcoming powerlessness. Interdependence is transforming unhealthy dependencies. At the core is a shift from *fear* to *love*. It is the most significant change in all of human history and the beginning of the height of the human journey. It is a shift to a win/win world based on caring and abundance, and driven by information technology and changes in our wealth-creation system.

The creation of this new world, which has already begun, will likely be the most enjoyable part of your life. Out of tens of thousands of years you have the privilege of being alive in what we will soon know as the most exciting time in human history, a time of human awakening.

Regardless of who you are, you have tremendous opportunity in the years immediately ahead. We are entering a period in which you and your family will have the opportunity to learn and grow significantly; attain substantial material and nonmaterial wealth, and contribute enormously to a sustainable society. You will have the chance to experience the world and meet many new and diverse people.

THE HISTORICAL PRECEDENCE

Alvin Toffler, in *The Third Wave*, breaks history into three eras: the Agricultural Age, the Industrial Age, and the Information Age. As we make the transition from one era to another, history has shown that all of our social institutions are replaced. It has also shown that these eras come in with a bang, defined as *breakpoints* (Land and Jarman 1992). With breakpoints, trends and pressures build for years and decades with little substantive change. People become convinced that nothing is changing—"it's all talk." The old institutions become gridlocked and ineffective as citizens lose confidence and become increasingly frustrated, angry, and disillusioned. Then, all at once, there is a social breakpoint, and all of society is thrust into the new era when the old social institutions begin to be replaced.

We saw breakpoint in the transition from the Agricultural Age to the Industrial Age in the United States with the American Revolution. In Russia there was the Russian Revolution and in France the French Revolution. Globally, in all of what would become the industrialized world, we made the transition from monarchy to representative government. As depicted in Figure 1–1, we saw the global abandonment of serfdom and slavery and the shift to employment as our system of work. One-piece customization gave way to mass production as our system of production. Formal religion gave way to newtonian science as the science of the era. The extended family was replaced by the nuclear family as our family structure.

All around the world in what would become the industrialized nations, all of the Agricultural Age social institutions were

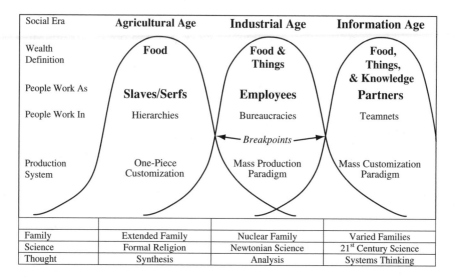

Social Era	Agricultural Age	Industrial Age	Information Age
Wealth Definition	Food	Food & Things	Food, Things, & Knowledge
People Work As	Slaves/Serfs	Employees	Partners
People Work In	Hierarchies	Bureaucracies	Teamnets
		◄— Breakpoints —►	
Production System	One-Piece Customization	Mass Production Paradigm	Mass Customization Paradigm
Family	Extended Family	Nuclear Family	Varied Families
Science	Formal Religion	Newtonian Science	21st Century Science
Thought	Synthesis	Analysis	Systems Thinking

FIGURE 1–1   Abbreviated Age-Wave Chart

not merely changed, they were systematically replaced (see Figure 6–1 for more detail).

Today we see the same transition as we shift from the Industrial Age to the Information Age. In work and business we are making the transition from being employees to being owning partners, from bureaucracies to virtual networks of teams, and from controlled economies (organizations of employees controlled by bureaucrats) to free market economies of real internal customers and suppliers within organizations. At the same time, we are shifting from mass production, which thrives on homogeneity, control, and stability, to mass customization, which thrives on diversity, freedom, and chaos. In science we are shifting from the mechanical, analytical newtonian worldview to the new synthesis-based sciences of chaos theory, complexity, and quantum physics.

In regard to social power we are seeing a shift from masses of people being passive cogs in an Industrial Age machine controlled by managers and politicians to people being fully empowered as proactive owners, responsible for and in control of their work and lives. In social organization we are witnessing the death of representative government as we daily participate in the creation of a new, more liberating, and collaborative form of democracy based on synergy. The new system is moving us beyond the limits of taxes, politicians, and bureaucracies. It is a system of synergy in which order in society comes as a natural by-product of our system of work, human organizations, and human interaction. Social order is produced as individuals and organizations work to meet each other's needs as interconnected and interdependent owners, partners, customers, and suppliers.

SOCIAL EVOLUTION OR SOCIAL ENGINEERING?

We are witnessing the end of representative government, companies, the nuclear family, employment, managers, unions, and far more as the norms in society. Sound implausible? Sure. Think, however, of a French aristocrat in 1780. Imagine trying to explain that every institution in his agrarian civilization (see Figure 6–1) that had existed for hundreds of years would be replaced. There would be no more serfs, monarchy, aristocrats, or extended families as the norms and power. It would be overwhelming and unbelievable. He would have a hard time even imagining a world operating without those age-old institutions. However, it did happen, and today it is happening again.

What I demonstrate in the following pages is that the new civilization and worldview are already easing their way into our lives and that the *successful* trends burgeoning in the world scene exhibit traits conducive to the new worldview.

I am not proposing a utopia for you to "sign up for" and attempt to live by, and I am not proposing any socially engineered solutions or political dogma. What I am doing is showing you a *perspective* that will allow you to see what is already coming at you with lightning speed and inundating you with opportunities. But you must *see* these opportunities, or they will fly right past you. I want you to see them, use them, and thereby prosper with this New World.

THE SHIFT TO INFINITE KNOWLEDGE POWER

As we enter the Information Age, a shift has occurred in work and wealth creation that propels all of the other changes. For millennia, we have lived in a world in which the creation of *things* is what has generated wealth. But now the creation of *knowledge* is the primary generator of affluence, and this is changing our world and worldview forever.

Today, the vast majority of value added to human lives no longer comes through tangible things. It comes through knowledge, ideas, intellect, and brainpower. Even with tangible things, the knowledge content far outweighs the value of the physical thing. For example, for the $500 one paid for a 200 megahertz 586 Pentium microprocessor in 1997, the knowledge content far outweighs the handful of sand from which it is made. Likely only a fraction of a penny of the $500 goes toward the cost of the sand. This has not always been the case. A typical product in the Industrial Age had a very large percentage of its value in the material good itself. Coal, as an extreme case, had nearly its full value as it was taken from the ground. In the Industrial Age, the people who owned the raw materials and processing facilities for oil, coal, and steel were the world's wealthiest people. Today, however, we do not see great fortunes being made with sand mines. Instead the people who control the knowledge control the wealth.

An example of this transition can be seen with a comparison between IBM and Microsoft. IBM for decades was the premiere corporation in the world. Many people considered it the world's best company to work for. Consultants rated it the world's best-managed company. For years it reigned as the most profitable corporation in the world. Though IBM led us into the information revolution, its profit and growth had come from the manufacture of computers and other hardware—material goods, *things*. In the late 1970s, at the beginning of the personal computer revolution, IBM contracted with a fledgling corporation called Microsoft. Microsoft produced the software operating system for the IBM PC, and IBM focused on the "important" stuff—the hardware. Yet by 1992, in a little over a decade, the stock market value of Microsoft had *surpassed* that of IBM. Microsoft had also replaced IBM as the leader of the information revolution. IBM had billions invested in hardware, factories, buildings, machinery, and equipment. It had 400,000 employees, decades of experience, and history. Microsoft, on the other hand, had only 11,000 brains, producing only thoughts, ideas, and *knowledge*.

Another example of the knowledge-power shift can be seen in the value of companies. Throughout the past couple of hundred years, the Industrial Age, hard assets determined the value of a company. Today, however, when companies buy other companies they routinely pay far more than the value of the hard assets. For example, in 1988 when Philip Morris bought Kraft for $12.9 billion, the hard assets of Kraft were only $1.3 billion as determined by Philip Morris's accountants. The other $11.6 billion was all knowledge value—brand equity, ideas in employees' heads, and market prowess (Peters 1992).

THREE PILLARS OF THE NEW CIVILIZATION

The transition to knowledge power is unleashing several unstoppable forces in work and wealth creation. These forces are changing our world forever, including all of our social institutions. The following three are the building blocks for a win/win wealth-creation system:

1. A shift from finite wealth, which operates on win/lose rules, to infinite wealth, which has the potential to operate on a win/win norm.
2. A shift from a competitive, seller-controlled society to a collaborative, buyer-driven society.
3. A shift from a marketplace dominated by employment to one in which individuals own the specific work they perform and are compensated directly by customers for the value they add.

TOWARD INFINITE WEALTH AND WIN/WIN

In the Industrial Age, the power that propelled wealth creation and society was *dollar wealth*. It took lots of dollars to finance equipment, facilities, and employees to make money. In the Agricultural Age *violence* and *brute force* powered civilization (Toffler 1990). There is a fundamental difference between the power of violence and the power of money versus the power of knowledge. Violence and dollar power are finite, whereas knowledge is infinite. This means that for the first time in history we are shifting to an era of infinite wealth!

When we consider the microprocessor, we humans have taken a small amount of physical resource and amplified its value perhaps 50,000 to a million times. We have produced, in effect, unlimited wealth through knowledge power and intellect. When we benchmark using the cost and performance of the first computers or even computers 20 to 30 years ago, compared with the cost and performance of today's computers, we have perhaps amplified the value of the sand as much as one billion times. Through the power of knowledge and intellect we have created something with greater value per ounce than gold (Pilzer 1990). The alchemist's dream is at last achieved!

The most striking trait of infinite knowledge power is that it can be leveraged across many people so that they all win at the same time and from the same idea. For example, one gun (representing violence power) or one dollar (representing dollar power) is finite and can be used by only one person at a time. For that reason in the past one had strong motivation to tightly hold onto whatever power (money and guns) one had and not to share it with anyone (Toffler 1990). We therefore had competition over finite wealth. Thus the two primary powers that have propelled civilization throughout all of human history have motivated us to create adversarial win/lose, competitive wealth-creation systems.

The power of knowledge, however, is such that one idea can be used simultaneously by 50 or 500 or 500 million people. All of these individuals can win, and because of synergy they can win more individually by sharing knowledge than by not sharing it. Instead of competing over finite wealth, we can collaborate to create infinite wealth whereby everyone wins. Stephen Covey, Marianne Williamson, Tom Peters, and Scott Peck share their ideas in books, and millions of people use their ideas and win with more growth, increased wealth, and happiness while these authors win millions for themselves.

Rich Devos and Jay Van Andel, the two cofounders of Amway, developed a system in which partners win by collaborating and sharing their knowledge and successes with other partners. The result is an organization that has created more millionaires than any other organization in history. For their part, in 1994 the two billionaires, Devos and Van Andel, were the fifth and sixth wealthiest people in the United States. Bill Gates, Microsoft founder and CEO, established an employee stock ownership program (ESOP) at Microsoft, a pure knowledge business containing no tangible product. Gates shares the wealth opportunity with Microsoft employees and encourages knowledge sharing and collaboration within Microsoft, producing thousands of millionaires. In 1994, 33% of Gates's 11,000 employees were millionaires, and two of these were billionaires. In 1995, Paul Allen of Microsoft ranked as the fourth wealthiest person in the world with $5.3 billion, and Steven Ballmer ranked thirteenth.

Gates helped other people win by sharing ownership and wealth opportunity in a knowledge business and thus won for himself. He has been the wealthiest person in the world for much of the 1990s. In 1997 he was worth more than $36 billion, ranking as the wealthiest person in history. Gates is dealing not with guns and dollars but with knowledge, a power derived within an individual's brain. Because of the infinite capacity of knowledge power, Gates wins more by creating a win/win system in which the wealth-creation opportunity and knowledge are shared. In the heart of the Industrial Age and the Agricultural Age, one never found this type of wealth sharing, because material-based power and wealth were finite.

Larry Ellison, CEO of Oracle, another multibillion-dollar software producer, has helped create hundreds of millionaires through his Oracle ESOP. Because of his wealth sharing initiative, Ellison was the twentieth wealthiest person in the United States in 1995. In a sort of cascading effect, some of the millionaires Ellison helped produce have gone out and started their own companies and ESOPs and produced a list of their own millionaires. For example, in 1993 Tom Siebel, one of Oracle's employee millionaires, went out and started his own company, Siebel Systems, Inc., and produced 40 millionaires in three years.

In company after company we hear of teams, teamwork, collaboration, partnering, learning organizations, and far more. We hear of collaboration between competitors, with suppliers and customers, with employees, and with unions. As we make the transition from competition to collaboration we see books appearing with titles such as *Co-opetition, Collaborating to Compete,* and *The Death of Competition.* In the Win/Win Era of infinite wealth, the more we help others win, the more wealth we create for ourselves.

Kevin Kelly in *New Rules for the New Economy* (1998) shows how the New Information Age economy operates on win/win rules of abundance as opposed to the scarcity of the Industrial Age. He explains a concept called the fax effect where each fax owner wins as others purchase fax machines. He says,

> Consider the first fax machine. . . . It was worth nothing. . . . The second fax machine to be made immediately made the first one worth something. There was someone to fax to. Because fax machines are linked in a network, each additional fax machine that ships increases the value of all of the fax machines operating before it. . . . When you buy a fax machine, you are not merely buying a $200 box. Your $200 purchases the entire network of other fax machines in the world and the connections among them—a value far greater than the cost of all the separate machines. Indeed the first fax machines cost several thousands of dollars and connected to only a few other machines. . . . Today $200 will buy you a fax network with $3 billion.

This is a reversal of the finite wealth of the Industrial Age where, as Kelly shows, value comes from scarcity: diamonds, gold, oil, steel, and coal. When things became plentiful in the Industrial Age they were instantly devalued. As an example, carpets, when handmade, were rare and very valuable, but once they were produced in volume, they lost their value (Kelly 1998, p. 39). Kelly says, "The logic of the network flips this industrial lesson upside down. In a network economy, value is derived from plentitude, just as a fax machine's value increases as fax machines become ubiquitous. Power comes from abundance. Copies are cheap. Let them proliferate."

TOWARD A CUSTOMER-DRIVEN WORLD AND THE GOLDEN RULE

During all those millennia while the manufacture of *things* was central, we lived in a seller-controlled society. Henry Ford arrogantly bragged that we customers could have a car any color we wanted as long as it was black. We were happy to buy his black cars because it was a whole lot better than walking or riding a mule. Managers, executives, bureaucrats, and CEOs were the sellers, and they dictated what buyers would get, when they would get it, and at what price. The seller, not the buyer, was king and the one to be served by society.

In the seller's era of Ford's day, both the end-user consumers and the workers served the company's and society's managing elite. It was a period in which the managers and executives were *elevated* in social, financial, and political status, education, and power. Their needs were met better than those of the common consumers and workers in society, who, after all, were (and still are) the same people—the masses. Being in the privileged position of seller was the ultimate position in society, as reflected in the nearly universal desire to climb the "corporate ladder." If the customer is defined as the one to be served, then the "social customer" during the seller's era has been the managing elite.

Bureaucrats used mass production and mass marketing "push" systems to *push* products onto what were interchangeable customers. For example, my wife and I recently endured a high-pressure pool salesman who spent three hours selling us on a $12,000 aboveground swimming pool, which we told him at the outset we had no interest in. We continually tried to define our needs only to hear at the end, "Well, it's a numbers game. I pitch the same to everybody, and a percentage will buy." In the "sales era" the seller's job was to convince you that you needed some product, whether you needed it or not. The measurements used by management to track success were internally driven measurements that had little to do with customers. In fact, many things were done to hurt customers in order to make the bureaucracy's month-end quotas. For example, in push mass production systems prebuilt "batched" inventory must move regardless of customer needs. You may need "x," but we have "y" in stock, so this is what we will try to convince you to buy.

Today the marketplace is reaching the breakpoint at which the buyer becomes the one to be served. Consumers have more choices each year spawned by knowledge power and technology. For example, in 1980, 2,689 new grocery and drugstore products were introduced. By 1991, this number rose to 16,143 (Peters 1992). Many suppliers worldwide are seeking to meet any need we have. They are vying for our dollars, courting us, wooing us, bending over backwards for us, trying to anticipate our needs, thinking from our point of view. It's as if they are actually *caring* for us. We are shifting from a "sales era" to a "service era" (Williamson 1992) in which the seller's job is to empathize, understand, anticipate, and meet the buyer's specific, individual needs.

We are shifting from the bureaucrat-driven push system of mass production to the customer-driven pull system of mass customization (Toffler 1980; Davis 1987; Pine 1993). Suppliers, such as Motorola, while still mass-producing pagers, tailor each unit to meet specific customer needs. The company pulls from 29 million variations of pagers and produces the exact pager you desire within minutes of receiving your order (Pine 1993). At Levi's Personal Pair an individual's personal measurements are electronically sent to the factory. Tailored jeans are then produced from 10,000 combinations of sizes (Peppers and Rogers 1997). The notion of "careless" batches of thousands of products being pushed onto customers is being replaced with one customized product at a time being "carefully" pulled by customers to match their exact needs.

Through cellular manufacturing, entire "push" factories are being broken into dozens of customer driven, mass *customization*–based "pull" minifactories called manufacturing cells. These factories once "batch processed" or mass-produced then mass marketed thousands of identical products and "pushed" them onto the public.

At Milwaukee Electric Tool in Milwaukee, Wisconsin, liberated self-directed teams of individuals work in cells without supervision, pulling products one piece at a time to meet a customer's specific needs. Other organizations have combined customer-focused cells with self-directed teams, team incentive systems, and profit centers to produce, in essence, nimble customer-focused businesses within businesses.

In school systems such as Snow Hill Primary in North Carolina, learning is tailored to each student's unique intelligence through child-centered learning based on Howard Gardner's *Multiple Intelligence* (1993). Snow Hill has moved from the "factory school" with rows of desks and all students' hearing the same boring, mass-produced lecture, regardless of needs or special gifts. Led by people like Paul Browning and Gail Edmondson, the school system has moved from pushing rigid education on children through discipline and control to a system of caring and love whereby children pull learning at their own pace, because they are passionately engaged and having fun learning.

The global quality and customer-focused movements of the 1980s and 1990s were just the beginnings of a shift to caring for others. Just as people like Gates, Ellison, Siebel, and Devos are winning by helping others win, by sharing wealth-creation opportunity and knowledge, others are winning big by helping us move into a buyer-driven society. Tom Peters in 1984 published *In Search of Excellence* to share his ideas. Peters ignited the customer-focused movement and allowed billions of people globally to win while making millions for himself. The book stands as the largest-selling business book in history; more than 4 million copies have been sold in ten years. In 1996 Peters commanded $80,000 per day to *share* his ideas with an audience.

People like Sam Walton of Wal-Mart have won big by helping buyers win with low prices, high quality, and good customer service. For years, Walton reigned as the wealthiest person in the world. Even after Walton's fortune was split among his children, combined they still held the world's top slot with $23,450 billion in 1995. The billionaire Nordstrom family, with their retail stores famous for customer service, ranked among America's wealthiest people.

The global quality movement is also part of the shift to a customer-driven world. Edward Deming sparked this movement using knowledge power as he taught the Japanese his statistical quality concepts in the 1950s. We saw the full impact in the 1970s when

Japan's superior quality in the automotive industry nearly put some of the big three automobile manufacturers out of business and eroded market share permanently. We also saw it in the electronics industry, in which today there are few, if any, American manufacturers of devices such as televisions, VCRs, and video cameras. In 1995 we saw those like the Milliken family of Milliken Textiles and the Marriott family of Marriott Hotels, both famous for quality and service, on the Forbes list of America's wealthiest billionaires.

In summary, we are witnessing a shift from authoritarian and bureaucratic control of the wealth-creation process to the individual and the customer controlling wealth creation.

TOWARD INDIVIDUAL OWNERSHIP OF WORK AND HUMAN LIBERATION

During the industrial material era there was a division between "ownership" and work, with employment being the primary means of working and creating wealth. Whether in socialist or capitalist countries, the worker, as employee, does not have direct ownership of the specific work he or she performs. Part of the shift to a win/win world and a customer-driven society involves liberation of workers from the *bonds* of the controlling bureaucracy and managing elite to become real *owners* of the *specific* work they perform. With the real value for customers now coming from knowledge and knowledge coming from the brains in persons' heads, we are evolving to the point at which the individual, by default, owns the means of production. Toffler says, "Today the most powerful wealth-amplifying tools are the symbols inside workers' heads. Workers, therefore, own a critical, often irreplaceable, share of the means of production" (Toffler 1990, p. 233). In an economic environment in which wealth comes from brains, it is only natural and more effective for organizations to evolve into systems in which individuals actually own the *specific* work they perform.

Knowledge-based wealth creation and employment-based work simply are not compatible. In the Industrial Age, people making and moving things created wealth. Wealth creation could be tracked and therefore controlled easily. Motivation through regulation, supervision, and punishment could increase the number of tangible things one produced. Employment-based work therefore was feasible. Today the company attempts to own the thoughts in workers' heads. But how can a person's thoughts truly be controlled?

The trends toward personal ownership and liberation of work are apparent in the innovations of organizations worldwide with variable compensation systems, empowerment programs, and much more. What we are witnessing is no less than the *mass privatization* of work—a *privatization* of wealth creation on a much more profound and elemental level than traditional capitalism has ever embraced. It is a shift to individuals owning their individual work and having the freedom to work as desired to meet the needs of other people. We are moving toward a new wealth-creation institution, the mass privatization enterprise, which is replacing the company and bureaucracy as the primary wealth-creation institution in society.

Because the individual owns the specific work performed it is "private work," and because the masses of people in large global organizations are private workers, the system is called "mass privatization."

Mass privatization is a system of human organization whereby the individual worker, or a small team of workers, owns the substantial share of the *specific* work performed. Individuals are interconnected through advanced information technology. They are also interdependent through partnerships with other individuals, organizations, or teams of private owning partners. The organization is structured so the individual wins when he or she helps others win. It is a system with no managers, employees, unions, salaries, wages, bureaucracy, or hierarchy.

To end our deficits, the person who controls wealth creation must also own the thoughts. This is the individual, and the system must come through private work. This work must be connected for leverage and synergy; hence mass privatization. With mass privatization there is natural alignment between ownership and the means of production, because the person who owns and controls the thoughts also owns and controls wealth creation.

Most companies in recent years have implemented some form of variable compensation system or empowerment program. With variable compensation, an individual's compensation varies on the basis of the value he or she adds. Just like a business owner's, the worker's compensation varies from day to day or week to week or month to month. Individuals, in effect, receive a percentage of the wealth they create and therefore have some *privatized* or personal ownership of their work. With variable compensation, organizations hope to approximate some of the incentives and pride found in owning one's own business.

The road to the privatization of work has a long history, as is defined in detail later. Starting near the middle of this history we see employee stock ownership arising, a system in which employees own shares in the company. It has progressed to include profit sharing, whereby employees receive a percentage of the total company profits, and bonus programs whereby employees receive a bonus based on some criteria. There is also gain sharing, in which a group within a company receives a percentage of the gains made by their specific unit. With at-risk pay, employees are guaranteed only a portion of their previous salary or wage but are entitled to perhaps substantial additional income based on the profits generated by the team or local group. With employee product royalties, an employee receives a royalty on each sale of a product or service he or she helped create. These are only a few out of many private ownership programs being tried in organizations.

Lincoln Electric, a 100-year-old manufacturer of welding equipment, uses a form of private ownership. At Lincoln, a worker's income reflects directly the amount of work performed, quality produced, and value added. In 1991 the average production worker's income was about $50,000 (compared with less than $20,000 for most production workers). Lincoln sees its workers as a collection of entrepreneurs. The more the individual wins, the more the company wins. Located in Cleveland, Ohio, the rust belt of the United States, Lincoln Electric has flourished when others have dropped by the wayside.

Nucor Steel has a similar personal ownership system. At Nucor, the average production worker in 1996 earned $53,000. Nucor had grown from a $20 million company in 1970 to a $2 billion company by the early 1990s, largely because of its personal ownership–based pay system. This success occurred as the Japanese put many U.S. steel manufacturers out of business because of ineffective operations.

Amway is another example of this trend. It is an organization that sells products relatively similar to those available in retail stores. Individuals own their one-person dealerships and are exponentially rewarded for any growth they can create for the company by selling their products. As stated earlier, Amway has produced more millionaires than any other company in history.

To further show that economic success is moving toward private ownership of work and away from managerial hierarchies, consider the following facts. In the early 1990s, on any given day, 8,000 people moved *into* self-employment. During the same period, on any given day, 250 managers and 1,500 employees *lost their jobs!* In 1994, the fastest-growing segment of the economy was the one-person enterprise.

Along with private ownership systems, most companies have implemented some form of worker empowerment or human liberation system such as self-directed teams. These are teams devoid of supervision. At the heart of any democratic country there is a degree of freedom and liberty supported by the right of ownership. Like countries, as organizations move toward democracy, they also are moving toward more individual liberty and freedom of workers supported by the individual's right of ownership. Billionaire Ross Perot founded and built EDS on the basis of empowered and liberated knowledge-based *project teams*. At EDS, the project team has replaced the bureaucratic structure. In return, Perot is one of the wealthiest billionaires in the country. At Johnsonville Foods, self-managing teams and a variable-pay profit-sharing system have helped the organization grow from a $7 million company in 1981 to $130 million by 1991 (Peters 1992).

WINNING BY HELPING OTHERS WIN

As can be seen with the examples of Devos, Van Andel, Perot, Nucor, and the others, we are shifting to an era in which to thrive economically we must *care* for and help other people win. The more people we are able to help, the wealthier we become ourselves, both materially and nonmaterially. We must also consider that 46% of the 129 wealthiest people in United States in 1995 who acquired their fortunes through their work and not inheritance did so in knowledge-based businesses, through privatized work, or with a commitment to customers.

The cases listed above are not isolated incidents. They are part of a rapidly growing trend. Intel in 1996 paid out $620 million in profit sharing to 40,000 employees. Mary Kay Ash is CEO of Mary Kay Cosmetics, a multibillion-dollar cosmetics company that offers private work opportunity to women. In her book *Mary Kay, You Can Have It All* (1995), Ash says her highest goal is helping women everywhere achieve their full potential. Tom Melohn, CEO of North American Tool and Die, says in *The New Partnership* (1994), "If you reach out and genuinely care for your fellow employees, there is no limit to what you can accomplish." After buying NATD, Melohn radically changed operations, making honesty, trust, respect, and caring core values of the company, basing this policy on the assumption that people want to do a good job. Although NATD was in trouble when Melohn purchased it, within 12 years NATD's pretax earnings increased 2,400%. The return on investment moved to top the 10% of the Fortune 500, sales grew by 28% per year, stock value increased 47% per year, and productivity increased 400%.

Hal Rosenbluth, CEO of Rosenbluth Travel, in *The Customer Comes Second* (Rosenbluth and Peters 1992) shows a similar philosophy of caring for workers and customers. Rosenbluth Travel has grown 7,500% in 15 years. We see similar philosophies and results in Anita Roddick's The Body Shop as defined in her book *Body and Soul* (1991), Ricardo Semler's Semco as defined in his book *Maverick* (1993), and Jack Stack's Springfield Remanufacturing Corporation as defined in his book *The Great Game of Business* (1992). Then there is Percy Barnevik's ABB (Asea Brown Boveri), and Nordstrom's focus on customers as defined in the book *The Nordstrom Way* by Robert Spector and Patrick McCarthy (1995).

TOWARD A WIN/WIN WEALTH-CREATION SYSTEM

Perhaps none of the aforementioned persons is 100% benevolent and perhaps none is a 100% win/win, customer-driven believer in private work. In fact, some, such as Gates and Ellison, are known to be fierce win/lose competitors. Ellison is famous for quoting Genghis Khan's statement, "It's not sufficient that I win; others must fail." The U.S. government sued Gates in an antitrust suit for unfair competitive practices. Walton and Wal-Mart have been criticized broadly for systematically ruining small business owners in small towns.

Undoubtedly, there are contradictions and incoherence in our actions and thinking. However, it is not necessary that we do everything 100% consistently to evolve from a win/lose to a win/win wealth-creation system. In fact, it's rather silly to think that we could evolve from one system to another without some slow progress and mixing of the two systems and worldviews. The first Industrial Age steam engines were used to pump water onto Agricultural Age water wheels to run factory drive shafts, as opposed to using the steam engines to drive the shafts directly.

New wealth-creation systems, social systems, and worldviews are not born fully matured and complete. They evolve slowly with various pieces developing independently, confusing the old with the new. They build momentum; the various new pieces begin to integrate and build on one another until breakpoint is reached. After breakpoint, the systems continue to evolve. Therefore if we expect to understand the frantic change occurring around us today we must synthesize and integrate the developing and incomplete trends into a coherent whole. By synthesizing the trends we learn to see that some things are leftover residual activity or success from the outgoing system and other things are part of the new, incoming system.

Today most leaders and organizations still operate *primarily* in win/lose adversary relationships in one form or another. However, if we look from certain perspectives we can see the win/win trends developing, growing, and evolving. Clearly there is a long-term trend from the ruthless robber barons of the Industrial Age, who sought to control and get as much as they could from everyone they could, to the more customer-focused win/win entrepreneurs. Today's customer-focused entrepreneurs more than ever seek to help themselves by helping stockholders, customers, workers, and suppliers.

THE RISE OF A WIN/WIN CIVILIZATION

As shown in Figure 1–2 the shift to knowledge power is the foundation on which an entirely new civilization is arising. Knowledge power is already producing the pillars and building blocks of this new civilization, which are as follows:

- Infinite win/win wealth
- A buyer-focused society
- The privatization of work

In past decades, partial success with just one of the three concepts has been shown to be quite effective, as demonstrated throughout this chapter. Individuals looking to win big for themselves tomorrow stand an excellent chance of achieving substantial wealth

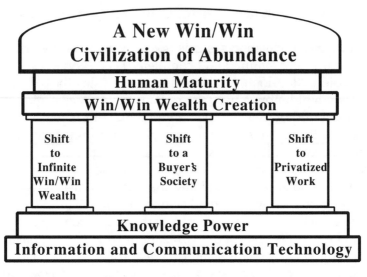

FIGURE 1–2   The Rise of a New Civilization

if they embrace all three concepts, not merely because they want to win, but because helping others is simply the right thing to do.

The three knowledge-based building blocks form the pillars that support a new system of win/win wealth creation. The new wealth-creation system is literally causing humanity to mature and see a broader reality that has always existed—we win by helping others. For the first time in human history, practical necessity depends on our exercising a new version of the golden rule, which is treating others the way *they* want to be treated.

Atop this entire structure is emerging a new win/win civilization—a civilization that is leading to a new social order beyond representative government, taxes, politicians, companies, employees, and control. It is a new civilization propelled by the *synergy* of six billion fully participating individuals, one in which success comes from *caring* for others, *sharing* with others, and exercising individual freedom. It is a new civilization with new social institutions for the Win/Win Era.

AS GOES WEALTH CREATION SO GOES HUMAN MATURITY

A civilization's wealth-creation paradigm and system determines its citizens' maturity and forms their perception of human nature. For thousands of years we have operated from a win/lose competitive paradigm not because it is our universal "human nature" but because humanity's level of maturity has been determined by our wealth-creation system. As we mature we are learning that by collaborating we can produce synergy and create infinite wealth whereby we all win far more than we would if we were competing with one another.

As we evaluate the traits that make up human nature or human maturity we find that they fall in one of two categories. They come from either a love paradigm or a fear paradigm. From love we see traits such as creativity, generosity, caring, sharing, nurturing, mercy, compassion, understanding, friendliness, empathy, helpfulness, consideration, cheerfulness, confidence, intuition, understanding, forgiveness, and abundance. We also see the desire to help others, for synthesizing, collaborating, producing synergy, learning, changing, improving, and growing. From love we see a strong connection to our children, friends, relatives, humanity, nature, and the universe.

From fear we see greed, selfishness, hatred, scarcity, "survival of the fittest," laziness, competition, envy, jealousy, violence, and fear of diversity and change. We also see such traits as being closed, distant, uncaring, distrustful, inconsiderate, and resentful as well as the desire to analyze, divide, separate, conquer, and control.

For thousands of years great spiritual leaders and philosophers have put forth lofty notions of a win/win and love-based human nature. We, however, could not fully accept and consistently actualize a love-based nature in our daily lives because it was in conflict with the practical reality we experienced each day. If you have little or no food on the table and someone is trying to take what you do have, it is difficult to focus on such lofty notions. One feels compelled to focus on meeting practical needs. Tangible things, such as food and shelter, are what we considered the fundamentals of wealth in the past as we focused on the more basic of human needs. Even those who are relatively wealthy have been nurtured in a worldview in which *fear* is the wealth-creation norm. Most material wealth has come from fear-based activity.

In the past, our wealth-creation paradigm, the making, mining, and growing of things, and our wealth-creation systems to make, mine, and grow these things propelled our *perception* of human nature toward fear. This is because these "things" were considered finite or scarce, and thus wealth was finite. We therefore had to *compete* with one another through win/lose means for scarce wealth, attaining it much of the time at the expense of others. Because of finite wealth, our wealth-creation system has been one driven by win/lose behavior, making *competition* the very core of human civilization. Wealth creation has therefore driven us to more fully develop the *fear-based* traits of our perceived "human nature."

What would happen to human nature if, through advances in knowledge, wisdom, information technology, human maturity, and technology we created a new win/win organizing system for work? What if we found that we could create more wealth for ourselves by collaborating with more diverse people and that the more people we helped, the more wealth we created for ourselves? What would happen if year after year and decade after decade, the people using win/win collaboration tapped an infinite source of wealth, continually becoming wealthier while those who continued the immaturity of win/lose competition slipped further and further into the lower economic class? What if on every level and in all segments of society we began to see the win/win reality developing and working directly before us, in small, medium, and large ways, and the more we saw, the larger it grew? What would happen if each time we participated in win/lose activity we lost more than we gained when we participated in win/win activities?

What if we discovered that the world's problems from gangs to drugs, to greed, to violence, terrorism, war, low self-esteem, and more are caused by limited paradigms or hurts inflicted on us by a competitive win/lose environment—in other words, adaptations to win/lose wealth-creation systems? What if these hurts are healed as we begin caring for one another? What would happen if the power of wealth creation and a six billion person collaborative, customer-driven free market began healing humanity?

An awakening would occur as our worldview shifted and we rapidly began to mature. We are witnessing the beginnings of a transformation from a perceived fear-based human nature to our true nature; *love*, which is based on an infinite and abundant wealth reality.

If fear-based wealth creation has driven humanity, against its true nature, to do the evils that it has done, then there are no limits to what we can do as wealth creation becomes aligned with humans helping one another.

To facilitate your seeing what I describe, I take you a few miles in my shoes, so that you can experience with me this evolution of thought. I then expand more completely on the concepts involved. My journey is one about work because we create wealth through our work. Our civilization rests on our system of work, and as this changes so does everything else.

PART II

Gridlocked Wealth Creation

2

A Personal Journey of Discovery

A Study in the Mysteries of Wealth Creation from the Front Lines

*Most managers and workers in today's enterprises are cogs in
obsolete machinery. They sometimes have a vague feeling that
the machinery needs scrapping and replacing, but they do not
know what to do about it. . . . We are in the early phase of a revolution that will fundamentally transform enterprises around
the planet. The transformation is a paradigm shift of immense
magnitude.*

—James Martin, *The Great Transition*

THE MAKING OF A NONCONFORMIST

I grew up the second of three children in a middle-class black family
living in rural Virginia. My father owned a construction business,
and my mother worked as a secretary with the state government. In
1965, Virginia instituted a voluntary school desegregation policy. At
age nine, my brother and I were the only two black children to integrate the public elementary school system of Boydton, Virginia.
Although I scarcely met with angry mobs, water hoses, or police
dogs, I did notice an abrupt change in my station in life.

I had been one of the "good," smart kids at the black school, but
at the white school I was suddenly a loner to be avoided. My class
was a harsh, hard, and abrasive environment filled with tough country boys. I responded to the challenge by becoming tough and somewhat callous. I tuned out much of the harshness around me, as when

29

my fourth grade teacher asked me not to sit with one white boy at lunch because it made him sick to eat with a black kid. I ignored her comment and sat with him the very next day.

I can't say that the five years at the new school traumatized me in the sense that I was in any pain and anguish. I simply toughened as it became impossible for me to feel inferior to *anybody*. I was vaguely aware, at that age, that the black people around me felt apprehensive toward white people, but with what I was seeing, there wasn't a thing intimidating about those trifling people. If I sensed people responding to me in a weird way, I concluded that there must be something wrong with *them*, and I tuned them out.

I began to feel comfortable being different and going against the grain. I actually began to thrive on others' teasing me for being a nonconformist. I began to question many norms, including the traditional rigid, factory-like school system with its petty rules, boring mass-production mode of teaching, and obsessive focus on analysis. From the fourth to the twelfth grades I simply refused to participate. They wanted me to exchange my creativity and love of learning for obedience, grades, and conformity, so of course I paid them no heed.

After my elementary school experience, questioning authority and tradition or seeing with nontraditional paradigms was not an issue for me. The impulse to conform to mindless customs and rules rarely occurs to me. And the superior, intimidating white "bogeyman," which was quite real to those who came before me, such as my grandfather, was exposed as merely a laughable impostor.

It probably is useful to mention the story of my paternal grandfather and my great-grandfather. In 1900 my grandfather was born to an unwed teenage couple. The boy was of Scottish descent; the girl was the grandchild of former slaves. The two married others, and my grandfather lived with his mother. For some reason, however, when my grandfather was a teenager his natural father took custody of him. My grandfather lived with his father and his father's family as the "yard boy," but it is clear that the father undertook to surreptitiously raise his son and guide him. The stereotypical qualities of Scottish descent, "thrift, industry, and ingenuity" were apparent throughout my grandfather's life. To this day, my wife says that the only ethnic stereotype she's ever found to apply to me is the one about Scots and their money. I *do* despise waste and wasted potential, and this is a primary problem of Industrial Age wealth creation.

THE WORK JOURNEY BEGINS

At age 13, when I began to work as a laborer in my father's construction company, I began to notice that something was wrong with work or people or both. Every summer day for five years I'd wake up with my dad at 4:30 A.M. to have enough time to go to the workers' houses and wake them up. Throughout the workday, my dad spent his time forcefully directing, pointing, and showing people how to do things quickly and efficiently. Day after day, year after year, he showed the same things to the same people.

Those five years taught me a lot about hard work, challenge, pain, fun, and life. I did a lot of thinking about work and workers. After all, I was a laborer, and a laborer has a lot of free brain time. Why did we have to wake up adults each morning as though they were children? Why did my dad have to keep telling them the same things over and over for years? Why was there no motivation, no drive, no passion, no life, and no engagement? Why were some of these men walking zombies? I witnessed the same malaise in the farm workers in the Virginia tobacco fields where I spent a couple of summers.

I thought that maybe "walking zombies" were just the type of people found in construction and farm work, but my mother had told me many horror stories about state government. There was gross negligence and incompetence; people went weeks, months, and years without doing any work at all.

Before working with my dad, I had acquired a solid understanding of the value of work from the seemingly endless list of chores that my mom had available for my brother, sister, and me. I used to think she sat around all day trying to think of work for us to do. It provided me with an appreciation of work and reward. Working in my father's business and performing my mother's chores around the house provided a solid work foundation. It was the beginning of a wide variety of work experiences and the start of a journey of discovery.

COLLEGE

On August 28, 1975, I went away to college, a black school in central Virginia. The first week of college was rough. Students had to get their college identification cards, meal tickets, books, and a host of other things. I decided to get my meal ticket first. The line was 50 yards long. It was 8:00 A.M., so I figured it would move fast. By 9:00 things were moving very slowly, and by 10:30 I finally made it to the front of the line. The drowsy-eyed, officious clerk asked to see my college ID. I told him that I didn't have it yet. With a ho-hum sigh, he said, "You'll have to go to Foster Hall and get your ID before you can get a meal ticket." From the way he said it, I could tell that he was sick of telling freshman idiots like me the same thing over and over. I wanted to ask him why they didn't put up a big sign saying, "Meal tickets dispensed only with ID. Obtain your ID first," so that people would not waste two and a half hours standing in the wrong line. After all, it didn't take a genius to figure out the effectiveness of a sign. I thought to myself, "Oh, no! Officious government workers!"

Foster Hall was even worse. The IDs were being produced on the top floor of a tall, old building with no air conditioning. It was August in Virginia. When I opened the door to the fourth floor to see a line 70 yards long with people packed in the eight-foot-wide hallway, the temperature was 85 degrees. Two hours later it was 95 degrees. When I got to the front of the line, the student workers moved as though they were in slow motion. They reminded me of the zombies in the movie *Night of the Living Dead* as they moved in a sort of dazed state, distant and detached from the present, their work, and me, the customer. They made no eye contact and seemed to look right through me, as though I wasn't even there. While processing my ID they talked to other workers about personal issues, which slowed them down even more as the line grew longer. I had seen this "zombie-clerk syndrome" in employees before and have many times since.

Throughout the week I faced many zombie-clerks and stood in many long, wrong lines, wasting a lot of time. Why was there such lack of intelligence in the system? Why were there no posted instructions? Why didn't people care about their work? Why were these people dead? During the next four school years, I saw many more examples of these problems, with many people not doing their jobs. For example, in my four years there, 1975–1979, a relatively large percentage of my electronics class time was spent studying vacuum tubes. Why, in 1979, an era of personal computers and electronic chips, was anybody spending any time on vacuum tubes?

Teachers gave the traditional factory-style, boring lectures, much of which was out of date and out of touch with the real world. Students put in as little effort as possible and cheated to get grades.

The school continuously lowered its academic bar because the students would not even attempt to clear it.

Being a pole-vaulter, I understood clearing bars very well, but the four-year experience with my college coach did little to help my opinion about people and work. The head coach had recruited me to attend the school and pole vault. I quickly found that my coach was a talker, not a doer. He gave me the runaround for a couple of weeks about getting the pole vault equipment set up. I finally decided to do it myself. When I found the vaulting pit, it was torn, old, ragged, and hard. I found some old poles, but none my size. I spoke to the coach about the equipment he'd promised me a year earlier, when he proposed that I attend the school. I received only slippery answers and more false promises. I figured that I had all I was going to get, so I knuckled down and began working with what I had.

Five months later I was in the hospital with a broken neck from a weird landing on the hard, old pit. This wasn't so bad, since I had made the decision to use the pit, but coach didn't call or visit me in the hospital. He had forgotten to list me on the track roster, so I wasn't even insured by the team's insurance policy.

I recovered with no permanent damage and successfully pole-vaulted for three more years. In four years of pole-vaulting, I received coaching advice on a total of five occasions. It was always the same advice. As I ran down the runway, planted the pole, and began going up and over the bar, five times in four years I heard the words, "Over the bar," come from across the track field.

Why wasn't the coach doing his job? It wasn't as though we pole-vaulters did not contribute to the team and his success. In our second year the three pole-vaulters won first, second, and third places in the championship meet. We clinched the CIAA (Central Intercollegiate Athletic Association) conference title for our track team. It was our coach's first championship in his 25-year career. However, we pole-vaulters languished for lack of coaching.

DEFENSE DEPARTMENT

My second year into college, I started working for the U.S. Department of Defense. The waste boggled my mind. When I walked into one of the many, many warehouses filled with people and goods, I saw desk after desk and row after row of what looked like hundreds of office workers. They were bored, half-asleep, and half-alive. Many had nothing to do. Some had their heads propped on their arms on their desks. In the section where I worked, we spent a large percentage of our time repairing other employees' personal property because there was not a lot of official work. We averaged two, maybe three hours of work per day, at a nice, slow pace. The rest of the time was spent debating, playing racquetball, or working on personal property.

NOTE: THE ACTUAL NAMES OF COMPANIES WHERE I'VE WORKED ARE NOT USED IN THE REST OF THIS CHAPTER. INSTEAD FICTITIOUS NAMES ARE BEING USED.

RESPECT COMPUTERS, INCORPORATED

After two years working at the defense department and while still in school, I landed a job with Respect Computers, Incorporated, in the field engineering division. A year later, I accepted a permanent position as quality engineer at a Respect Computers manufacturing plant in New York State. This was the beginning of a 20-year journey in quality improvement and organizational change.

Respect Computers was a tremendously empowering environment. In fact, out of all of the things I've done in life, the work at Respect Computers was the most enjoyable. At Respect Computers, I had the opportunity to experience firsthand the tremendous productive power of creative freedom and empowerment. I loved going to work. Workdays were the same as holidays or vacation days. I used to say I couldn't believe they paid me to have that much fun.

Respect Computers was viewed by the world as probably the premier corporation in the world. It was the model for companies worldwide. Consultants wrote about it continuously. Only one of every 1,000 applicants was hired. Wall Street loved it. It had been one of the most profitable corporations in the world for many years. It was consistently rated as the best place to work in the world.

Going into Respect Computers I thought, "These are some of the smartest people in the world. With their profit, growth, and success, for sure I'll see how work is done right. How else could they have gotten where they are?" Yes, they were some of the most intelligent people in the world, but this means little, given the state of the world of work.

I heard a recurring theme from many different people throughout the company. "How do we possibly make money?" The waste was so enormous that it was apparent to virtually everyone that something was gravely wrong. I worked six years at three different Respect Computers manufacturing plants and one field location. I interfaced with many Respect Computers locations nationwide and worldwide. The single biggest waste factor was the huge number of people who did nothing, added no value, or even subtracted value. This showed up not only in wasted salaries but also in insane decisions that were being made regarding products, resources, customers, and materials.

There was the lost $30,000 piece of test equipment that nobody cared about. There were customers who could not get a replacement printhead for their nonfunctioning printers. They were repeatedly told that it would take months to obtain replacements that were available at the time. There were rooms full of scrap, hundreds of thousands of dollars' worth, in the receiving inspection department because poor shipping containers were used, and there was no corrective action. There were presentations in which none of the product quality engineers knew what was going on with their product lines.

One department in which I worked had four engineers and a manager. The manager was completely out to lunch, never offering advice. There was no guidance, no coaching, no involvement, no direction, no nothing. For the year that I reported to him, I did not know of a single thing that this manager contributed or accomplished.

Regarding the other people in the department, one middle-aged engineer had a chip on his shoulder about work and was simply determined that he was not going to do any. And he didn't. A second engineer was very timid and lost in the political maze of the company. The third engineer was the senior engineer in the department. He did nothing; he had no responsibility that I knew of. He had written a few procedures, but hardly anyone ever looked at them. The department, as a whole, simply was missing in action. Although this was one of the worst departments I'd worked in at Respect Computers, it was not far from average. My personal estimate, at the time, was that Respect Computers could cut 75% of its workforce and not miss a beat. Seventeen years later Respect Computers *had* cut 50% of its workforce with profits higher than ever.

In addition to this, I was simply astonished at the number of goofs, buffoons, and idiots in management. Respect Computers had a "respect for the individual" concept. They were so sensitive to the treatment of employees that they sacrificed competence for niceness. This was not all bad, but the negatives, particularly the bureaucratic method of implementation, far outweighed the positives.

The "respect for the individual" concept had been grossly distorted. There was so much freedom and "respect for the individual," that if one did not want to work, one did not have to. The situation became disrespectful to the individuals who *did* work. Work was shuffled around to the people who would work. Joe and Jane were receiving the same pay, except Joe was working one hour per day and Jane was working fourteen. Joe's presence cost the company money, whereas Jane's made money. Although overworked "real workers" would always pick up some of the slack, most of the needed work simply wasn't done, and nobody cared. Respect Computers was making plenty of money; it was growing like a weed; customers were happy. Consultants wrote books about Respect Computers as if it were Valhalla. Who cared about the tremendous waste and wasted potential? The customer was, after all, happy and willing to pay for it. "If it ain't broke, don't fix it," was the attitude.

Then there were the self-interested shysters. As a quality engineer, I worked on one printer that had many quality problems. The production manager had his sights set on the fast track and had told me, privately, that he would do anything it took to get there. We were having functional problems with the printers as the quality inspectors tested them. This was bottlenecking production and holding up shipments. The production manager called my second-level manager and requested relief. Without conferring with me on my product line, the second-level manager told the inspectors to stop checking the failing parameter. A couple of hours later, when I heard what had happened, I told the inspectors to start back-checking the parameter. Again behind my back, the second-level manager told them to discontinue the inspection. I found out later and called the field service department to notify them of the situation. When confronted by field service, both managers denied what they had done.

My time at Respect Computers was a period during which I vented some rage. I was judgmental and quite angry at what I perceived as other people's lackadaisical approach to work. I was in quality control, which requires one to judge others' work. I was a bureaucrat in a position of power and able to do something about what I perceived as laziness. I was a one-person terror, working 80 hours per week to build some accountability and responsibility into the system. To put it mildly, I kicked some butt. I played the game of controlling bureaucrat as well as it could be played. Though this effort was fun and yielded relatively good product-quality results and many awards for me, I now know it to have been a waste of time.

THE DREAM OF A MORE NATURAL, FAMILY-CENTERED LIFE

I was on a personal five-year plan when I started at Respect Computers. Having given considerable thought to the concept of work while in college, I had concluded that being an employee simply was not for me. After all, one should work to live, and not live to work, right? At least as long as we see work as separate from living, which it is not and can never be. Working as an employee one spends approximately 54% of one's waking hours away from one's family and passion, usually doing a passionless job for which the reward does not reflect the value one adds. At the time I saw a clear division between working as an employee and living.

I had decided to work for five years, then move to the mountains, build a log cabin powered by a small-scale hydroelectric power plant, and build a family-centered life—a life in which most of my family's needs would be met through the passion and love of family as opposed to external lifeless bureaucracies and zombie-clerk employees. I planned to home school my children because of my boring experience in the mass-production factory school.

Though I basically perceived work as something done by an employee, deep down my values were grounded in a "private" work and family-centered paradigm. My mother had been the only employee in the history of my family; my father, grandparents, and ancestors since abolition all had made their livings in their own businesses or farms.

Starting at Respect Computers on a $19,000 per year salary, in five years I had saved more than $100,000. Everything was on track, except I had missed one minor detail: I did not have a wife. I left Respect Computers and was off in my travel trailer, traveling the world, hang gliding, canoeing, wind surfing, scuba-diving, and searching for a wife. I was like Cane, the Buddhist priest, wandering, learning, and discovering.

In 1986 while traveling, I read half of a book titled *The Third Wave* by a fellow named Alvin Toffler. It helped me make sense of my work experiences and my work values, and I began shifting my paradigm regarding what I had witnessed in work.

LIFE AS A CORPORATE STOCK INVESTOR

During my nomadic period, as I invested in stocks and mutual funds, I discovered just how distant and out of touch the real owners of corporations were. I tried to make mental connections between the $40,000 of Respect Computers stock I had just purchased and the fact that I actually owned a piece of Building 101 in Charlotte, North Carolina. I simply could make no connection in my mind between where I had worked, the people I knew, what they were doing, and the stock certificates I was holding. It was simply not real to me. As an investor, I was interested in what most investors and I consider to be long-term gain, six months to three years. Of course, by any real standard, the long-term well-being of a company is much longer.

With the system of ownership in our wealth-creation system, corporate stock ownership, most owners couldn't care less about the true long-term well-being of the company. With the owners of the company giving little to no thought to the long-term well-being of the company, one could hardly expect management, employees, or anybody else to care very much. I can recall thinking of these companies as "ownerless enterprises." In essence, nobody owns them. Employees own a paycheck and care about little more. Management owns a bigger paycheck, some of them caring about the next quarter and the year-end results for their fragmented job. Management cares only as much as its personal interest is involved. The owners think of little more than a few months out, or a few years at most.

When something goes grossly wrong and harms society enormously, usually no one is held responsible as the corporation files bankruptcy, vanishes into thin air, and leaves the taxpayers holding the bag. I had discovered, as an investor, that the public corporation, the heart of our wealth-creation system, is, in essence, an ownerless system in which ultimately no one is responsible, and that few people really care about the long-term health and well-being of the organization.

CHECKMATE

In 1986, opportunity struck, and I started a business. For a few years, I had been searching for a wife. I found it crazy that in Alvin Toffler's

Information Age, I was having such a hard time connecting with her. After all, the only thing that separated us was information. I decided to start an on-line computerized personal-advertisements system— CheckMate. The personal ads were different from those in newspapers because they were 600 words long and included photos. The computer could hold thousands of photo introductions and allow customers access indefinitely. I invested $50,000 in equipment and start-up costs. I quickly met my wife and we married, but business success was a lot tougher. I accepted a position with a defense contractor, Central Aircraft, while my wife and I operated the business.

CENTRAL AIRCRAFT

After the empowerment of Respect Computers, the rigid bureaucracy and centralized control of Central Aircraft was like going from the freedom of hang gliding to the rigid regimentation of boot camp. At Respect Computers, there was a great deal of individual ownership, for those who desired it, because of less work fragmentation. Central Aircraft had work divided into smaller pieces. The work was controlled less by the individual than by management. It was less interesting, less real, less empowering, and a lot less fun. Decisions were made as far toward the top of the organization as possible. Although Central Aircraft was more controlled and exhibited less tangible waste than Respect Computers, the wasted potential was far greater.

Central Aircraft's customers were paying a huge price in poor quality and high cost because of this waste and wasted potential. It did not much matter to Central Aircraft's customers, because they were only other defense contractors, who just passed the cost to the defense department. The bureaus within the defense department didn't mind because they would simply pass the cost to the taxpayer. More spending by a given bureau meant a bigger budget next year for that bureau. This waste would possibly even mean a salary *increase* for bureau managers because the more resources they managed, the higher were their salaries.

The problem was that the people making wasteful decisions at all levels stood to lose little by perpetuating waste. It wasn't *their* money, and they didn't own a significant piece of the company or bureau. If they owned stock in the company, their contribution was so small that it did not affect their return on investment. In many cases the decision makers even stood to gain from the waste. This applies to most companies, not just defense contractors.

With tightly controlled military specifications it was difficult to change things. It created an antichange, status quo environment. With change, one risked attracting the attention of government auditors. On the other side, there was no positive benefit to the company or individual to counter this risk. The last thing a defense contractor wants is an auditor snooping around. It was, and still is, a system based on stability. Seven years after the military adopted the concepts of total quality management and continuous improvement, I have seen no real change away from stability.

Central Aircraft could not change because its customers, other defense contractors, could not change, and the customers could not change because of the defense department. Individuals like me could not make changes, because management was locked into the stability of the company. No one could change because everyone would have to change for one person to change; there simply was not enough in it for these ownerless bureaucrats to desire changing or improving.

At Central Aircraft work was boring, lifeless, and tedious. People were clock watchers. They had good ideas, but the company was simply not interested in any kind of improvement. Most employees had given up and were just going through the motions, as do all good zombie-clerks. Employees repeatedly said, "How can management be so dumb?" Management controlled and defined most things. Not being at the level of detail of the employees, management lacked the information, perspective, and time to control and define the details intelligently. On the other hand, management viewed employees as idiots in light of their poor participation.

Central Aircraft wanted to turn me into a zombie-clerk like the people I'd seen at the defense department warehouse with their heads propped on their desks. At Central Aircraft, I probably averaged a couple hours of work per day, and that two hours, in my opinion, added no value. Central Aircraft was undoubtedly the most boring experience of my adult life. I did, however, learn a lot about the current state of work, people, and bureaucracy.

I tried for a year to encourage change and improve productivity and quality. Eventually it was communicated to me through a conversation between my manager and his manager, the director of quality, that Central Aircraft was not interested in fixing anything that was "working," regardless of the waste or poor quality of the work. I interviewed for a position with TOPS Printers, Incorporated, and was out of Central Aircraft within three weeks.

Central Aircraft not only desired zombie-clerks but also would not tolerate anything else. The message I received, not in so many words, was that Central Aircraft did not want me to do anything but show up promptly for work each day, go to and come back from lunch on time, and be there for eight hours. From their perspective, I was merely filling an affirmative action slot.

I began to see that the problem was larger than controlling managers or lazy employees. Individuals and organizations are locked into a mutual death dance of low productivity, low creativity, poor quality, poor communication, and boredom. The Central Aircraft bureaucracy is interlocked with those of other defense contractors, the military, and the Federal Aviation Administration, the human resources bureaucracies, the union, environmental, and other governmental bureaucracies, and customer and supplier bureaucracies.

At the individual level, senior management is locked into middle management and employee inertia and vice versa. Departments are locked into other departments and traditional ways of doing things, and the entire system is locked into gobs of regulations pertaining to affirmative action, harassment, family leave, "mil-specs," worker compensation, COBRA, OSHA, the environment, Social Security, state and federal taxes, and on and on.

The entire system is stuck because our entire system works based on relationships of dependence and bare tolerance. It is the "G" word—gridlock! (Certainly not limited to Washington politics.) Gridlock, I discovered, is everywhere. I saw it at Respect Computers and at Central Aircraft and discovered more of it everywhere I went. Stability, which had been so good in an Industrial Age, had transformed into this grotesque gridlock. We were entering an era that required continuous, chaotic change but were being held by the structure of stability that had got us where we were.

As at Respect Computers, at Central Aircraft the real waste again showed up in crazy, insane decisions that were being made regarding product, resources, customers, and material. One example was Fiber Optic Mil-Spec-347, which we debated for hundreds of hours because we simply could not call the person who wrote the specification to obtain clarification. Doing so might have drawn the attention of auditors. I came to understand why the military was paying thousands of dollars for a hammer. The enormous cost of military products is not so much the result of fraud and abuse as it is the result of waste, rigid bureaucracy, gridlock, and disengagement.

CHECKMATE

In the meantime, my home business was moving at a snail's pace. I did well in companies, producing tremendous savings and productivity improvements for them, but could not muster a profit out of a small "mom and pop" operation. How could companies be so stupid and tremendously wasteful in their decisions and actions but be successful? I was quite confused. The problem is that the lone entrepreneur lacks the supporting structure and momentum that an established company provides. As a manager once said, "Cash flow and profit cover a multitude of sins."

Lack of momentum presents lone entrepreneurs with a "Catch-22" situation. They need the resources of an organization with momentum—the financial power that comes from the sale of current products. They need the cash flow to cover the many mistakes and trial-and-error experimentation required. I was discovering why most entrepreneurs fail. Their enterprises do not have the momentum of an established bureaucracy.

I was discovering that most new things fail and that it would be only through trial and error that I would get anything to work. I was learning this the hard way. Trial and error with limited capital was extremely time consuming. We were implementing what worked and discarding what didn't, and it was taking forever. For years I thirsted for a method to move faster with limited dollar capital.

There was a bigger Catch-22. Companies were too rigid and gridlocked to produce the intelligence to meet customers' rising expectations, and lone entrepreneurs lacked the momentum and power. I began dreaming about ways to combine the momentum and power of a large bureaucracy with the freedom, intelligence, and agility of an entrepreneurial venture. This became my paradigm, the reality for which I searched. It was a dream out of the practical reality of profit and loss.

TOPS PRINTERS, INCORPORATED

At TOPS Printers I found more of the same top-down management and strong central control as in Central Aircraft. At least TOPS

Printers sought improvement, but they wanted it dictated by the few people at the top; the workers and engineers were considered too stupid to solve problems.

TOPS Printers, more than any of my other employers, demonstrated the Catch-22 of our centrally controlled wealth-creation system. Unable to get employees to make the "right" decisions and do the "right" things, senior management made the employees' decisions for them. This practice was flawed because management did not have sufficient time, detailed information, or intelligence to do the job well. The distrust and contempt for the individual was a self-fulfilling prophecy. The combination of a strong command and control system and a view of people as incapable, stupid, or a liability caused the workers to live up to that image and reinforce it. TOPS Printers had taken a group of intelligent people and made them stupid through their system of organization. This was not new; I'd seen it before and would see it again and again. The following represents a typical example of the ineffectiveness of management-controlled decisions not unique to TOPS Printers.

For the X8000 program, management at the vice-president level decided that it needed to begin reviewing all engineering changes because the manufacturing, design, and quality engineers and the production planners were not competent enough to do the job properly. As quality manager I happened to be present when one hot engineering change was being processed. The engineers, who all worked closely with the product line, took a couple of minutes to review thoroughly and sign off on the change. Quickly and efficiently, they made a good decision based on all the facts. Later I was in a meeting with the vice-presidents when the same change was delivered to them for their sign-off. It took more than an hour for them to sign the change. There was much misinformation, lack of information, and confusion. The vice-presidents looked like stumbling clowns at a circus because of their ignorance of the details. In the end the decision they made was the right one, but it was poorly made because of their insufficient knowledge of the facts. They were too far from the action to be attempting to make detailed decisions.

What had happened at TOPS Printers was that management had taken ownership of activities they deemed to be poorly performed. As management did this, workers more and more gave up ownership of their responsibilities. The more the workers pulled back, the more management said, "I told you so. We can't trust them; we must do this ourselves." In the end, the workers at TOPS had fulfilled management's belief that they were limited, incapable, and stupid.

Over time, management divided jobs into very narrow slivers to allow maximum control from the top. Most people just accepted this division. I knew that there were more productive and enjoyable ways to divide work. From my empowerment experience at Respect Computers, I knew that work could be divided so that there was more ownership and fun. Although Respect Computers had its own problems with waste, Respect Computers' empowering "respect for the individual" concept had shown me that there was another way to divide work.

With just one year of experience as an associate quality engineer at Respect Computers, many times I dreamt up concepts overnight and had them implemented by 10:00 A.M. the next day. Nine years later, as the TOPS Printers quality plant manager, it would take me six months to implement one of the same successful concepts. It now took political maneuvering, strategic planning, and great effort.

As TOPS' quality manager, I had less real authority than I did as a Respect Computers associate engineer. At TOPS Printers, I had a nine-year track record of success with 25 people reporting to me. At Respect Computers, I had zero people reporting to me, one year of experience, and no track record. The difference in authority came from the way work was divided. At Respect Computers, I was the product quality engineer for the 3268 printer and had responsibility for quality on the product for the entire process. I was free to do whatever I wanted as long as I got results. At TOPS Printers, for the P9000 printer, no one person had full responsibility for the entire product from supplier to customer. A couple of people in the quality department had responsibility for suppliers; one had line support, and another had field support. Not only that, but no single quality department had ownership for the whole product; quality support was housed in several different departments.

The only person with vision of the entire quality process on any product was the vice-president of quality. I guess this is where the term "super-vision" comes from. In divided, ownerless work, the person seeing from the higher vantage point has better vision over the entire system. Respect Computers had discontinued the position of supervisor decades ago. At Respect Computers, lowly quality engineers had "super-vision" over their entire product lines and were therefore their own supervisors. It was clear to me that ownership and control had everything to do with how work was divided; the narrower the division, the less ownership was possible.

What I usually said at TOPS Printers was, "There is only one quality engineer here, the vice-president. The rest of us are just quality clerks." Again, I was trapped by another company that wanted no more than a zombie-clerk.

TOPS Printers began to reveal something very new to me. I began to discover that the personalities, insecurities, and weaknesses of the individuals in central control were limiting factors to wealth creation. Their beliefs about people's ignorance and limited capabilities were something in their heads, not reality. These beliefs caused people to become what those in control expected. A person in central authority limits others by his or her incoherent beliefs, misperceptions, insecurities, and weaknesses. Today I believe that many managers' beliefs about others are a reflection of their beliefs about themselves—their insecurities, weaknesses, and fears.

This limiting aspect of management worked in the Industrial Age because broad and high levels of organizational knowledge and intelligence were not very important nor were they desired. Rather, management's job was controlling and limiting the intelligence of an organization. As at Respect Computers and Central Aircraft, at TOPS Printers waste and wasted potential showed up in stupid decisions that were being made regarding product, resources, customers, and material. For example, I witnessed a situation in which ten inspectors spent a full year sorting out irrelevant cosmetic "imperfections" on the X8000 printer, "imperfections" that would not have mattered or even been noticed by a customer.

CHECKMATE

Back at CheckMate, I was still seeking a way to move faster in my business. Many people who wanted to form business partnerships approached me. Their proposals, however, required shared ownership of my business. I did not want to give away a piece of my company and the freedom that went with it, nor did I want joint ownership. Forming a partnership would have helped me leverage resources and move faster because more people would invest their time in the project. I would not have been paying hard, tangible dollars for every minute of work. However, I felt the trade-off wasn't acceptable.

I was continuously contrasting being an owner by night against being an employee by day. Looking back upon it, I was learning more about work by experiencing the stark contrast between the two than anything else I could have done. The waste in bureaucracies was so plain to see. I wanted that momentum and those resources in my business so badly I could taste it.

INSECURE MOLDING

As I continued my journey I went to work for another company, Insecure Molding. By then I was quite skeptical about what I would find at any company. I knew that something was gravely wrong with our entire work system.

While at Insecure Molding, I worked on selling a Statistical Process Control (SPC) program to senior management. SPC is simply a tracking program that lets one know that a manufacturing process has changed and could produce defects. The advantage of SPC over traditional quality control inspections is that SPC lets you know ahead of time that defects will be produced. Traditional inspection is an after-the-fact system. After defects are produced, they are impossible to catch and sort out. What is produced is what will ship to customers regardless of after-the-fact inspections. The difference between SPC and traditional inspection is the same as that between driving your car with and without a gas gauge. With a gas gauge you know when your fuel level is getting low and you might run out of gasoline; without a gauge, it's a blind guessing game. It's one of the concepts that caused the Japanese to excel at the global quality movement. Even though SPC has been around since 1922, in all of my visits to different companies around the Untied States and the world, I can count on one hand the number of companies that really use it.

At Insecure Molding, with our SPC charts we were quickly able to determine when a manufacturing process had changed and defects would be produced. Hours ahead, we were able to detect when defects would be produced. The quality control department had a detection-based quality control program based upon after the fact inspection that missed many defects. At best, it would catch some defects hours after they had been produced.

Even when the quality department caught defects, the production operation rarely sorted out all of the rejects, or even cared. I kept a running log of all of the incidents and repeatedly provided management with copies of this report. The production superintendent flatly told me that SPC would never be implemented there. "The president started the company and built it into a 60 million dollar company without SPC, and he does not need it now," he said. Many people told me that the president ran the company and that following his lead and his ideas was what was important.

The production superintendent was right. I could hardly believe what I was experiencing. A business owner, "entrepreneur" was not interested in profitability and growth unless they resulted from *his* ideas. We had conducted experiments and found solid data showing improvement. Scrap could be cut by huge amounts, quality would be increased significantly, customers would be happier, and profitability would increase. But all I was getting was indifference.

I learned that there are many reasons why people are in business. Some of these reasons have to do more with satisfying an internal personal insecurity, weakness, or need than making a profit or satisfying customers. I learned that even though a company is privately owned, it might not be profit driven on the basis of logic, data, facts, intuition, or anything else. I was learning that insecurities (and we all have them) and the limited perspectives of individuals in positions of central control are primary factors that limit the creation of wealth. The higher up an individual is in an organization, the more amplified the individual's weaknesses or insecurities become in restraining the organization.

I began to see that one person having authority over another weakens the vision, intelligence, and capability of the entire organization. Because we all have insecurities and limited perspectives, I began to doubt the entire concept of employment, hierarchy, and bureaucracy. I began to question the employee-management system of control. I wondered whether the management of people had become an impractical means to create wealth in Alvin Toffler's Information Age.

In my own business, I began trying to remove myself more and more from blocking others but had no easy answers and little success. I somehow knew that more than anything else, to thrive in the Information Age, a system of organization was needed that would make everyone an engaged owner and leader, a system of true liberation. We needed a system that would remove any position that would limit individuals' capability or motivation.

Through a great deal of political maneuvering, eventually I was able to implement SPC in an Insecure Molding plant a few miles away from my original location. I was able to start a company-wide total quality management program. For one part of one product alone in three months using SPC we reduced scrap $500,000 per year by reducing the defect rate from 15% to 3%. Insecure Molding had hired a new vice-president of manufacturing, Phil Taylor. We worked in the one plant to implement SPC and some other programs. Within one quarter, the plant was operating in the black, leading the company's profits for the quarter. The total quality management program produced $2,000,000 in the first year, but it died because it did not have the president's support. Seeing that quality improvement was a losing cause at Insecure Molding, I left the company.

Although there were people in Insecure Molding with more SPC experience than I had, they would not even attempt to implement it. I have seen this in every company for which I've worked. People had the answers to many problems but were not willing to risk their jobs by going against the grain. They would not fight the politics or the bureaucracy. On the other hand, why should they? After all, there was and still is nothing in it for them. Most people realize that they are being paid a flat salary or wage simply to do what they are told—not to do what they believe in.

CHECKMATE

At CheckMate, we eventually hired a few employees. One, Tracy Teaford, was creative, bright, and inventive. After my experience with Respect Computers, I was a heart and soul believer in empowerment and had an empowerment philosophy within CheckMate. Tracy thrived in this environment. I had started the business with the goal of maintaining a very-low-cost, affordable service for all to use. Tracy came up with the idea of markedly increasing prices. She believed the fee for membership should have been $195 rather than the $35 we were charging.

Our sales showed that we probably needed to increase prices to become profitable. We began to experiment with increased prices, trying $45. We were risking a lot of money, because it took weeks to see the results. The initial responses did not seem to be good. However, we knew from history that the initial responses are not reliable. We became nervous and directed Tracy to lower the price, but she was certain that we should hold out. Her intuition told her that raising prices was the right action to take. We still told her no. Against our directive, she maintained the higher price. We found out a week later and were furious. We explained that it was *our* money being risked, not hers.

We thrashed her for this "insubordination" just as any good authoritarian bureaucrats would. We lowered prices to the original setting. There was not enough data to tell whether the price increase worked. Tracy eventually left our employ. At some point, we did eventually increase prices. We tried $45, then $55, then $75, $99, $150, settling at $195. We found that $195 had a perceived value in line with what the customer was receiving.

At $35 customers had undervalued and underutilized their memberships. We also found that $195 was the perfect balance for sales rate and profitability. At $35, 20% of the people who received sales packages joined. At $195, 9% joined. If we sent out 400 sales packages in a week at $35, we grossed $2,800; at $195 we grossed $7,000. It was the difference between profit and loss.

Tracy was right, but I hadn't trusted her intuition. "In God we trust; all others bring data" was, and is, the creed of the controlling bureaucrat. It was not *her* money being risked. My central control of decisions cost me a lot. Perhaps it cost me that business. What if there had been an organizing system within CheckMate that allowed Tracy to invest some of her money into her decisions? She could use intuition, and she would share in the gain or loss. This would have been a win/win situation for all. Instead we all lost.

Tracy had experienced the same disempowerment that all employees routinely experience. I had tried empowerment in an inherently disempowering organizing structure. It was sham empowerment, just as it is in every other company and bureaucracy.

MORE AND MORE COMPANIES

I went on to work at several more companies, large, medium, and small. I saw more of what I'd seen many times before. To date, I have worked in or with companies in the automotive and computer industries, defense, cosmetics, nuclear energy, aerospace, farming, construction, machining, plastics, rubber, and retail. I have worked in government, dating services, and the stock market. I have worked in the United States, Japan, and Mexico and with many people and companies elsewhere around the world. I have worked with most of the fad management programs of the past 20 years.

I worked as consultant, manager, engineer, writer, supervisor, business owner, production worker, and maintenance technician. In my business I'd done it all from customer service to accounting, marketing, sales, production, and company president. I had seen a very **broad** and **detailed** spectrum of work and wealth creation from many perspectives and the common theme never changed—waste, wasted potential, little *real* change, and lots of veneer hype.

THE STATUS OF WEALTH CREATION

I had discovered the status of work and wealth creation to be in very poor condition from virtually all perspectives. It is one of relative weakness, gridlock, dependence, apathy, frustration, waste, and **enormous wasted potential**.

Artificial Laws of the School

In *The Seven Habits of Highly Effective People* (1989) Stephen Covey speaks of laws of the school versus laws of the farm. The laws of the school are artificial and manipulative. They are based on veneer, surface appearance. One can cram for tests and get high grades without learning anything. One can present statistics in a way to show a preferred reality. One can present a surface picture showing that an outstanding job is being done when in reality one is just a slick salesperson presenting fragments of reality. "We want to put on a good front." On the other hand, the laws of the farm are natural and substantive. Either you plant your crops in time or they do not yield results. You reap what you sow. There is no way to whitewash the results or cram for the test at the end. Our Industrial Age wealth-creation institutions work primarily upon the weak laws of the school. This includes schools, companies, representative democracy, politics, courts, government agencies, and far more. In our weak world of work, appearance counts far more than reality and veneer far more than substance. Organizations look great on the surface with profits, growth, nice buildings, and accelerating careers. However, just beneath the surface lies the rot and stench of dysfunctional systems, wasted potential, horrible injustices, pathetic, insecure dictators, and brain-dead wealth creators.

Gridlocked Free Market

Free markets are supposed to squeeze out waste, inefficiencies, and weaknesses. They are not working because they are locked in by the mutual death dance of low productivity, low creativity, poor quality, poor communication, and boredom. The control and stability of the centrally controlled organization has mutated into a death grip on wealth creation. Virtually all that defines a company, including politics, self-interest, factional fighting, bureaucracy, employees, apathy, central control, and more contributes to this death grip.

The people at the lower levels have solutions to problems but do not or cannot contribute those solutions. Each day, nationwide and worldwide, the answers to hundreds of billions of problems, as well as many potential opportunities, lie idle in employees' heads. This condition equates to hundreds of billions of dollars in waste and **trillions of dollars in wasted potential.** In a society of deficits as large as ours, in which the primary wealth creator is knowledge, this situation is simply intolerable.

With our norm of gridlock, things change only when they have to. Patience is the primary virtue customers, suppliers, employees, managers, and all stakeholders must have to survive within the system. Patience with roadblocks, patience with the rigid hierarchy, patience with management ineptitude, patience with poor quality and service, patience with waste, patience with employee incompetence, and on and on.

Entitlements

Most people have a sense of entitlement—employees, welfare recipients, subsidized farmers, artists, and companies receiving subsidized government training. People feel entitled to get what they've always gotten regardless of contribution or conditions. "I should be paid just for showing up for work." "The organization and society owe me something." "I should get raises each year regardless of performance and market conditions." Seniority is one of the most sacred entitlements. In our entitlements-based system of work, personal responsibility and contribution mean little.

System of Dependent Victims

We are stuck in a system of gridlock in which most people, from CEOs to front-line workers, feel like helpless, dependent victims being swept along by a raging current. We have a system of mass victimization because employment is a system based on relationships of *dependence* as is explained in detail later.

Passionless Wealth Creation

There has been a common thread wherever I've gone. Most people are disengaged from their work. They go through the motions with little passion, little love, and therefore little life. Most people start out with passion, but the system of red tape, central authority, and gridlock beats it out of them. The veneer laws of the school wear them down. People evolve to one of many types. Some put on a good show, get good results on paper, add little value, and climb the ladder. Some people simply don't care. Others are angry and frustrated. Some are dogmatic believers in authoritarian control. Most have simply given up; they work for a paycheck and do what they are told. In general, companies and employees are going through the motions; no company even comes close to its potential.

Poorly Aligned Structures

There is poor alignment throughout our wealth-creation system. People's interests in many cases run counter to those of the bureaucracy and the other stakeholders. Alignment is the degree to which all stakeholders' interests—customers', investors', suppliers', partners', and coworkers'—interests directly coincide and are in harmony (Naisbitt and Aburdene 1985).

Constipated Free Market

The free market of the Industrial Age has not focused on the win/win of meeting customer needs. Instead it focuses on the win/lose of *beating the competition* at meeting customer needs; being just a notch better than the competition regardless of what customers want, regardless of the waste, regardless of the wasted potential, regardless of our systemic and collective social deficits. Our progress therefore is retarded. Organizations are not focused on what is possible with their resources or on reduction of waste and wasted potential. There are huge deficits between customers' expectations and quality delivered, but there is no problem because there is no threat from other slow-moving bureaucratic competitors.

System of Limited Personal Growth

Instead of a system that inherently encourages the growth of individuals, the present system of ownerlessness, supervision, and regulation structurally inhibits growth of the individual and personal responsibility. Like that of a child under the supervision of an overly protective, micromanaging parent, growth is stunted. The result is immaturity and low emotional and spiritual intelligence (McDermid 1995).

Wealth-Limiting Bureaucrats

People in central positions of authority today are halting the driving forces of the free market, holding back advances, and limiting wealth creation in the name of stability and control. Bureaucrats today are preventing the free market from advancing.

Stifled Employees

In survey after survey, most people working as employees say: (1) They do not like their jobs. (2) Their job utilizes only 10% to 20% of their potential. (3) They would prefer to be doing something else.

Frustrated Individuals

Company after company desires no more from its employees than being "zombie-clerks." In fact, companies demand that employees be no more. Where there is passion, it is driven out. Where there is creativity, it is stultified. Where there is diversity, it is forced to conform. Where there is growth, it is stunted. Where there is challenge, it is restrained. Where there is thinking, it is lobotomized. Where there is risk, it is avoided. Where there is relative stagnation, it is embraced. As the Japanese say, "The nail that sticks up shall be pounded down."

Continuous Improvement

The past decade has seen continuing improvement within bureaucracies as managers try to move bureaucracies beyond their natural limits. As documented in book after book, and throughout this book, one failing or mildly successful fad management program appears, nudges the paradigm, makes some improvement, then disappears. Employees have become fatigued with "program of the month" meandering. Managers void of vision grope in the dark from one program to another. Scott Adams, through his *Dilbert* cartoon series, has become a millionare showing managers to be stumbling fools and clowns. Though meandering has increased organizational effectiveness in the past two decades, we have only tapped the smallest fraction of available potential. "Even a blind hog gets an acorn once in a while." Employees and customers still are not getting their needs met as they desire. Most employees still dislike their work. And most bureaucracies are still grossly ineffective at tapping the potential at their disposal. With continuous improvement we are attempting to cross a chasm in small steps. Alone and void of vision, continuous improvement is a bankrupted long-term policy. In the short term, however, managers look great while killing the goose that lays the golden eggs.

Zombie-Clerk Employees

As one senior employee recently said after years of progressive fad programs and a new one that was aimed at making him productive, "I haven't worked in 20 years, and I'm not about to start now." Though fads show the direction of change, they have barely scratched the surface of the wasted potential in companies.

THE DISCOVERY

Somewhere in my journey, I discovered the problem. It was not government workers, construction workers, or bureaucrats. Nor was it company presidents or lazy employees. All of these were symptoms of deeper problems.

The problem was, and is, our entire system of organizing work and wealth creation. Our system of organizing work, at its core, is based on ownerless representation, divided work, authoritarianism, bureaucracy, subordination, low intelligence, and stan-

dardized compensation. It is based on impersonal relationships of dependence, mistrust, adversarialism, and misalignment. Underlying all of this, it is a system of control based on fear.

The very foundation and structure are based on *control* by a few brains and therefore low intelligence. The system, one of "tolerable bondage," is based inherently on disempowerment and suppression of ideas.

At their core bureaucracies are organizing systems with extremely limited perspectives. Work is fragmented into specialized departments, jobs, divisions, and titles, and no one understands the whole. Then through adversarialism we fight for and try to get each other to understand our fragmented perspectives. The present system is simply not geared for a knowledge era of generation of diverse ideas. It is not geared for the wealth production of an Information Age.

What I continually heard through the 1980s was, "Customers are content, companies are growing and profitable, people are being employed, taxes are being paid, boom times are here. So what if there is waste and wasted potential? If it ain't broke, don't fix it." In the 1990s I continually heard, "We are continuously improving ahead of the competition. So what if customers' needs are not quite met or employee potential is stifled—who cares? As long as we stay ahead of the competition at meeting our customers' needs and profit grows each year, so what?"

I'll tell you so what! The competitive paradigm is dead, that's what! What happens to your organization when new types of organizations appear and focus strictly on customers' needs with the primary purpose of helping others? They are so highly focused on customers' needs that they do not even see or care about competition. In fact, competition does not exist from their perspective. What happens when their workers, who are intelligent business owners, collaborate to meet people's needs with high levels of synergy, creativity, speed, and customization? What happens as teams and individuals synergize to tap near-genius levels of potential daily while working to help others? Will anyone be buying your inferior products at higher prices made by your brain-dead *employees*? Will you have time to develop your employees to grow into collaborative business owners? Will you as an employee have the time to develop the thinking, partnering, leadership, and collaborative skills needed to feed your family in the new economy?

Breakpoints happen very fast. Most plantation owners never recovered their leadership positions in society as they were forced through breakpoint to the industrial revolution. Most on the agrarian side of the shift felt great pain as their entire civilization was lost.

As you read this, millions of individuals are connecting and building the foundation and infrastructure for a new way of working through the Internet and *infant* information superhighway. Millions are doing the healing work required to collaborate and produce synergy with others. What are you and your organization doing? Are you merely playing at progressive wealth creation and personal growth? Are you in denial regarding your personal and organizational progress? Do your "laws of the school" graphs and numbers look great, but deep down you know of the waste and wasted potential lurking beneath the surface?

For more detail on the journey of discovery, see *Journey of Discovery* and *Broken Wealth-Creation* at the WinWinWorld.net website at **http://www.winwinworld.net**

3

Companies Are Controlled Economies

Employment Is Socialized Work

Hundreds, perhaps thousands, of consultants and business leaders are pushing for what they see as dramatic reform. They want to re-engineer the corporation, . . . empower the workforce, . . . give workers a sense of ownership. . . . These are all worthy objectives and are definitely steps in the right direction. What frustrates me is that they all reach a certain point in both theory and their application and suddenly they hit a wall. They never reach the logical conclusion to their own argument. . . . They are looking for answers within a system that does not work.
—Roger Terry, *Economic Insanity*

Imagine a society in which you have no guaranteed freedom of speech and no right to privacy, in which tapping your phone or secretly videotaping your every move is legal and is done. Envision an economy in which all customers internal to the society are controlled centrally by bureaucrats and in which wealth creation is socially owned—one in which the individual is not allowed to own the fruits of his or her labor. Imagine a place where there is no freedom of market choice and all of your suppliers operate as monopolies and are chosen for you by autocrats in the bureaucracy. Imagine a place where regardless of the contribution you make, your reward stays the same and you are rewarded the same or less as those adding less or even no value in the society.

In this society the bureaucracy, as in a welfare system, pays for the services provided to you. Imagine a culture in which people tap only a small percentage of their passion and are relatively disengaged, in which giving mediocre effort and service to customers internal to the society is the norm. Imagine a society in which internal customers wait in long lines to have their needs met; one in which customer and supplier relationships are mostly ones of indifference or are even adversarial. It is a society in which the organizing system consistently suppresses individual creativity and initiative. Imagine a system of secrecy in which the central bureaucrats in power tightly hold information. They strategically use information as propaganda to put the best spin on things from their perspective and for their gain and comfort. No, I am not talking about the former Soviet Union. I am describing the internal operations of the company or *controlled economy* in which you likely work.

As I revolved from one company to another trying to find someplace that would make sense, it occurred to me that "the company" and all bureaucracies are controlled economies. **Controlled economies are organizations in which the wealth-creation process of trade between individuals and groups is controlled. They are organizations in which internal suppliers and customers do not have freedoms as owners, because they do not own the specific work they perform and therefore must be managed and controlled by others in *superior* positions. Controlled economies are the very foundation of our Industrial Age civilization, socialist and capitalist alike.**

For me, the great irony of our age is that we and the Russians lived in abject terror for a generation, spent money to the point of bankruptcy, and endangered the existence of life on earth to debate a moot point. Our respective economies were and are Tweedledum and Tweedledee. The answer to the debate lies entirely outside both paradigm boxes, which are in fact the same paradigm box—Industrial Age society. We both had the right ideas, but we bungled them in different ways. Capitalists in the United States believed that private ownership was the key to growth and prosperity but then structured private enterprises to severely limit ownership. Socialists in Russia believed that the worker should own the means of production but structured ownership so that control was limited to a smaller, more corrupt, and incompetent horde of fat cats than ever before, and they paid the price.

The controlled economy has been the wealth-creation engine for Industrial Age civilization and has been the core of our system for organizing humanity. In the West the controlled economy has existed primarily in the form of the company. However, controlled economies come in all forms of bureaucracies, including hospitals, government agencies, schools, nonprofit organizations, and even entire countries, such as the former Soviet Union.

Companies, like all bureaucracies, are in essence miniature Soviet Unions. They are bastions of dictatorship, systems that operate structurally almost identically to the former Soviet Union. All controlled economies, regardless of size, operate on the basis of the same principles, systems, and values. This controlled environment is the primary reason that most people dislike work and live for Friday and freedom. The primary difference between wealth creation within the traditional company and in the Soviet Union is size. There is nearly a point-by-point, item-by-item match between the principles, systems, and values of the company and the former Soviet Union. If there were a company as large as the former USSR, it would be almost identical to that country. We do not live in a free marketplace. Rather we are languishing in disparate autocratic socialistic entities in which our pioneering, entrepreneurial intelligence is systematically crushed.

This chapter shows the following startling revelations about our "free market" economy: (1) approximately 95% of all customers are controlled centrally by bureaucrats; (2) only 5% to 10% of wealth is privately created, 90% to 95% is socially created; (3) fully 90% to 95% of wealth is *controlled* by 5% to 10% of the people. All of this occurs because our economies are made of collections of controlled economies. Let's step back and look at the weak principles of the controlled economy and where and why it evolved this way.

For a detailed, point-by-point analysis of why and how companies are in essence miniature Soviet Unions see *Companies Are Controlled Economies: The Hopelessness of Miniature Soviet Unions in an Information Age* at the WinWinWorld.net website at **http:// www.winwinworld.net**

CONTROLLED CUSTOMERS WITHIN A FREE MARKET

In a typical transaction of product to consumer, most people consider there to have been only one supplier-to-customer transaction.

The supplier is the company and the end-user consumer is the customer. Assume that there were 20 people in the supply chain who worked to make the final product. In a controlled economy all 20 of these people are brought together and seen as a single entity—the supplier or the company. This is an illusion caused by the socialized and monolithic perspective of the controlled economy.

Whenever work or knowledge flows from one person to another, there is a transaction as value is added and wealth is created. There are therefore not one but many supplier-to-customer transactions, and there are many customers. Controlled economies disguise these supplier-to-customer transactions, hiding them so well that it has taken us 200 years to discover them. Today organizations are beginning to apply internal-customer and inverted-pyramid concepts whereby each worker in the company is seen as a supplier and customer to other workers.

The internal supplier and customer concept is not so much a discovery of what has been or is but is recognition of the direction we are taking. We are attempting to move toward a free market *within* the enterprise in which the customers, not bureaucrats, do the driving—a system of real internal suppliers and customers.

Because the people performing the work are the ones creating the wealth, management adds no value to the wealth-creation process. They are the glue that holds the work of an organization together and they provide motivation and leadership, but perhaps there are other ways of motivating, leading, and gluing. Let's theoretically remove management and hierarchy from the picture. What is left is work being performed and people adding value as work flows from one person to another and wealth is created—in essence, real customers and suppliers. There is, however, something still wrong with this picture. As work and products flow from one person to another, money or some form of consideration should be flowing in the reverse direction. But it does not.

CASH FLOW IN CONTROLLED ECONOMIES

In controlled economies, money is controlled and flows from external customers up the vertical hierarchy to be artificially redistributed as standardized compensation to the owner's representatives, the employees. This distribution method allows money to be the "fear-based" controlling glue that holds together the misaligned and fragmented pieces of work. These are the economics of trickle down inherent to systems of centrally created wealth. This lack of money flow from individual customer to individual supplier is the primary factor that causes us to lose sight of the fact that the workers are suppliers and customers. To correct our problems of misalignment, money or some form of consideration must flow directly from customer to supplier as work flows in the opposite direction.

MONOPOLIES WITHIN A FREE MARKET

Another factor that helps disguise suppliers and customers within controlled economies is the lack of freedom of market choice. Controlled economies work internally on the basis of monopolies. Traditionally, employees have had no say regarding their internal suppliers, the other employees within the organization. Employees are hired by management and work where and with whom they are told. They can complain to management about a poorly performing supplier, but management usually has more important and less painful things to deal with. If service is poor to internal customers, there is little recourse for the internal customer. The norm in companies is for service from internal suppliers to be extremely poor, with many internal customers' needs going unmet for years.

As we looked at the former Soviet Union, we saw pictures of empty store shelves, long lines, poor service, and poor quality. In general, within the old Soviet Union the normal mode of practice was that people internal to the society did not have their needs met very well. All controlled economies have this problem within their organizations because of the constipation of wealth flow. For example, for 18 years a production person at Insecure Molding tried to get a $5 wrench. It would have allowed him to do one of his jobs twice as fast and to save hundreds of dollars per year. He was told by his supplier (his supervisor) for 18 years that the money was not in the budget.

Processes are systematically not defined, preventive maintenance of equipment is systematically not done, and details of work are not covered. Support is systematically not provided by internal suppliers to internal customers; systems are usually not capable. People eventually tire of fighting the bureaucracy and give up. Patience with waste and gridlock is our real world, even after decades of continuous improvement. In general, within companies we have become accustomed to the neglect of dozens of critically important needs.

People who demand better service or demand that their needs be met are labeled troublemakers. We have become accustomed to the fact that it will take months and years to meet our needs. The norm is "Relax, don't get so excited. It's not your money. It's just a job." The supply chain in both systems is systematically unable to deliver.

"You can't manage everything" is what one manager told me when I showed him that we were paying 50% more for pens of less value than pens from another external supplier. He was exactly right, and that is why controlled economies are obsolete. There is simply too much detail for a few bureaucrats to manage and too many employees' needs to meet. Companies have the equivalent of the long lines and empty store shelves of the former Soviet Union, as internal customers go for years without having their needs met because we centrally control the wealth-creation process. This is true even in the most progressive controlled economies with horizontal business units, self-directed teams, empowered employees, gain sharing, and the like whereby companies seek to decentralize authority and ownership. Because of control, which is at the core of controlled economies, they cannot go far enough to get the job done, even with the new and most progressive programs. I know, because I have been there and done that.

THE LIBERATION OF CUSTOMERS

As middle management and supervisors disappear, as hierarchies flatten, pyramids invert, and companies shift horizontally, the trend in controlled economies is toward free markets within organizations with work flowing from one person to another as consideration flows in the opposite direction.

Internal customers are beginning to have some say regarding their internal suppliers with progressive management programs such as 360-degree surveys, internal customer surveys, peer evaluations, internal supplier and customer value chains, and inverted pyramids. In self-directed teams, horizontal business units, and team-based organizations, employees are beginning to have some say in supplier and partner selection through 360-degree surveys and peer evaluations. At W. L. Gore and Associates people wander around the company until they find partners and customers who want to work with them and stay only as long as they add value for these people. As we move toward intrapreneuring and smaller profit centers at the team level, cash is beginning to flow in the opposite direction of workflow.

As we metamorphose toward mass privatization, employees are beginning to be seen as the customers *they* are. The internal customers are gaining control of their supplier base and are starting to have freedom of market choice. In addition, cash is beginning to flow horizontally.

All the aforementioned fad management programs are free-market based. Although changes in controlled economies show the trend and direction, they do not and cannot come close to tapping the potential required for a knowledge economy. This is because the very core of what they are, *controlled* economies, prevents free-market initiatives from really working—from reaching their natural conclusions.

For more detail on the parallels between the company and the former Soviet Union, see *Work and Money Flow, Monopolies, Beyond Controlled Economies, The Trends toward Holistic and Private Work, Core Demands of the New Wealth Creation* at the WinWinWorld.net website at **http://www.winwinworld.net**

ADAM SMITH, THE DIVISION OF LABOR, AND FRAGMENTATION

As I made my journey through controlled economy after controlled economy, I saw the same trends common throughout. Many wasteful, insane, and limited-perspective decisions were being made daily regarding products, resources, customers, and materials. There is a question to be asked concerning all of the waste and wasted potential within organizations.

If those making the decisions to produce the waste were in their own private businesses and paying the *entire* cost and reaping the *entire* benefit, and seeing the *whole* picture, would there be the same waste? The answer is no.

Herein lies a big chunk of the problem. The work of controlled economies is divided into narrow fragments. Various people and narrow, fragmented departments perform specialized segments of the divided work. Because of these divisions, the specific person performing the work cannot own it.

Two hundred years ago, at the beginning of the Industrial Age, Adam Smith wrote a book, *An Inquiry into the Nature and Causes of the Wealth of Nations.* Smith defined the Industrial Age wealth-creation system. He presented a concept called division of labor. According to this concept, work is divided into areas of specialty and batch processed to mass-produce the same thing over and over. On the first page, Smith goes to the very heart of the matter. Using the example of pin manufacturing, Smith explains that an uneducated person making as many pins as possible in a day produces between one and twenty pins. If, however, the pin-making labor is divided into ten small operations performed by ten uneducated people, the ten people can collectively produce 48,000 pins, or 4,800 per person.

We took people from an Agricultural Age, directly from the fields, or one-piece, "whole" craftwork and put them on fragmentation-based assembly lines. In the Agricultural Age, individuals performed whole work, such as growing their own food or making one customized horseshoe at a time or one made-to-order cabinet at a time. Individuals went from this to performing narrow "slivers" of work, such as inserting the same bolt into the same hole thousands of times each day and never seeing an end product. We divided work into such narrow slivers that people lost perspective of what they were doing, of the end product, and of its function.

For more than 200 years, the division of labor within controlled economies has increased productivity. Consistent with the newtonian worldview, the science of the Industrial Age, we viewed work as something that could be divided and subdivided into its smallest elements and then artificially aggregated back together. The glue with which we attempt to patch and hold this fragmented work together is *control*, which comes through supervision, pay for time, management, procedures, regulations, talk, performance evaluations, punishment, and propaganda. A serious problem, however, is that glued, fragmented work leaks massively; many pieces fall through the cracks between individuals' fragmented jobs.

The concept of the division of labor is the heart of the organizational structure that has powered the Industrial Age—the bureaucracy. Bureaucracy is far more than a synonym for "red tape," rigid policies, or the operating system of the former Soviet Union. It is the very foundation and structure of our entire civilization. Most institutions, whether governmental, nonprofit, or privately owned, are based on this organizing system. Bureaucracy is a system for organizing by bureaus or departments of specialty. Bureaucracy is the organizational structure for vertical integration of the work of a business under one central authority and dividing it for control. It is the operating system for the entire industrialized world, socialist and capitalist countries alike. It permeates every segment of advanced civilization. It is a structure for organizing information and the work of people and therefore wealth creation.

Bureaucracy is the bedrock and framework of huge, powerful organizations. It has created tremendously forceful advances in human growth. Nonetheless, we currently associate the word *bureaucracy* **not with strength and power but with clumsiness, inefficiency, stupidity, and ineffectuality. This alone should be enough to tell us that something is gravely wrong with the foundation of our wealth-creation system.**

Today the bureaucratic trend is reversing, even in hard-core manufacturing, as companies shift to programs such as manufacturing cells, one-piece flow, mass customization, just-in-time production, lean manufacturing, business units, profit centers, reengineering, and horizontal organizations. With all of this activity the division of labor and bureaucracy are literally being undivided and despecialized. Some products have gone from taking weeks to go through five, six, or seven specialized departments (machining, premolding, molding, assembly, and inspection) and 15 people within these departments to one person. The one-person product-focused cell performs all work on the product. This is a direct reversal of Smith's division of labor.

> *Fundamentally, reengineering is about reversing the Industrial Revolution. Reengineering rejects the assumptions inherent in Adam Smith's industrial paradigm—the division of labor, hierarchical control and all appurtenances of an early stage developing economy. . . . We say that it is time to retire those principles and adopt a new set.*
> —Michael Hammer and James Champy,
> *Reengineering the Corporation*

The lean manufacturing approach takes three- to four-day Kaizen events to suck a single product line out of several vertically integrated functional departments of specialty. The product line is placed into a one-piece, flow-manufacturing cell that produces entire products. Sometimes a self-directed product team is established at the same time, along with a team-based incentive system. In essence, a small business is being created that comprises a small team of semi–business owners. All of the work of the product line is performed by this small business.

Having led many Kaizen events and participated in more than I'd care to admit, I can attest to the significant performance improvements from making work whole. Within the Kaizen events, organizations routinely see 50% to 80% improvements in many performance measures—productivity, cycle times, on-time shipments, lead times, scrap, external failure rates, and more.

For more detail on the reversal of division of labor and related concepts, see *The Trends toward Holistic and Private Work*; for more detail on fragmented work, see *Trillions of One-Dollar Problems* at the WinWinWorld.net website at **http://www.winwinworld.net**

"PUBLIC WORK" AND SOCIALIZED WEALTH CREATION

We wanted to fragment work in an Industrial Age so that it could be centrally owned, planned, and controlled from above. There are two reasons for this, as follows:

1. The wealth-creation process in the Industrial Age has been capital intensive. To create wealth one needed lots of dollars to purchase expensive equipment and facilities and to hire lots of people to mass-produce for mass markets. Because most people were not wealthy, only a minority of people could afford to own the wealth-creation process. This minority needed a system that allowed them to own and control the work of hundreds, thousands, and even hundreds of thousands of people from a single, controllable point. Divided work and bureaucracy were the answer.

2. It has been natural in the Win/Lose Era to want to control as much power and wealth and as many people as possible. It was and is a norm of "control or be controlled." When we shifted from the Agricultural Age to the Industrial Age, power shifted from being confined within bloodlines to being available to anyone who could amass enough wealth. The wealthy, however, needed a system for owning and controlling the work of others. The answer came in dividing other people's work and vertically integrating it under one person's ownership and central control—hence bureaucracy.

Divided work was a foreign notion to those with an Agricultural Age paradigm. My great-uncle, the grandson of a freedman, farmed all his life with a mule and a few acres of land. He was clearly a relic of the Agricultural Age. I heard him say on several occasions that he could not understand how people could possibly perform "public work." Until recently, I never quite understood what he meant by "public work." At the time, I was 14 and working as a laborer in my father's privately owned construction business. I did not perceive this as "public work."

With the division of labor within companies, work is publicly owned. Although a company owned by an individual may be privately owned, the person performing the work does not own that work. That work, therefore, is not privately owned.

In companies, the fragmented work of many individuals is collectively brought together into one whole. It forms one business and is owned by the company. The company is owned as a single entity, a collective whole, by one person or a group of people. The word *collective* is defined as the bringing together of individual pieces into one whole. (The words *public, collective, communal, social* as in socialism, *shared*, and *cooperative* all are synonyms.) In a company of a thousand employees, the work of a thousand people is brought together and owned by one person or a group of shareholders. This is collective, public, or even *socialized ownership*. It is just as collective as socialism, whereby the work of a nation, such as the former Soviet Union, is brought together and collectively owned by all of the people.

Whether the company is owned by one person, many people, or even collectively by the people performing the work, the company being owned as a "collective whole" disallows work from being owned by the specific individual performing it. This makes work within a company public or socialized by any logical standard.

My great-uncle was correct; any divided work not owned by the individual doing that work is "public work." In a conversation with a production worker regarding whether work within a private company is socialized, he said, "But in socialism, the state bureaucracy owns the work and everything else." I asked him, "Who owns the work you do, you or the company bureaucracy?"

The term *private ownership* commonly refers to private ownership of the entire enterprise. Little attention has been paid to whether the work and wealth creation within the enterprise are publicly or privately owned. In the former Soviet Union, private ownership was disallowed. In a society of ownerless clerks, one would expect to have productivity and growth problems in a customer-driven era.

What do we find when we take a close look at our supposedly privatized free-market economy? We find that there is not much more private ownership of wealth creation than in the former Soviet Union. In fact, there is hardly any private ownership of wealth creation at all. Because wealth is created through the work of people and employees perform most of the work, most wealth is created through public or socialized work.

THE MISALIGNMENT OF FRAGMENTED PUBLIC WORK

We divide whole work and artificially aggregate the fragmented public pieces through control. The result is a poorly aligned organization or economy.

Alignment is the degree to which an individual's interests directly coincide and are in harmony with those of other individuals in an organization as well as those of the whole organization and other stakeholders. It is also the degree to which diverse people who have differing visions, values, thinking, or life purposes are able to synthesize these into a harmonious, coherent, collective whole.

As depicted in Figure 3–1, the interests of the various stakeholders (suppliers, customers, stockholders, managers, various departments, employees) in controlled economies point in many different directions. For example, most controlled economies desire "getting more out of people" but wants to pay them as little as possible in order to be more profitable and stay competitive. The net result of poor alignment is a control-based win/lose system in which one individual gains when another loses.

The more narrowly work is divided, the more controlling glue is required, and the less alignment is possible. The more holistic the work, the better is the alignment. Also the more holistic the work, the less it can be controlled from above and the less central control is required.

Serfs in the Agricultural Age did not have an external quality control inspector controlling the quality fragment of their work. The serfs had authority over the entire process from production to consumption. Because serfs and their families lived on their share of the

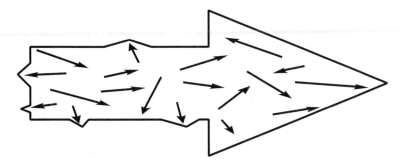

FIGURE 3–1 Poor Alignment within Organizations

crop, there was natural alignment regarding the serfs' growing the best-quality crop. Therefore, no quality "controlling" inspector was required to assure the serfs' work, but there were tax collectors to ensure the nobles got their "fair" share.

Today inspectors and other checks-and-balances systems are disappearing as work becomes whole and begins to be privatized. As we near breakpoint, organizations are developing new compensation systems in which individuals receive a percentage of the wealth they produce. These systems include gain sharing, at-risk pay, team-based pay, bonus systems, pinpointing, profit sharing, and many homegrown systems. Companies such as Nucor Steel and Lincoln Electric have production operators who receive as much as $80,000 per year for work for which most manufacturing companies pay $20,000 per year or less. Most of the income for Nucor and Lincoln workers comes from a percentage of the value they add above a set baseline. These companies perceive an abundant reality and an expanding pie, and they have been highly successful doing so.

For more detail on Nucor, Lincoln, private work concepts within organizations, and the transition to private work, see *The Trends toward Holistic and Private Work* at the WinWinWorld.net website at **http://www.winwinworld.net**

A LIFE IS A TERRIBLE THING TO SELL

The defining trait of poorly aligned public work is *standardized compensation*. This is compensation for which, regardless of the value one adds, one is paid a flat salary or wage. One therefore is paid for one's time and not for one's value or the value one adds. It is a system that devalues the individual. One sells one's time just as a prostitute does. Prostitutes passionlessly *rent* their bodies for money. Employees passionlessly *rent* their lives for money.

According to Webster's dictionary a prostitute is "one who *deliberately* debases, devalues, or lowers oneself or one's talents for money." How many of us as employees do not come close to fully utilizing our talents? How many of us work on things for which we have little passion or in which we do not believe or outright oppose just for the money? Do we do what the boss wants, knowing it to be wrong, just for the money? How many of us prostitutes come close to utilizing our potential as employees? Very few! Like other prostitutes we must do the "practical" thing to meet our needs of daily living. One sells part of one's life to another and is detached from the outcome of one's work in order to pay the bills. This is prostitution. It is a paradigm of relatively low emotional and spiritual intelligence. This is not bad, but is merely another sign of our level of maturity and the positive direction of our growth. After all, I would rather be an employee than a serf or a slave.

From the organization's perspective, the problem with human rental property is one of motivation and responsibility. Most prostitutes are not very passionate or engaged in their work, and this includes employees. As we move into the knowledge era, in which wealth is created through the generation of diverse ideas, the disengagement and newtonian separation of one's mind, spirit, and body are completely intolerable.

THE INSURMOUNTABLE PROBLEMS
WITH PUBLIC WORK

The following problems with public work and controlled economies make the Industrial Age system too weak for an Information Age:

1. Misalignment. Poor alignment is the norm of public work. There is inherent misalignment between individuals, the organization, and other stakeholders. Individuals are routinely put into situations in which they gain when the organization loses, and they lose when the organization gains.

2. Low responsibility and motivation. Because there is no ownership and people are paid for their time and not their value, there
   is little negative or positive consequence for one's actions. Individuals therefore are not highly motivated, because their actions
   are either paid for by others or rewarded to others. It is a system
   with an inherent level of low responsibility and motivation.
3. Blindness. Public work is a system lacking in perspective and
   thus wisdom and intelligence; it is a system of poor vision, near
   blindness, and limited realities. Each individual sees, works,
   and experiences wealth creation from very narrow and fragmented perspectives; no individuals see or have a good understanding of the entire wealth-creation process.
4. Adversarialism. Public work is a system based on division or
   fragmentation; each individual sees from a different, narrow
   perspective. Combining fragmentation with competition makes
   the system adversarial at its core—production against quality,
   design versus process, management versus employees.
5. Waste. There are huge amounts of waste and wasted potential
   as work slips through the cracks of the fragmented and glued
   public work.
6. Knowledge work. Public work has too little capability to handle the intangible knowledge work of the Information Age. In
   the Industrial Age, most fragmented work occurred through
   the making and moving of things. Work was easily measured
   and tracked. However, my profitability as a knowledge worker
   cannot be tracked if as an employee I am sitting in my office
   thinking, doing brainwork, or developing ideas. Knowledge
   work must be whole and privatized for its profitability to be
   known.

The division and public ownership of work, therefore, result in
billions of foolish decisions being made each day around the world.
Billions of wasted dollars and priceless wasted potential are inherent
to our system of work, and our deficits grow larger.

The narrow and limited perspective of public work, low intelligence, and the inability to handle knowledge work are critical points
but far too complex to fully explain here. For more detail, see *Profit
and Loss from Fragmented, Divided Public Work, Intangible Wealth
from Fragmented Public Work, Divided Public Work and Low Intelli-*

gence, Fragmented Work, Reality and Quantum Physics at the WinWinWorld.net website at **http://www.winwinworld.net**

REPRESENTATIVE CUSTOMERS ARE NOT REAL CUSTOMERS

When you purchase a product from Wal-Mart, you take a couple of seconds to inspect it. When you get it home, perhaps you inspect it more as you install it. When Insecure Molding sells personal computer backup-tape cartridges to Perspective Supplies, a receiving inspector at Perspective Supplies inspects the incoming product. The inspector is a customer. However, because he is not paying his own real dollars, the receiving inspector has a poor perspective of what is important and what is not. On the basis of experience, the inspector knows that if something gets past him that does not meet official specifications he could be in hot water. Having little idea of the end use of the part, the inspector's motivation is to reject anything for the slightest imperfection.

Perspective Supplies' receiving inspector had repeatedly rejected tens of thousands of protective cases for data cartridges supplied by Insecure Molding. Using a magnifying glass, the inspector had rejected the cases for two or three very tiny air bubbles (virtually invisible with the naked eye) on the bottom leg of the data cartridges. As a consumer who purchased Perspective Supplies data cartridges I had never once looked at the case much less thought of inspecting it with a magnifying glass. As a paying customer I honestly did not care about the case as long as it protected the tape and did not have any obvious cosmetic defects. As a customer, I was more concerned with the irritating and possibly damaging noise that the cartridge made while in use. My Sony cartridges did not make this noise.

Insecure Molding was focusing its limited resources on solving a nonproblem, the bubbles, while the end user's real problem, the noise, went unresolved. Insecure Molding thought it was being customer focused by paying attention only to the needs of the next customer in the chain, the inspector. The problem was that the receiving inspector was not a real customer; he was not paying his money for the product. He was a representative customer who saw only a sliver of the wealth-creation process, and his self-interest was tied only to this narrow, nonaligned sliver. However, because he was in a position of power, the inspector caused the entire supply chain to shift limited resources away from the real customers' real concerns. I have seen inspectors and many other public workers effortlessly jerk entire companies and supply chains around like flies on the end of a whip—making them non–customer focused in the name of being customer focused. Each day around the world supply chains made of many nonowning representatives within many companies waste millions of dollars on things that mean nothing to end users. At the same time they are ignoring the important things. People, like inspectors, do what is in their narrowly focused best interest or face the wrath of insane and convoluted organizing structures.

Companies and supply chains that focus on being directly customer focused when selling to representative customers without at least attempting to collaborate on end users' needs miss the boat of the customer-focused concept. The problem is that no departments or representatives within or outside controlled economies have the perspective or motivation to collaborate on such details.

THE WEAKNESS OF A REPRESENTATIVE FREE MARKET

With our present wealth-creation system, we have a representative free market that corresponds to our representative government. It is part of an entire Industrial Age civilization. With a representative government, politicians represent the owners of the country. In companies, employees represent owners of the company. A representative free market is one in which the majority of customers and suppliers are representatives of real owners and are not themselves the owning customers and suppliers.

Public work, after all, is representative ownership. An employee is paid for her time to represent the owners of a company, just as a politician is paid for her time to represent the owners of a country. Our free market is weak because people are simply much less effective and efficient when they are spending and receiving someone else's money and when interests are not aligned. We easily see and understand this weakness within representative government today. We complain about our representative politicians, but most of us as employees act with equal levels of self-interest, disengagement, narrow vision, lack of passion, and patience with waste and wasted potential in our jobs.

For more details on the representative free market, see *The Personal Journey Continued* at the WinWinWorld.net website at **http://www.winwinworld.net**

CONCLUSION: CENTRALIZED WEALTH CREATION

Most trade in the United States and the industrialized world, perhaps as much as 95%, is intracompany trade. This is trade that occurs as work flows from one worker to another within a controlled economy. The customers and suppliers in these companies are controlled by central planning bureaucrats (managers). It then follows that the United States is probably only about a 5% free-market economy. Instead of being 99.999% centrally command and control, as was the old Soviet Union, the United States is probably 95% command and control. That 5% to 10% of the people *control* 90% of the wealth in our society confirms this probability. It also is validated by the fact that we likely have as many bureaucrats per capita as the Soviet Union had. When we tally all of the managers and supervisors within companies and government agencies (state, local, and federal), the numbers are also likely to be close.

Overall our "fleet-footed" free market is not so free. At microlevel, where people work and wealth is created, we have socialized public work, and centralized bureaucrats control the work. At the median level, the level at which organizations exist and trade with one another, we have a representative free market in which ownerless representatives buy, sell, and trade for organizations. At macrolevel we have a federal government that regulates our system of centrally created wealth. This is in addition to the fact that government directly participates in the wealth-creation process in education, transportation, health care, postal service, and more. We can hardly classify ours as a free-market economy. In reality, we have a society of miniature Soviet Unions partially regulated by a central government.

By any reasonable definition, we must classify our national economy as a central command-and-control economy based on the degree of wealth creation controlled. We have for the past 200 years operated with a system that I call *centralized wealth creation*. This is a system in which the control of wealth creation is centralized under the authority of *relatively* few people.

The controlled economy is the primary social institution that underpins our system of centralized wealth creation. However, our government also is part of our centralized wealth-creation system. In this system, wealth is created in vertically integrated bureaucracy-based organizations and is redistributed to the masses in society through wages, salaries, and taxes.

THE END OF THE COMPANY

As I synthesized the age-wave concept, breakpoint science, the incoming Information Age, the poorly performing fads within bureaucracies, my journey of experience, the realization that companies are weak, miniature Soviet Unions, and that our economy is relatively a central command-and-control system, I was led to the following conclusions:

- Our wealth-creation system, which is based on controlled economies and employment, is too weak for an Information Age in which knowledge is the dominant source of wealth and brains within people's heads are the primary means of production.
- The company and controlled economy will soon cease to exist as the *primary* wealth-creation institution in society, and employment will soon cease to exist as the *primary* means of working.

Slow, continuous improvement, reengineering, reinvention, or reform of public work is not practical without a long-term vision and integration of various concepts with that vision. Though these and many of our other fad programs all take us closer to mass privatization, they are based on the wrong foundation and therefore are quite ineffective. Using only continuous improvement is about as effective as trying to improve plantations in 1858, when the industrial revolution was about to make them obsolete. (There were empowerment and incentive systems tried on plantations near this point [Ball 1999].) There is too much misalignment in the system for it to work. It is no more practical than the reform efforts in the Soviet Union. Those diligently working to "continuously improve" their companies are the Gorbachevs of the West as they attempt to empower people within an organizing structure based on control and disempowerment. Open-book management and empowerment programs are comparable to glasnost—both are the opening of controlled economies. Like Gorbachev, their efforts, though mostly ineffective, are leading us toward breakpoint. Just as Tom Peters (1992) predicted, "thirty-nine of forty managers will be fired."

The collapse of the central-planning monster in the Soviet Union is a forerunner of what is happening in today's corporations and will accelerate in the years directly ahead. As Peter Drucker said, "the Fortune 500 is over" (1992). The controlled, obsessed public work institutions of the Industrial Age lack the capacity for the levels of liberty, ownership, intelligence, and synergy necessary to power today's and tomorrow's civilization and have become dysfunctional relative to our needs. With work lying at the core of our institutions, if our system of work is dysfunctional, nothing else will operate properly.

Within the coming years, the company as we have known it will be all but gone. Companies will either be metamorphosed or crushed and assimilated by the incoming customer-driven free market.

> *As a result of these developments . . . the corporation as we have known it for eighty years will have largely disappeared, its few survivors mostly huddled in dwindling market niches. Those in competitive markets that delay, in some cases even refuse, the process of becoming virtual corporations will be swept away, their remnants seized, reorganized properly and absorbed by fast moving modern competitors.*
> —William Davidow and Michael Malone,
> *The Virtual Corporation*

Some say that it is improbable for change to happen so quickly. The Soviet Union, however, did something far-fetched. No one in 1989, 1990, or even July of 1991 would have guessed that the Soviet Union would disappear overnight, but by the end of 1991 it was gone. Southern plantations and slavery disappeared equally as fast. An entire wealth-creation system was wiped out overnight. Paradigm shifts, breakpoints, and social change stop for no one. Even the most powerful quickly become extinct with the advance.

The end of the company does not mean that people will cease to work together in single buildings with direct person-to-person contact. People will have a choice of working from home, from a single building, from their automobiles, from various locations, from a remote location, or from a combination of these places. People will, in fact, have closer working relationships with more people than ever. The end of the bureaucracy-based, controlled economy does not mean that we will no longer work in organizations. In fact, we are moving toward a society of interconnected organizations.

The end of the company means that the new wealth-creation process will require systems and organizations so different from those of a company that the new institution can no longer be classified as a company by any reasonable definition.

There will be no management, no employees, no central stock ownership, no central control or planning, no bureaucracy, no departments, no salaries, no wages, and no traditional division of labor. The new organization for an Information Age can best be described simply as a community.

The end of companies, controlled economies, and employment as the primary way we work does not mean that there will be no more employees or companies. There will likely be companies, but most people will not work in them. In fact, employees are destined to become the new underclass in society.

PART III

The Emancipation of Capitalism

4

Collaborative Free Markets within Organizations

The Rise of the Mass Privatization Structure

Times such as ours have always bred defeatism and despair. But there remain, nonetheless, some few among us who believe man has within him the capacity to meet and overcome even the greatest challenges of this time. If we want to avoid defeat, we must wish to know the truth and be courageous enough to act upon it. If we get to know the truth and have the courage, we need not despair.

—Albert Einstein

In 1990, after years of effort moving at a snail's pace to make Check-Mate work, things were going great. We had a profitable business. Our sales had held at a 9% hit rate for two years. As long as this figure held, nothing could hurt us. Years of data showed it would take more than an earthshaking catastrophe to make that figure drop. My wife, Linda, and I confidently decided to relocate our small mail-order business to the peaceful Blue Ridge Mountains of Virginia, as we'd planned for years. Two weeks after I announced leaving my day job, it happened. All in one week, Iraq invaded Kuwait, news of recession broke, President Bush and Congress were gridlocked on passing the 1991 budget, and the federal government was on the verge of shutting down. The country went into shock, and our sales hit rate did not simply drop; it plummeted to zero.

The pressure was on, and after I had struggled for years with the paradox of waste and gridlock within traditional companies versus the weakness of building momentum in a small, start-up venture, the answer became clear. Panic and the threat of financial ruin from my business allowed me to see past my paradigms. While reading about Jay Forrester's vision of private work in *Reinventing the Corporation* (Naisbitt and Aburdene 1985, p. 50), I felt as though I'd been shot through the forehead with a brain-piercing, revolutionary epiphany.

We needed a completely new system for organizing work. We needed one that combined the power, size, and momentum of a bureaucracy with the creativity, flexibility, passion, and intelligence of a mom-and-pop operation. Within the bureaucracy, momentum and size were right, but alignment was missing; the opposite was true of "mom-and-pop shops." The kind of alignment we needed in organizations could come only from more ownership throughout the supply chain so that all stakeholders' interests pointed in the same direction. The wealth creators needed to own the specific work they performed and be compensated on the basis of a percentage of this wealth. We needed privatization within the organization on a mass scale, hence mass privatization.

The mass privatization structure creates a win/win condition in which the more one individual wins, the more other stakeholders win.

MASS PRIVATIZATION DEFINED

Today we face the greatest move toward personal responsibility, ownership, and personal power in all of human history. When we synthesize age wave theory with changes in work, business, science, information technology, organizations, and wealth creation, we see a new work and wealth-creation institution emerging—the mass privatization enterprise or community.

I define mass privatization as a wealth-creation organization or community in which individual workers, or a small team of workers, own the *specific* work they perform. These private owners work in partnership with other private owners. Networks of small virtual teams (teamnets) form chains of customers linked through information technology to form powerful global enterprises (Lipnack and Stamps 1993). Teamnets are flexible enough to customize at the individual level while producing *en masse*, hence mass customization. Partners are bound together through a com-

pelling vision and mission and through the alignment that comes from an organizational structure based upon win/win compensation. Internal to the organization, suppliers as partners are compensated directly by their customers. Likewise, internal customers pay their suppliers directly. There are no managers, salaries, bosses, hierarchies, employees, or central controls.

Is mass privatization socialism? No! In socialism the *individual* worker owns nothing. Is it capitalism? No! In capitalism the individual worker does not own the *individual work* performed. Though socialism purports to be a system in which workers own the means of production, and capitalism espouses the right of the individual to own an entire business, neither system supports the *individual's owning the means of production for his or her own work*. Both systems are, however, based on the central control and ownership of work.

Mass privatization is a more coherent wealth-creation paradigm than either socialism or capitalism; it comes from a higher vantage point. It synthesizes the best values of both systems (individual liberty and worker ownership) and ignores the negative methods (authoritarian control and the centralization of ownership). Mass privatization is a wealth-creation organizing structure that both socialist and capitalist would likely embrace. They would both feel as if their views had been proved correct and valid. Ironically, there is also the possibility that either of these people would find mass privatization total heresy.

ORDER ATTAINED THROUGH ALIGNMENT RATHER THAN CONTROL

For centuries humans have attained order through control. However, we confuse control with order. Ask any typical manager and he will tell you that people need to be managed; there have to be rules, laws, and punishment. Control, however, is merely one means to attain order. Alignment is another, more advanced, means, and there are others beyond alignment that we will discover as we mature. For our level of advancement, however, we must have either control or alignment to attain order, as shown in Figure 4–1.

The less an organization is aligned, the more control is required. The more aligned the organization is, the less control is needed. No one, after all, has to monitor the local family-owned, mom-and-pop convenience store to assure the owners are making the best decisions

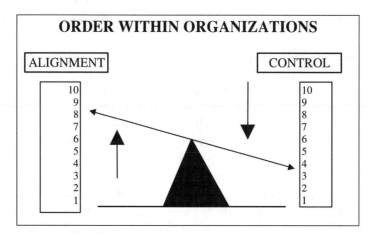

FIGURE 4–1   Order from Alignment Rather than Control

for their business. The problem with order from control is that there is little commitment or engagement on the part of the workers. For today's level of human maturity, alignment is mandatory before empowerment, liberation, and self-direction can effectively occur. Empowerment within organizations without alignment produces disorder, as people's arrows of interest point in various directions. By not understanding the broader, synthesized picture of where change is headed, some companies are trying faddish self-directed team and empowerment programs without alignment. The result is a mess—again I speak from experience. Others, however, are providing alignment in the form of variable-compensation systems such as gain sharing and team-based pay.

Though we need mass privatization, it does seem to be a contradiction in terms (as does the term *mass customization*). Private work is work owned by one person. It would seem, then, that the only way there could be mass work within a single organization would be if it were to be publicly owned. The difference, however, is that today's information technology is beginning to allow individual private workers to network together to form organizations from remote locations—virtual organizations.

CHAOS THEORY: THE SCIENCE SUPPORTING ALIGNMENT

Margaret Wheatley, in her groundbreaking bestseller *Leadership and the New Science* (1992), shows how organizations today operate on principles derived from newtonian science of the seventeenth century, which assumes a fragmented and mechanically controlled universe. The new sciences, such as chaos theory, quantum physics, and complexity theory, have overturned almost all of this old science. Chaos theory and complexity theory show that in complex systems far better order is produced through self-organization than through control.

Neither Wheatley nor myself is the first to discover chaos theory in wealth creation. Adam Smith, in *The Wealth of Nations* 200 years ago, identified the "invisible hand" as the driver of free markets. Smith's invisible hand is chaos theory. Smith showed that free markets and free individuals are best at meeting other people's needs. As people work as liberated agents they automatically provide a system of order.

In the late 1980s, when I lived in Southern California, I sometimes compared the central control of companies with the chaos theory that produced order on Southern California streets, roads, and freeways. Thousands of decisions are made each second regarding turning at intersections, merging at freeway on and off ramps, changing lanes, and pulling into traffic from stop signs. Do I go or do I wait, do I turn or do I not? Decisions are made at the *local level* and based on personal judgment, experience, intuition, creativity, and yes, ownership. Who is better to make the decision regarding whether or to stay or go than the person whose life, family, and personal property are at stake? We make tremendously complex decisions in split seconds with only a glance. We synthesize the speed of oncoming traffic, the distance, our acceleration potential, pedestrian traffic, and many other factors and make correct decisions 99.999999999999% of the time. Out of millions of miles traveled each day in Southern California, there are only relatively few accidents. I used to wonder what would happen if a few bureaucrats controlled all this activity. Suppose they had a massive computer system and attempted to control every decision made by every person on all the roads in Southern California!

As I watched the complexity of decisions being made by just a few cars in my immediate vicinity, I knew the impossibility of the task. There would be thousands or tens of thousands of accidents each day. However, the bureaucrats would track the numbers and declare success with a 98% accident-free rate. Maybe they would eventually install a "continuous improvement" program, improving from 98% to 98.05% over a couple of years and again declare success while patting themselves on the back while thousands of people are being injured and hundreds killed daily. Yet companies worldwide consider the pitiful continuous improvement model perfectly acceptable while external and internal customers receive a mere fraction of the value, service, quality, and customization potential available.

Within companies, "accidents" take the form of human needs' not being met. These are the accidents that destroyed the former Soviet Union. Perhaps the most striking similarity between a company and the former Soviet Union is the degree to which both of these controlled economies consistently failed to meet the needs of the people internal to them. In the end, external customers and all of society pay an enormous price for the wasted potential of control. We pay in poor quality of products and services, a lower standard of living, reduced quality of life, and many other deficits.

Chaos theory is the key to the mass privatization organizing system. Chaos theory has a component known as the *strange attractor* that produces order while giving significant freedom at the individual level. Schools of fish move in harmony while each fish has the freedom and autonomy to go its own way. For the fish, the strange attractor is the safety of numbers and the perplexing patterns created by hundreds of moving fish, which confuse predators.

In organizations the strange attractor (Figure 4–2) acts as a powerful magnet that naturally aligns all stakeholders' arrows of interests. This is not done through force or control but through each individual's own free will, through self-determination, as each individual wins for himself or herself by helping others win. It is done through alignment. In the mass privatization paradigm the win/win knowledge-based structure and compensation system and the caring, shared vision, values, and passion of the individuals within the organization produce alignment and operate as the powerful

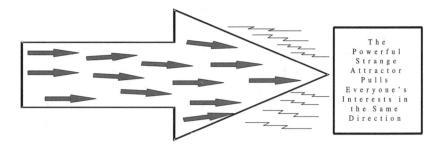

FIGURE 4–2 Alignment in the Mass Privatization Enterprise

strange attractor. In mass privatization I make more money by helping others; the more people I help, the more money I make.

THE TRENDS TOWARD MASS PRIVATIZATION

As my business was sinking and I thought more about mass privatization, I was struck by a jolting thought: mass privatization is what
the market has been demanding. It is where all of the faddish, frantic
business change and hype have been headed over the past 30 years.

The new wealth-creation enterprise is easy to visualize. As
shown in Figure 4–3, all one needs to do is evaluate what business
has been for the last hundred years, compare it with the progressive
changes over the last few decades and years, synthesize the trends,
and extend these trends a few years.

THE HISTORY OF ORGANIZATIONAL OWNERSHIP

As we look over the past hundred years, we see a very specific and
clear long-term trend from centralized wealth creation and controlled economies to decentralized wealth creation and free-market
economies, or mass privatization. Early "smoke-stack" companies
vertically integrated the entire supply chain into one huge self-
contained, controlled economy under the ownership and control of
one person. This was the ideal toward which capitalists strove.

When the Industrial Age, or mass production era, was in its
prime, corporate chiefs such as John D. Rockefeller crushed their

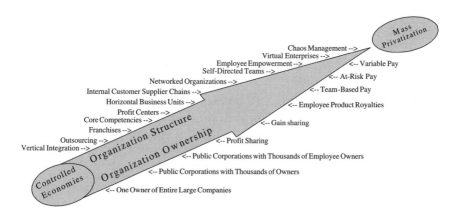

FIGURE 4–3 The Trends toward Mass Privatization

entrepreneurial rivals, drove them out of business, purchased the remains of their businesses, and then hired the former entrepreneurs as controlled and controlling bureaucrats within their companies. The name of the game was to control as much of an *economy* as one could. One of the many entrepreneurs driven out of business and vertically integrated into Standard Oil was forced to become a bureaucrat controlled by Rockefeller. He commented, "This is downright undemocratic, it's an infringement on my freedom." He was exactly right. With vertical integration entire small businesses were bought and broken up. Their resources were put into defined departments or bureaus of specialty (e.g., marketing, production, sales, engineering, quality, and accounting). Vertical integration turned owners into representatives and entrepreneurs into bureaucrats.

Vertical integration disguised customers and suppliers in the supply chain as employees. The Industrial Age was based on the idea of vertical integration. Henry Ford had a factory that was miles long. It had iron ore on one end and automobiles rolling off a production line at the other end. Ford even owned iron mines and rubber plantations.

The history of the ownership of companies at the height of the Industrial Age was one in which an owner like Ford owned the entire supply chain. Over time, free-market forces compelled dilution of ownership into the hands of more individuals through stock ownership. Rather than one owner, there were thousands. Then came employee stock ownership—programs whereby employees owned percentages of companies or even the entire company. Later came profit sharing and franchises. There has been an explosion of variable-pay private ownership or value-added compensation programs. These programs allow individuals to own more directly a percentage of the wealth they produce. They include gain sharing, at-risk pay, team-based pay, and incentive, pinpointing, and bonus programs.

The steps from control to liberation were not necessarily desired by companies and owners. The market demanded them. For example, a public corporation could raise the capital needed to seize opportunity much faster than could a company that attempted to maintain sole ownership and complete control. Through natural selection, the public corporation became the norm. Today it is natural selection that will cause the end of the controlled economy and the rise of the mass privatization organization. Companies like Nucor

Steel and Lincoln Electric have thrived while many in their industries have gone under. A five-year study by the National Center for Employee Ownership concluded that companies with employee ownership and participation financially outperform companies that do not have these two qualities. This is because nonowning employees simply cannot meet customer needs as well as do participating owners.

THE HISTORY OF ORGANIZATIONAL STRUCTURE

Regarding vertical integration, what is occurring today is devertical, or horizontal integration of controlled economies as we move to the horizontal mass privatization structure (see Figure 4–3). Starting with owners such as Rockefeller who owned the entire supply chain, perhaps the initial step toward horizontal integration came with outsourcing. With outsourcing more owning suppliers were introduced into the supply chain. External companies (owning suppliers) rather than controlled bureaucrats performed more of the work of the supply chain. Today no global company owns more than a fraction of a total supply chain; the work of most supply chains is performed by many different suppliers. This shift has occurred because it is more profitable to control less of the wealth-creation process. Companies either horizontally integrated or went out of business. "To be in control today is to be out of control" (Peters 1992).

Perhaps the next big step was franchises. Kentucky Fried Chicken has 10,000 restaurants with many thousands of small-business owners. Franchising involves introducing more real owners in the wealth-creation process in order to expand rapidly to meet customer needs. However, the operations are somewhat outside the control of the founding organization. The other option is slow growth and tighter control. Price Club was the first company to pioneer the brilliant wholesale warehouse concept. It seemed destined to dot the entire U.S. landscape with Price Club warehouses. However, in 1993 it was announced that because of a decrease in earnings, Price Club was merging with Costco. The decline was caused by slow expansion when an onslaught of competition from Sam's Club, Price Savers, Pace, Costco, and the like entered the wholesale warehouse business. The Prices stated that the reason for the slowness and ultimate fall was the moderate pace of expansion that was prudent and necessary to ensure that management had tight control over operations. Today, tight control over operations is a sure road to decline. Again, "to be in control is to be out of control."

In recent years, there has been a flurry of activity toward horizontal integration of controlled economies, including core competencies, profit centers, business units, horizontal organizations, self-directed teams, virtual organizations, network marketing, contract employees, lean manufacturing, and more. All of these concepts move us a step farther away from the control of vertical integration and toward the liberty of free markets. With some of the programs, downsizing is causing many people to leave the bureaucracy to become business owners. With the collapse of the mainframe computer, IBM lost approximately 200,000 of its 400,000 employees. Many of these former bureaucrats and employees are now building and selling computers in their own one-person computer retail stores. The crushing weight of the free market is forcing bureaucrats back into the horizontal supply chain—an exact reversal of vertical integration.

We are emancipating capitalism. Vertical integration turned entrepreneurs into bureaucrats and clerks; horizontal integration turns clerks and bureaucrats into entrepreneurs. Vertical integration might have been mandatory in the mass production era because mass wealth and mass physical resources were required to produce wealth. However, with knowledge as the primary wealth creator, vertical integration is obsolete. Individuals own the knowledge in their heads. By default individuals today own the means of production.

BOOKS AND FADS SHOW THE TREND TOWARD MASS PRIVATIZATION

Books document trends, activity, and thinking in society. Before 1980, the number of business books showing new, progressive thinking and activity was relatively small. It was a period of long stability, and there was little need for new business theories, thinking, or activity. There has been steady growth in business books since the early 1980s, and the growth exploded within the last few years. Since 1990 many new publishers of leading-edge progressive but widely accepted business books have entered the market, including Berrett-Koehler, Executive Excellence, and Butterworth–Heinemann.

It is imperative to understand that each book concerning business or social change represents thousands of hours of thinking, researching, reading, and collaborating focused on a specific issue.

Today's explosion of progressive business books from hundreds of publishers represents virtually all that is presently occurring in business, organizations, and society. When we stop analyzing and step away from the trees to see the forest, things come into focus and mass privatization is clear to see. We are discovering a completely new wealth-creation paradigm one building block at a time.

The key is to be able to synthesize the material being produced and make a holistic picture of the trends. When viewed collectively, the trends almost completely define the mass privatization paradigm. Box 4–1 shows a small sample of the books published in the last few years regarding organizational and social change. Many of the book titles stretch beyond the content of the book. For example, the thought expressed in the title *Businesses without Bosses* is exactly where wealth creation is going. The author, however, does not advocate a new form of business whereby managers and hierarchy do not exist. Although many of the books lack the substance implied in the title, the titles and hype nonetheless show the demand of the market and where we must ultimately go—what controlled economies are unable to completely deliver. A mere review of the titles provides an excellent indicator of the direction and degree of change.

In 1990, when the mass privatization concept clicked in my head, I knew through intuition that it was the answer to our gridlocked system of work. After the weakness I'd witnessed in companies and my own business struggles, I knew that personal ownership was the only way out. In the years while writing this book, I have watched as others discovered bits and pieces of the mass privatization paradigm. I would write about a concept such as alignment, infinite wealth, the death of bureaucracy, or democracy within business, and two months later I would find an entire book on the subject. Because that occurred repeatedly in all segments of society, the evidence for the mass privatization concept became overwhelming. Box 4–1 lists books that point toward mass privatization and a win/win world. This is an abbreviated list limited to only five books per category. A more detailed list is provided under *A Synthesis of Business Book Publishing* at the WinWinWorld.net website at **http://www.winwinworld.net**

The activities documented in the books are being tried in many organizations around the world. If we could take all the activity and synthesize it into one organization, we would have mass privatization.

BOX 4–1   A Synthesis of Business Book Publishing

From Controlled Economies to Free Market Economies: *The End of Bureaucracy, The New Management, Managing without Management, Intrapreneuring, The Age of the Network*

The Shift to Democracy within Organizations: *The Democratic Corporation, Business without Bosses, Democracy in Small Groups, The TeamNet Factor, Virtual Teams*

The End of Rigid and Traditional Jobs and Work: *The Virtual Corporation, The Virtual Community, Jobshift, Virtual Organizations, Going Virtual*

The Move toward Private Work: *GainManagement, The New Pay, Strategic Pay, Wave 3, Compassionate Capitalism, We Are All Self-Employed*

The Dysfunction of Standardized Compensation and Employment: *The Cost of Talent, Violence in the Work Place, Breaking the Mold, The Unnatural Act of Management, Job Shock*

The Dysfunction of Win/Lose Wealth Creation: *When Corporations Rule the World, No Contest: The Case Against Competition, One World Ready or Not, The Death of Competition, Economic Insanity*

The Dysfunction of Controlled Economies: *Why Work Doesn't Work Anymore, Corporate Abuse, Tyranny of the Bottom Line, The Overworked American, The End of Work*

The Shift to Horizontal Integration: *Horizontal Management, Lateral Management, Liberation Management, Demass, Toppling the Pyramids*

The Shift to Knowledge-based Wealth Creation: *Rise of the Knowledge Worker, The Knowledge Evolution, The Knowledge Economy, The Knowledge Value Revolution, Post-Capitalist Society*

The Shift to Intelligence Organizations: *The Intelligent Enterprise, Creating the Intelligent Organization, The Living Organization, The Learning Edge, The Strategic Management of Intellectual Capital*

The Shift from a Sales to a Service Paradigm: *Customers as Partners, Stop Selling Start Partnering, Customer Bonding, Raving Fans, Customers for Life*

From the Mass Production Era to the Mass Customization Era: *Mass Customization, Future Perfect, Differences That Work, Valuing Diversity, The One-to-One Future*

The Shift toward Internal Customers Controlling Wealth Creation: *The Customer Comes Second, What America Does Right, The New Partnership, Chain of Customers, The Human Equation: Building Profits by Putting People First*

The Shift to Spiritual Intelligence in Work: *The Seven Spiritual Laws of Suc-*

cess, *The Soul of Economies, Work as a Spiritual Path, Reawakening the Spirit at Work, The Seven Habits of Highly Effective People*

The Shift to Emotional Intelligence in Work: *Putting Emotional Intelligence to Work, Working with Emotional Intelligence, Emotional Intelligence at Work, Working Beneath the Surface, The Six Pillars of High Self-Esteem*

Radical and Abrupt Shifts in Organizing Systems: *Breakpoint and Beyond, Paradigms, Paradigm Shift, Shifting Paradigms, Discontinuous Change*

The Win/Win of Business Ecology: *Business Ecology, The Bottom Line of Green is Black, The Ecology of Commerce, Lean and Clean, Green Gold*

The Shift to Intuition and Creativity in Work: *Intuitive Imagery, The Competitive Power of Constant Creativity, Corporate Creativity, Imagization, Artful Work*

The Massive Reinvention of Work: *Recreating the Workplace, Recreating the Corporation, Reinventing the Factory, Reinventing the Corporation, The Reinvention of Work*

Toward the Synthesis of Whole Work: *Corporate DNA, Seeing Systems, Corporate Tides, Reengineering the Corporation, Lean Manufacturing*

Toward Win/Win Leadership: *Jesus CEO, Stewardship, A Higher Standard of Leadership, Fusion Leadership, Beyond Counterfeit Leadership*

The Shift to Collaboration: *Organizing Genius, Shared Minds of the New Collaboration, The Power of Partnering, Power Partnering, Breakthrough Partnering*

Organizing Wealth Creation on the Basis of Twenty-first Century Science: *Leadership and the New Science, Strategic Thinking and the New Science, Complexity and Creativity in Organizations, Rewiring the Corporate Brain, Quantum Leaps*

Building a Win/Win World through Wealth Creation: *Building a Win/Win World, The Fourth Wave, The New Paradigm of Business, Visionary Business, Framebreak, The Spirit in Business*

From Finite Wealth to Infinite Wealth: *Creating Affluence, Unlimited Wealth, God Wants You to Be Rich, Friction Free Economy*

The Power Shift to Workers and Buyers from Information Technology: *Future Shop, The Death of Distance, How to Make a Fortune on the Information Superhighway, Digital Economy, GlobalWork*

A Shift to Passionate Work: *Working with Passion, To Build the Life You Want Create the Work You Love, Do What You Love and the Money Will Follow, Who We Could Be at Work, Making a Life while Making a Living*

The Shift to Alignment in Organizations: *The Power of Alignment, Reinventing the Corporation, The Great Game of Business, The Fifth Discipline, The Stake Holder Corporation*

We try bits and pieces of mass privatization by drifting from one fad program to another. This is because of our Industrial Age *analytical* bias. Analysis is a slow and piecemeal thought process that focuses on one thing at a time. We see the activity documented in these books as fad programs, which we try independently. Most fail within controlled economies for the following reasons: (1) mass privatization cannot occur piecemeal, (2) most managers have little vision of what is occurring as they drift from one fad program to another, (3) much of what defines a controlled economy directly opposes the new free-market programs. The very definition, foundation, and core of a controlled economy contradict these concepts.

Two common threads run through all of the activity and fad programs listed in Box 4–1 and Box 4–2. All these programs are customer focused or free-market based. If one simply listens to the terminology of the many management programs, one can easily hear the demands of the market and what controlled economies are unable to provide. The market is asking for a shift within the enterprise from employees to real business owners, real internal suppliers and customer chains, and real partners. Real profit and loss are being demanded instead of salaries, hourly wages, and standardized compensation. The market is dictating a move away from supervisors, hierarchies, regulation, and control to freedom, liberty, and opportunity for all. We might ignore one book or one fad program or even a handful. However, we cannot ignore it when the totality of business publishing and activity point toward mass privatization.

For more detail, see *Vertical Integration and De-Vertical Integration, Holistic and Private Work, Core Demands of the New Wealth Creation, The Emancipation of Capitalism Has Begun* at the WinWinWorld.net website at **http://www.winwinworld.net**

CUSTOMERS ARE THE DRIVING FORCE BEHIND HUMAN LIBERATION

The driving force behind the shift from controlled economies to free-market economies is the natural desire for human freedom. Because of our analysis bias, we seek to separate concepts such as human liberation from business. Today, however, the most powerful branch of the human liberation movement comes directly from customers as they seek more freedom, options, and choices from suppliers.

BOX 4–2 Progressive Management Programs
Showing the Shift to Mass Privatization

Shift from Public Work to Private Work: Gain sharing, variable pay, team-based compensation, at-risk salary, incentive pay for whole work, employee stock ownership, bonus programs, profit sharing, employee product royalties, management by objective

Shift from Vertical to Horizontal Integration: Core competencies, horizontal organizations, outsourcing, downsizing, temporary and contract employees, flattening the hierarchy, inverting the pyramid, decentralization, delayering, internal suppliers and customer chains, intrapreneurs, and reengineering

Shift from Bureaucracy-Driven to Customer-Driven Markets: Virtual organizations, networked organizations, democratic organizations, self-directed and self-starting teams, customer-focused and quality movements, customer-driven organizations, supplier and customer partnering, internal customer and supplier chains, inverting the pyramid, starburst and spider-web organizations, employee empowerment, organizations based on the new sciences, quality circles, continuous improvement, cross-functional teams, employment involvement, value-added work, mass customization, and time-based competition

Shift from Control-based Wealth to Wealth through Liberty: Worker empowerment, alignment, and vision, mission- and principle-based leadership

Shift from Fragmented to Whole Work: Lean manufacturing, just-in-time production, systems thinking, one-piece continuous flow, cellular manufacturing, total quality management, reengineering, business units, horizontal self-directed teams, and cross-functional teams

Shift from Brute Force Work to Knowledge-based Work: Learning organizations, intelligent organizations, knowledge workers, creative organizations, symbiotic organizations

Shift from Win/Lose Competitive Wealth Creation to Win/Win Collaborative Wealth Creation: Partnering, open book management, teams and teamwork, collaboration in work, trust and win/win in business, stakeholder management, wealth creation from increased emotional and spiritual intelligence, theory X and Y

The controlled economy is a system established for a seller's market from a sales paradigm in which sellers controlled the economy. Centralized wealth creation is a foundation on which a relatively few sellers can determine how, where, and when everyone else's needs are met—internal and external customers. We have, in fact, had a bureaucrat-driven market. In a seller's market, the seller mass-produces the same product for everyone regardless of the individual needs. The seller then charges the highest price the market will bear. It is a market in which lead times are long. Sellers produce in large batches at their own pace and convenience. Most customers are controlled by and report to the single, monopolistic seller (the bureaucracy). It is an economy of stability, standardization, and mind-numbing conformity. Quality is sacrificed at the expense of production and productivity. The seller's market organizing system is the foundation on which our industrial society rests.

A seller's market foundation is not inherently bad, just primitive, having been created 200 years ago. As we evolved from the scarcity of the Agricultural Age, buyers were glad to get whatever they could. Technology and human advancement were limiting factors. In 1800, typical Americans had fewer than 300 products to choose from in their hometowns. Things have changed. Today we have many suppliers and many choices. The average American has easy access to more than one million products and many suppliers for most products. An average supermarket alone carries 25,000 products. Wal-Mart superstores carry 110,000 different items (Snider and Ziporyn 1992). However, our advanced technology, our production and wealth-creation systems, and all of society still rest on a rusty, primitive, bureaucracy-based foundation—the seller's market.

Controlled economies might somewhat effectively manage a few dozen products and a few employees, mass-producing the same thing for everyone. Today we are asking them to effectively organize tens of thousands of products and people and to begin customizing for each individual customer.

It boils down to a matter of complexity. If companies were countries, we would easily recognize the absurdity of central planning. In 1989 General Motors ranked as the twentieth largest economy in the world on the basis of economic output. In fact, in 1989, 47 of the world's largest 100 economies were corporations, not countries (Ackoff 1994).

Today we know that countries are too complex to be run with systems of central planning and control. We spent trillions opposing centrally planned communism. We must come to understand that this is true of companies as well. How can we philosophically oppose a controlled economy such as Cuba or North Korea and

simultaneously support the systems of larger controlled economies such as General Motors, IBM, and AT&T?

Americans used to wonder why tens of millions of Soviet citizens supported a system that systematically limited their freedom and wealth opportunity. Yet we do exactly the same thing, because we believe in companies as our primary wealth-creation institution. This shows the difficulty of attaining perspective within a paradigm.

At its core, centralized wealth creation evolved for a low-tech, low-information, stable, stationary, illiterate, ignorant population with simpler and smaller systems. Today the population is educated, mobile, versatile, and informed. Society also has become more unstable, complex, interconnected, global, diverse, automated, and advanced. As things change and evolve from the primitiveness of an early-stage industrial economy, a seller's market foundation can be stretched only so far toward a buyer's market foundation.

If an economy truly had a buyer's market foundation, customers would control it (this includes internal customers, today's employees). Customers would have seemingly infinite choices and receive customized goods and services made specifically to their desires and receive them immediately with zero lead time.

With the advent of the customer and quality movement sparked by Japan in the 1970s and 1980s, the seller's market foundation has begun to crack. What the Japanese sparked has become a global state of chaos. At least one new progressive management program is introduced each week to better meet customer needs. With each failing program, the cracks in the foundation grow larger as customer needs continue to accelerate and go unmet. Though progress is being made, it is too slow and falls short of customers' needs. We normally do not notice this shortfall because we are not really concerned with meeting customer needs. Because of the win/lose competitive paradigm, we are concerned only with being a step ahead of the competition at meeting our customers' needs. Entire value streams involving dozens and hundreds of companies miss the mark regarding what customers really want (Womack and Jones 1996).

Today the information superhighway threatens to explode the cracked Industrial Age foundation and establish a new foundation. As it opens global markets and puts the mom-and-pop shops on equal footing with large corporations, the information superhighway becomes the foundation for mass privatization.

MASS PRIVATIZATION VIA THE INTERNET

For the task of restructuring companies and whole industries to survive in the super-symbolic economy is not a job for nit-picking, face-saving, bean-counting bureaucrats. It is, in fact, a job for individualists, radicals, gut fighters, even eccentrics—business commandos, as it were, ready to storm any beach and seize power.

—Alvin Toffler, *PowerShift*

Any time two individuals exchange information or knowledge there has been a trade and wealth has been created. If these people are not employees and not acting on behalf of an employer then this is a private trade. When the 3,000 private individuals of New Civilization Network (NCN) exchange information, knowledge, and wisdom (wealth) through their discussion forums, relay chats, or e-mails, this is mass privatization. This is true whether or not money exchanges hands, since there is consideration. Though NCN has some monetary trade, the structure as of this writing has not yet been established to facilitate monetary exchanges. As this structure is implemented the members of New Civilization Network will begin trading on a massive scale using many mediums of exchange, including knowledge, money, E-Gold (private capital), and electronic barter with both internal and external customers. NCN will then be a fully functioning mass privatization community of tens of thousands of private wealth creators complete with products and services for internal and external customers.

Today there are tens of thousands of people on-line connecting and openly building a new civilization based upon mass privatization organizing principles. Flemming Funch, founder of NCN with thousands of members, says he desires building the foundation for a new civilization. James North of the Uni-v.e.r.s.e. Network of a hundred members is busily building a mass privatization community. North says, "I'm here to see that the new civilization happens through mass privatization." There are tens of thousands of others equally as determined and leading the building of the new world. Debra Amidon has thousands of "private work" partners in her Entovation Network helping to develop the knowledge tools of the new win/win world. There is also Frank Wallace with Neo-Tech, Frederick Mann with Free World Order, Allen Says with The Internet Marketing Warriors, E-Gold, New Utopia, Landmark, Free-Market.net, Laissez Faire City, and hundreds of others (North 1999).

Sure, many of these people will have great failures, however, the planet has never before had billions of people with the freedom to connect and freely organize as desired—to experiment wildly and boldly, requiring little dollar investment capital but with huge potential returns. Out of the millions of failures there will be millions of successes, and through passion and trial and error these millions of successes will help bring about the new civilization.

FROM A MASS PRODUCTION TO A MASS CUSTOMIZATION WORLDVIEW

> *The mass production system has run out of steam on the threshold of the twenty-first century. Its downfall is the fact that the American marketplace is no longer made of interchangeable customers. . . . The old mass production system must be replaced. . . . While a hierarchy allows management to control a stable, predictable Mass Production shop, it is the exact opposite of what is needed to empower a flexible, responsive workforce that is faced with a constantly changing marketplace. Mass-Customized businesses thrive on flattened hierarchies that give autonomy to groups. Each of these groups shares information through communications networks so that each group is constantly aware of what it must do to respond to the new needs of the customer. . . . Believe it or not, flattening the hierarchy is the simple approach. The most drastic structural innovation is to shatter it into independent pieces.*
> —Joseph Pine, *Mass Customization*

The shift from a seller's to a buyer's market foundation is far more than a shift in production systems. It is a shift from the entire mass production foundation on which civilization rests. Everything from representative democracy to factory-style schools to manufacturing to our view of justice to civil rights to competitive sports is based on the outdated mass production paradigm. The shift from mass production will mean the end of all of these institutions. We are shifting to a customer-driven civilization based on a new foundation of mass customization. As shown on the age-wave chart (see Figure 6–1 in

Chapter 6), society has begun to shift from a mass production to a mass customization system of production.

Mass customization is exactly what it says: producing in volume but at the same time giving each customer something different according to his or her unique needs. With mass production everyone receives the same thing regardless of individual needs. Mass customization not only is a new system of production but also forms a new worldview. In this new worldview, our notions of fairness and equality are challenged as we come to understand that no two persons' needs are exactly the same. Equality, the cornerstone of representative democracy, in which all are created equal and must receive equal treatment, loses its meaning. It is a given in industrialized societies today that no person is superior to another. Equality is merely a mass-production notion, the goal of which is to give everyone the same average treatment. People, however, have very different needs. Mass production then means that people will not have their needs met. Mass production is based on homogenous averages and majorities because at its core it is based on reducing variation while stabilizing, controlling and mass-producing the same thing thousands of times. In addition, mass production not only does not need diverse brainpower but also cannot tolerate it.

The focus of mass customization is on meeting individual customers' unique needs. We are shifting to a new civilization that operates through customization, variation, creativity, chaos, and diversity. A mass customization era will thrive and flourish on diversity, diverse brainpower, and creativity. If suppliers are going to customize to meet infinite variations of customer needs, they will need an infinite diversity of creative intelligence to do so. The more variation the better. This can only come when widely diverse people, six billion strong, control the wealth-creation process. Comparing mass customization with mass production, we find the latter was and is controlled by one very small minority—middle-aged white men. It simply does not take a lot of diverse intelligence to ignore specific, diverse needs and mass-produce the same product millions of times.

Business managers and political leaders can be as brilliant as Einstein, as creative as Leonardo da Vinci, as results-oriented as Attila the Hun, as honest as George Washington, and have the political leadership skills of Lincoln and Jefferson combined. Still, centralized wealth creation would not be capable of meeting the market demands of a mass-customized market. The collective intelligence is too low and too limited. The complexity of the market and its size pit the brains of a relatively few bureaucrats against the individual, unique, unpredictable, moody, subjective, changing, and intuitive needs of billions of people.

There is only one force on earth with the intelligence, knowledge, flexibility, and capacity to manage wealth creation to meet these needs. This is the collective, diverse brainpower of the billions of individuals who own, plan, and control work and wealth creation at the local level.

The intelligence found in diversity is the trait of the new mass-customization era that not only will end racial, sexual, and human division but also will cause us to embrace and thrive on diversity. As mass customization flourishes through the freedom of mass privatization enterprises, we will begin to see the end of racial division and racism as people begin thriving on diversity as millions of fortunes are made. Those millions of minorities now seeking opportunity from a mass production system, through affirmative action or not, are on a hopeless quest.

The new civilization is one that at its roots will drive people to help, understand, and partner with others very different from themselves, because this produces more intelligence and wealth for themselves. Meeting others' needs is already driving wealth creation in an infant Information Age. As we continue down this path, wealth creation becomes the driving force for human understanding, tolerance, empathy, and harmony.

The shift from a seller's to a buyer's market, the shift from mass production to mass customization and the ramifications for human growth, and the end of racial division, human division, and hatred are subjects deep enough for books of their own.

For more detail see *Seller's to Buyer's Market Transition, Mass Customization, The End of Racial and Human Division, The Death of the Bureaucrat as Customer, Increased Quality to the Individual, Core Demands of the New Wealth Creation* at the WinWinWorld. net website at **http://www.winwinworld.net**

THE INTELLIGENCE NEEDED FOR MASS CUSTOMIZATION

With knowledge as the primary creator of wealth in the Information Age, business enterprises must have the ability to foster very high levels of intelligence and must themselves be extremely intelligent. A company in which one person reports to another and in which standardized compensation is provided is specifically designed to have the people toward the top do the thinking. There is fragmentation and a division of labor between thinking and doing. With a few people at the top doing the thinking and the masses at the bottom doing the actual work, we have a dumb organization. There simply are not enough brains thinking. Milliken, the textile manufacturer, like many in the South, at one point actually called its production workers "hands." As we move toward mass privatization, Milliken began calling workers employees and now calls its employees *associates*.

Though companies like Milliken have taken steps to become intelligent organizations, they, like all other controlled economies, can have only limited success. This is because of the inherent limitations of the controlled economy and the piecemeal approach to change. There are limits to which most nonowning *public workers* will engage their minds. There also are limits to the amount of thinking and creativity that a controlled economy can tolerate when variation is its enemy at heart. Ask any manager how best to produce quality or maintain order in a bureaucracy, and he or she will tell you that it is done by continuously reducing variation.

Because of the inherently low intelligence of controlled economies, in which the thinking is done at the top, the intelligence quotient of a company is only a fraction of the sum of all of the individual employees' IQs. It is a system in which $1 + 1 = 0.1$. Most of the intelligence of an organization lies with the frontline employees, simply because this is where most of the brains are. If one assumes, as most managers do, that managers are smarter than frontline employees, one finds that a company of 200 frontline employees with an average IQ of 100 points has a total frontline employee IQ of 20,000, not including any synergistic effect. A controlled economy with seven very smart managers with an average IQ of 125 and a CEO with an IQ of 150 has a collective management IQ of 1,025.

Including supervisors, engineers, and other specialists, the collective IQ of those doing the thinking, managing, directing, and controlling is 2,935. The IQ ratio between the "hands" and the "brains" is out of whack. The less intelligent (IQ 2,935) collective is thinking for, directing, and controlling the far more intelligent (IQ 20,000) collective. The subordinate, passionless, ownerless position given public workers renders the bulk of employee brainpower mostly useless.

Though steps are being taken to involve and empower employees, it is too little too slow. Customer needs are not met, and untold potential is wasted.

The Industrial Age operated with this dumb organization scheme because it did not take a lot of intelligence to mass-produce at the seller's pace and desire. It does, however, take a great deal of intelligence to produce at billions of individual customers' paces and desires. The dumb mass production–based controlled economy therefore is exactly the wrong organizing system and foundation for a knowledge era, in which ideas and knowledge create the bulk of wealth in society.

As we move to an era in which knowledge is the ultimate wealth creator, it is reasonable that organizations of the future operate as brains, because the brain creates knowledge. When my son, Travis, was five years old, he saw CheckMate's starburst (Quinn 1992, p. 148) organizational structure (Figure 4–4) and said, "Hey, cool. Neural connections!"

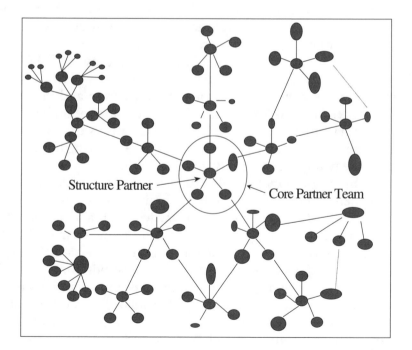

FIGURE 4–4   The Starburst Organizational Structure of Mass Privatization

At that point I knew the starburst was an appropriate organizational structure for a chaotic, knowledge-based Information Age. When we look at the neural network of the brain we see the same basic pattern as the starburst organization. This is no coincidence. The organization of the present and future must be a naturally evolving, learning organism. It must resemble the functions of a brain, including synergy, parallel processing, logical thinking, intuition, creativity, and freedom of thought and expression.

The brain is made up of about 28 billion neurons, or nerve cells. Neurons are tiny biological computers that, like personal computers, work through electrical impulses. They are capable of processing about 1 million bits of information per second. The brain uses what equates to about 6,000 miles of wiring for each neuron. Though neurons in the brain act independently, they also communicate with other neurons through a network of nerve fibers. Each person has about 100,000 miles of nerve fibers through the body (Robbins 1991). When we learn something, we create a physical connection between neurons called a *neural connection*.

Intelligence is determined by the number of paths of information between neurons. According to the National Academy of Sciences there are more possible connections in your brain than the total number of atomic particles in the entire universe (WOW!) (McCarthy, 1992). The more neural connections we have in our brains, the more intelligence we have to draw from and the more intelligent we are. The simple act of sharing information between two or more neurons creates intelligence. The same is true with people in organizations. Information technology is allowing humans to connect like neurons in a rapidly growing brain.

The brain uses what is called *parallel processing*, which is what gives it such power. Even though the brain takes a million times longer to send a signal than a computer switch, the brain can spread a signal to hundreds of thousands of other neurons in less than 20 milliseconds. Most computers operate on the basis of one-step-at-a-time serial processing, as does most of the activity within controlled economies. This is what makes bureaucracies and computers relatively slow. Parallel processing is simply the notion that several brains, neurons, computers, or computer-processing chips can work on a problem at the same time from different perspectives. When a number of people with aligned motives have aligned incentives to communicate openly, parallel processing and synergy can naturally occur in organizations and society.

Synergy, knowledge, and intelligence are created when neurons communicate with each other in a brain. Likewise synergy, knowledge, and intelligence are created when people communicate with each other within an organization or society. In the organization, as in the brain, the more neural connections there are, the more parallel processing there is. This means there are more communications and more intelligence; therefore more wealth is created. When aligned incentive for communication and connections is provided and enabled in a system such as mass privatization, the communication, gross intelligence, and wealth of the group increase.

When it comes to intelligence, diversity is the key component that creates intelligence. As Don Carew, coauthor of *The One-Minute Manager Builds High Performance Teams* says, "If two people on a team think alike, then one of them is not needed" (1995). If all brains in one network think basically alike, there will be fewer neural firings, less brain stimulation, fewer perspectives, and less intelligence created than in a network with more diverse brains. Fewer ideas will be produced, and the ideas will be less varied than in a network with more variety.

Organizations of the future must be designed for maximum development of neural connections. The system must have natural alignment toward building and creating more and better neural connections and diversity and have incentives for parallel, chaotic, free, and massive flow of information. As Alvin Toffler says, "When information flows, cash flows" (Toffler 1990).

The structure of a controlled economy inherently inhibits the free and chaotic flow of information needed for a truly intelligent organization. Companies as controlled economies cannot become intelligent organizations because of control. Even concepts such as open-book management can have only limited success in controlled economies. After all, at the core of a controlled economy is control, including control of information flow. It is critical to understand that control is the very heart of the controlled economy and bureaucracy. When enough control is eliminated to produce an intelligent organization, we no longer have a company by today's definition. We have mass privatization. Without control, there is no notion of management, employees, salaries, or any other of the very elements that define a company.

Because of control, even companies making a genuine effort to be intelligent organizations are tapping only the smallest percentage of their potential. Only through a system such as mass privatization, whereby individuals are free to and have the motivation to engage and dig deep, to freely connect, communicate, and collaborate with one another, can organizations produce the intelligence to meet customers' unique and customized needs.

5

The Workings of Mass Privatization via the New Sciences

The Organizing Structure for the Information Age

The world will not evolve past its current state of crisis by using the same thinking that created the situation.
—Albert Einstein

The company needs a complete metamorphosis to have the intelligence and motivation required to accommodate the demands of individual customers in a mass customization era. The changes are massive and comprehensive. They are so complete that by any reasonable definition, the company will no longer be a company once it has changed enough to meet customer demands. There will be no company left, and definitely not a controlled economy, once we

- Have changed compensation to have it flow from customer to supplier.
- Are truly customer driven and not management driven.
- Are true partners networked together in win/win arrangements.
- Truly have self-directed teams and horizontal, networked organizations.
- Truly operate on chaos theory.

There will be no company left because bureaucracy, employees, management, wages, salaries, and central control are what define a company. Two core components of the mass privatization enterprise differentiate it from a control economy—the compensation system and the organizing structure. People are compensated directly on the basis of the value they add for others as opposed to receiving standardized compensation for their time in the form of salaries or wages. People work in personal, partnered relationships as opposed to impersonal, subordinate relationships.

COMPENSATION SYSTEM

Compensation is structured in limitless ways within mass privatization. The methods include much of what is being tried today in companies—gain sharing, at-risk pay, employee product royalties, bonus systems, network marketing, team-based pay, variable pay, pinpointing, and much more. However, all mass privatization compensation systems have the two following key components:

- Individuals or small teams, in one form or another, receive compensation in direct proportion to the value they add or wealth they create for customers and partners.
- Individuals keep a percentage of the income they produce, and they accept losses incurred.

Mass privatization is a win/win system whereby the more value individuals and teams add for customers and partners, the more compensation they directly receive.

For more detail on private compensation systems, see *Private Compensation Systems* at the WinWinWorld.net website at **http://www.winwinworld.net**

ORGANIZATIONAL STRUCTURE

A company or controlled economy is public work, and public work is bureaucracy. A two-person bureaucracy in which one person reports to the other has the same negative traits as a 5,000-person bureaucracy. As Tom Peters (1992) has said, "Any organization with more than four people is a hopeless bureaucracy." When we analyze a bureaucracy by taking it apart, as depicted in Figure 5–1, we find

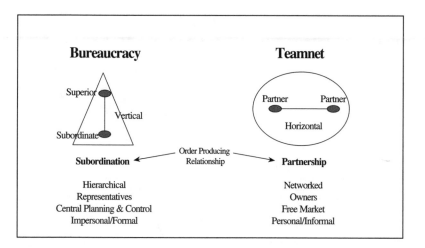

FIGURE 5–1   Bureaucracy versus the Teamnet Analyzed

an *authoritarian* relationship based on *domination* and *subordination*. The subordinate or "inferior" must report to the "superior" and be controlled because of the lack of ownership in the specific work performed. Without ownership there must be some means of accountability; in the representative bureaucracy, accountability comes through subordination.

At the core of the mass privatization organization (the starburst structure) are teamnets, or networks of teams (see Figure 4–4 in Chapter 4). These are virtual groups of partners who are overlapped and interconnected with other partners and teams. Teamnets come together, work on projects, disband, and reformulate as needed. The relationship that we find at the core of the teamnet is *partnership* (Figure 5–1).

Teamnets have the intelligence and flexibility of a mom-and-pop shop and the size, power, and momentum of a traditional bureaucracy. As depicted in Figure 5–2, when we synthesize the subordinate relationship we produce a full-blown bureaucracy. When we synthesize the partner relationship, we produce a teamnet, or starburst, organization.

With a teamnet, a structure partner forms a partnership with a core group of individuals to form the core team of the organization (see Figure 5–2). Core team members form their own team of partners, and each partner forms a partnership with his or her own team of partners. The starburst structure continues to expand until it

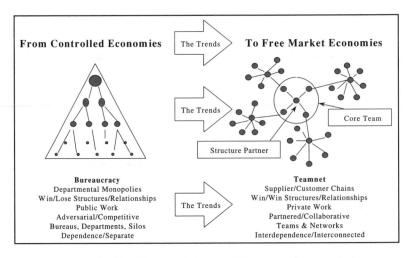

FIGURE 5-2 The Synthesized Cores of Bureaucracy versus the Teamnet

reaches a natural limit. There are so many chaotic connections between various teams and partners that they cannot be effectively depicted in Figures 4–4 and 5–2.

TEAMNETS AND THE "SYNTHESIS OF WHOLE WORK"

The teamnet concept has us moving toward a new, more powerful means of organizing work away from division of labor. I've labeled it the synthesis of whole work. Applied Computer of Anaheim, California, is a virtual enterprise. The virtual enterprise is a new organizational type based on extreme flexibility, core competencies, outsourcing, partnering, and constantly changing relationships (Davidow and Malone 1992). Ted Diab, owner and founder of Applied Computer, has completely reversed the division of labor and made work whole again. He is the only worker in his own corporation. He is marketing representative, salesperson, president, CEO, accountant, janitor, production line operator, test technician, programmer, field service representative, quality inspector, and friend all in one. In 1994 the fastest growing segment of the economy was one-person enterprises such as Applied Computer.

With his system of whole work, Ted gets to interact with all of the aspects of the wealth-creation process. With the divided work of controlled economies, all employees interact with mere fragments of the wealth-creation process. Margaret Wheatley writes the following in *Leadership and the New Science* (1992) regarding quantum physics, perspective, and employee interactions with work:

> In quantum logic it is impossible to expect any idea to be real to employees if they do not have the opportunity to interact with it. Reality emerges from our process of observation, from decisions we the observers make about what we will see. It does not exist independently of those activities. There-fore, we cannot talk people into reality because there truly is no reality to describe if they haven't been there. People can only become aware of the reality of the plan by interacting with it, by creating different possibilities through their personal processes of observation.

Charlotte Shelton, in *Quantum Leaps,* says in regard to quantum physics and organizations: "At the subatomic level, the parts do not determine the behavior of the whole. Rather, the whole determines the behavior of the parts." With newtonian-based analysis the parts determine the behavior of the whole (machines work this way). We try to make organizations work like machines through bureaucracy. With quantum-based synthesis the whole determines the behavior of the parts. Organizations naturally work this way regardless of how we try to control them as machines.

We, therefore, cannot get individuals in bureaucracies to behave as we desire because the whole organizing structure of frag-mentation, limited vision, limited motivation, and limited owner-ship motivates their individual behaviors. **Human organizing structures determine perspective and perception. Perspective and perception create reality, and reality motivates behavior.** Motiva-tion, reality, alignment, and organizations are all about perspective and this is what quantum physics is about. From what perspective is one experiencing a situation? In bureaucracy everyone's perspective is always "intentionally" fragmented. In mass privatization every-one is always coming from a whole organization's perspectives.

With bureaucracy we think by placing people in the right posi-tions with the right titles and job descriptions and proper checks and balances (all of the pieces of the machinery defined) the whole bureau-cracy will function properly. It never has and never will because the whole misaligned, fragmented system causes people to see different realities and behave in undesirable ways. The checks and balances work poorly because they are unnatural. Supervising people, auditing people, writing people up, and firing them are unnatural acts. Managers routinely go for years without addressing performance and behavioral issues because managing people is so unnatural.

Individuals within companies create wealth through their work. Because the whole process, including the details, is not within the perspective of any of the employees, including management, the resultant decisions and actions are far less than optimal. I have worked in manufacturing environments in which improper electrical assembly by a production worker could kill a customer. When I've mentioned this fact to production workers responsible for assembly, they've been shocked (no pun intended). After many years building the product, they were not aware of the gravity of their work. Likewise, managers have little idea of the real-world details of frontline work, though most think they do. Instead they live in a vague, abstract world of numbers, graphs, and charts that poorly represent reality. There also are segmented bureaus of specialty in which employees continually debate their individual perspectives, such as engineering, production, quality, marketing, and accounting.

Ted's work is powerful because from his perspective he sees and experiences the *whole* wealth-creation process. Because of his perspective, Ted is truly, deeply, and intelligently customer focused. It allows Ted and me to have a long-term relationship I classify as a partnership on the basis of Chip Bell's definition in *Customers as Partners* (1994). Bell says real partnerships must be based on abundance, trust, dreams, truth, balance, and grace.

Partnerships

- A customer partnership is a living demonstration of an attitude or orientation. Powerful partnerships are anchored in an attitude of generosity, a giving perspective in which there is pleasure in extending the relationship beyond simply meeting a need or requirement.
- Powerful partnerships are grounded in trust. Partners don't spend energy looking over their shoulders but take a leap of faith and rely on the relationship.
- Powerful partnerships are bolstered by a joint purpose. Although this purpose is rarely written down, each partner is enfolded in a vision or dream of what the association could be and a commitment to take the relationship to a higher plane.

- Powerful partnerships are coalitions laced with honesty. Truth and honesty are seen as tools for growth rather than devices for disdain. Partners serve each other straight talk mixed with compassion and care.
- Powerful partnerships are based on balance. In the pursuit of equality, however, one seeks stability over time rather than absolute encounter-to-encounter equilibrium.
- Powerful partnerships are grounded in grace. The spirit of partnership has an artistic flow that gives participants a sense of familiarity and ease.

Bell shows the kind of partnerships we must have in our wealth-creation relationships. I can trust Ted's advice 100%. The value Ted adds above what any controlled economy could ever produce comes from trust, honesty, and integrity—the wealth-creation norms for the new era. Ted's whole work is the foundation for the substantive laws of the farm in the new organizing system. There is no whitewashing of performance results with phony laws-of-the-school activity at the end of the week as employees and managers do. There is either a profit or a loss. There is also good reason not to kill the goose, long term, merely to get the golden eggs, short term, as many employees do. This is because Ted is very concerned about the very long-term health of his business.

Ted certifies his suppliers, as any large corporation would. He assembles, tests, and services his own computers. He qualifies components. His logo and personal computers look as handsome as Apple's, IBM's, or anyone else's. Without even knowing it Ted is on the leading edge of organizational change. His performance would make the most progressive companies appear decades behind. Ted has the ultimate horizontal and virtual organization. He has the ultimate gain-sharing system. He has the ultimate one-piece flow process using lean-manufacturing and just-in-time principles. With nearly zero inventory Ted takes an order for a customized computer, builds it, and ships it within 24 hours. He sees customers as partners, lives the seven habits of highly effective people, and works beneath the surface.

Without reading any fad business books, attending any seminars, or paying any consultants, Ted is doing the things larger organizations are paying consultants millions to teach them one fragmented piece at a time. Most companies struggle years and decades to make minor gains. Ted has done these things near their maximum potential because these things are natural to whole and private work.

Ted has unlimited flexibility, because he is a one-person virtual corporation. There is no way any fragmented organization can match Ted's service, quality, trust, or partnering. As the mammoth IBMs in the computer industry have downsized or gone belly up, thousands of Teds have sprung up. Most towns have at least one. Before development of the personal computer, the computer industry was vertically integrated like most others.

The tens of thousands of independent Teds are collectively mass customizing hundreds of thousands of computers and producing billions of dollars in income. Each outlet custom builds and ships one ordered unit at a time. Collectively they are likely shipping more units than some of the largest computer makers. At some point, these thousands of virtual corporations will begin to network with one another on the information superhighway for leverage and synergy, producing mass privatization. At present Ted's only disadvantage is price and name-brand recognition.

As Ted links with thousands of others into a single mass privatization community, he and the partners could agree to purchase X thousand motherboards, hard drives, and monitors per year on blanket purchase orders. They then would be able to match the prices of the large controlled economies. They also would have global name-brand recognition. They would be able to match price and brand equity with the big boys and would be far superior in all other aspects of business. This includes partnering and intraorganizational collaboration, customization, speed (lead times and response times), service, organizational intelligence, diversity, flexibility, perspective, wholeness, passion, trust, ownership, and far more.

As mass privatization organizations arise composed of thousands of Teds formed into teamnets, business units, and global communities, we move away from the newtonian division of labor. We shift to synthesis of whole work. This is where *whole* businesses come together to form larger whole businesses and then these wholes form even larger wholes. This is a quantum physics worldview. Division is about fragmentation; synthesis is about wholeness.

For more on the synthesis of whole work, see *Synthesis of Whole Work* at the WinWinWorld.net website at **http://www.win winworld.net**

As we view the situation with Applied Computer and thousands of people like Ted, we see that today we are very close to mass privatization. In the computer industry, we mostly lack the vision to pull the organization together.

If the mass privatization enterprise is so powerful, why has no organization gone all the way with it? Many organizations are performing bits and pieces and some are performing entire blocks of mass privatization, as documented in hundreds of books. A few organizations are very close to mass privatization. Some network marketing organizations are all the way there but only in sales and marketing. There are many mass privatization networks developing on the Internet that are operational and growing at lightning speed as shown in Chapter 4. You can join them or wait to become the plantation owners of the Information Age.

The question, however, still remains. If mass privatization is such a great deal for everyone, then why isn't there a mad rush to mass privatization? Well, why did plantation owners stay with plantations when industry was far more profitable and humane? In short, momentum, inertia, paradigms, complacency, low self-esteem, analysis bias, and the desire to control from fear, lack of vision, and limited technology all restrain us. However, as information technology reaches a critical breakpoint, we all will be thrust into the new system at the speed of light. When one organization in one industry either converts to or starts a mass privatization community, the entire industry will fall as dominoes, one company at a time. They will be forced out of business or forced to privatize. This precedent is occurring with virtual organizations such as Amazon.com, the world's largest bookstore. Barnes and Noble, Borders, and the entire industry are now rapidly going virtual.

THE AMAZON.COM MASS PRIVATIZATION REVOLUTION

Amazon.com has thousands of associates, private workers, who sell Amazon books through their associates' websites. These are true mass privatization partnerships where work has been made whole, as each partner is the owner of a whole business. Partners receive 15% on any specific book purchased through the partners' websites and 5% on each book purchased when a customer enters Amazon.com through the partners' sites.

The Amazon.com associate program is a tangible example of mass privatization. There are no managers and employees, salaries and wages, or policy manuals and rulebooks. Amazon.com is an established organization with thousands of virtual on-line bookstores operating as partnering associates. Each of these bookstores operates in individual niches—areas of special expertise. These partners are able to add value that simply could not be added by Amazon employees, any bookstore employees, or through any bureaucracy. This is true whether the bookstore's niche is win/win wealth creation, American Indian history, new age spirituality, model airplane building, rock climbing, romance, conservative politics, or any of a thousand other topics.

Mass privatization is about individuals being able to easily add value onto what an organization with momentum is already doing, while costing the individual and the organization virtually no investment capital. I found out about the associate program on January 10, 1999, and took twenty minutes to read the agreement and ten minutes to complete the application. Amazon.com approved the application and I had a functioning bookstore, with 4.7 million books for sale, up and running within 24 hours. There was no dollar investment capital required and my only investment was time.

The value that I add through my bookstore comes from recommendations regarding which books add value to the building of win/win wealth creation and a win/win world as well as how these books synthesize together. Likewise there are thousands of others with special expertise. In order for a traditional bookstore to offer a comparable service it would need to hire thousands of experts in thousands of fields. Even if they had the capability to hire these thousands of employees, which is impossible, there is no pool of employees to hire from for many of the niches. These controlled economies definitely could not develop this specialized, diverse, and nonstandardized expertise internally.

Without costing Amazon a penny of investment capital, Amazon has leveraged its position—reaching out to the free market for expertise that it cannot create through the control of bureaucracy. Amazon has won by increasing its sales, size, growth, and profits. Amazon associates have won by doing what they love while being compensated for it. Associates have also won by utilizing knowledge that they already have and leveraging on to what an established organization is doing, thus taking virtually no risk to start a business. Amazon customers have won by getting the passionate expertise and recommendations of the Amazon associates while receiving Amazon's huge discounts.

TED AND THE COLLAPSE OF TIME AND SPACE

Information technology, specifically the information superhighway, is the primary enabler of mass privatization. It has not reached the point at which it makes face-to-face communication *human* enough to compel mass privatization. We humans need real person-to-person communication to work together effectively from varied distant locations. Communication by means of telephone only uses one of our five senses—hearing. With the Internet we only have the written word and extremely limited use of hearing and sight through teleconferencing.

At some point in the near future Ted will have access to the tens of thousands of other Teds with direct face-to-face communication through the highly publicized information superhighway. Internet and teleconferencing technology will be integrated and more widely used. However, the information superhighway will also include the highly humanizing virtual reality and holographic technologies. These two integrated technologies will move us away from talking to one another through two-dimensional computer monitors to almost complete, person-to-person, three-dimensional communication, in which we fully use our senses of sight and hearing. Though mass privatization is possible today, virtual reality and holographic technologies combined with others will compel mass privatization. The information superhighway will be a synthesis of a vast array of information technologies, including the Internet, the World Wide Web, fiber optics, wireless technology, voice recognition, computer technology, virtual reality, language translation software, holographic technologies, telephone, television, interactive television, VCR, fax, and digital technology, and many more.

Ted and his partners will NOT be sitting in front of monitors talking to each other through a computer and computer screen. They will be having person-to-person contact through holographic, virtual reality, networked computer systems. Like *Star Trek*'s "holodeck," people will see and talk to others as though they are sitting in the same room, though they are thousands of miles away. The partners will appear to each other to be in the

same location, having a person-to-person conversation. Information technology is, in effect, collapsing time and space; it is allowing individuals to travel anywhere in the world and meet with anyone at the speed of light and at virtually no cost.

The information superhighway will have the ability to translate the speech of Ted's partners from all over the world so that many people from many countries can communicate. Your partner in Tokyo speaks to you in Japanese but what you hear is English.

TED IN THE YEAR 2020

Imagine the year 2020. One of Ted's partners, Jane, has a great idea for customizing their products for customers. At 7:30 A.M. Jane posts a meeting notice for the seven partners on her self-directed team and fifteen more from her broader business unit. She calls the meeting for 9:00 that morning and selects a secluded beachfront conference room on the Hawaiian island of Maui.

Eight of the twenty-two partners show up. With waves crashing all around, Jane presents data on a screen at the front of the room. She passionately explains how the idea has already improved her customer satisfaction and increased sales for her. The partners brainstorm with free-flow *dialogue*. Because each partner is eager to improve his or her own customer satisfaction and increase profits, the partners are open to new ideas—there is alignment. They seek first to understand and listen intently to one another. As the idea is presented, people add variations to the original idea, which may improve it even more. With synergy, the ideas build on one another. They are truly connected, synthesizing, and producing synergy.

After a short, informal 15-minute meeting, people sign off and are instantaneously back in their homes and offices. Ten minutes later some of the partners have already begun implementing the concept with variations. Some variations work and most fail. These eight partners have virtual meetings of their own with other partners who also try variations. Within 24 hours through parallel processing nearly all 10,000 partners have heard about the idea and 8,000 have tried it. After 24 hours, through the order in chaos theory and the interconnectedness of quantum physics, the idea has evolved through several variations.

Jane and 8,000 partners have implemented some version of Jane's original idea. Like a school of fish or flock of birds the entire synergy-based organization turns and moves in new directions with synchronous beauty and lighting speed as though guided by one brain. Without the rigid standardization of control and variation reduction of a controlled economy, we have a highly ordered economy based on broad variation, diversity, creativity, and individual liberty.

Ted's network is designed with a knowledge-leveraging compensation system, whereby an individual's income increases as other partners' incomes increase. Knowledge-leveraging compensation pools a small portion of each partner's income and divides it equally. In this system partners are highly motivated to communicate successes and failures to other partners. This pooling occurs at several levels—the team, the business unit, and globally within the organization. Because of passionate communication, gross income for the organization increases as individual partners' incomes increase, and customers are made happier. Everyone has won. In addition to knowledge leveraging compensation, there are many other reasons why partners want to share information with others. Trust, bonding, partnership, love, caring, friendship, strength of the network, and real teamwork all are driving forces behind information flow in mass privatization. People have also become aware of the win/win world that this behavior supports as the norms and values of most people have changed.

For more detail on the workings of knowledge leveraging compensation, see *Knowledge Leveraging Compensation, A System of Chaos Theory and the Synchronous Beauty of Calibrating on Variation* at the WinWinWorld.net website at **http://www.winwinworld.net**

Eight thousand partners plus tens of thousands of customers have won with one idea because of the win/win nature of knowledge power and the mass privatization system. Jane has won more by sharing the idea than withholding it. This is because others were allowed to produce synergy and synthesize their ideas with hers to build something that none of them could have developed alone.

Although the foregoing scenario may sound far off to some people, the fact is that the most practical part of this scenario already exists. By adding up the sales of the thousands of individual Teds who already exist, we already have an organization with billions of dollars in real sales through thousands of *private workers,* real growth, profits, and customers, and real products. All this exists without any division of labor, central control, operating procedures, petty rules, bureaucracies, managers, unions, or employees. All that is left is the alignment of these communities, the synthesis of the constituents of whole work.

Ted's 2020 mass privatization community operates as the brain itself, each person operating more or less like an individual neuron. Information technology works as neural networks and memory. Synergy and parallel processing are the core building blocks of the mass privatization paradigm.

As mass privatization expands, connects thousands of organizations, and produces a system of decentralized wealth creation, the global neural connections on planet Earth are about to expand exponentially in the coming years. With this degree of connection, it is easy to see the growth and intelligence potential ahead through the mass privatization paradigm.

For more detail on the practical workings of mass privatization, see *The Mass Privatization Enterprise, The Detailed Workings of Decentralized Wealth Creation* at the WinWinWorld.net website at **http://www.winwinworld.net**

MASS PRIVATIZATION IN HEAVY INDUSTRY

At this point you may be saying, "Perhaps I can see mass privatization working in service industries or assembly manufacturing, but what about heavy industry?" Heavy industry is already headed toward mass privatization with the long-term shift from vertical to horizontal integration. We have come from a past in which the entire wealth-creation process was defined and controlled. We have seen a gradual shift over time toward workers' controlling their specific work. We've gone from dictators such as Ford and Rockefeller, who had total control and ownership over entire supply chains (theory X management), to micromanagement, to theory Y management, to employee involvement, to empowerment, business units, core competencies, profit centers, and self-directed teams.

Leading-edge organizations such as Asea Brown Boveri (ABB) are at the forefront of today's continued decentralization, just as decades ago they were the first big manufacturers to go public. ABB manufactures products for power plants, power distribution, power transmission, transportation, and environmental controls. In transportation, for example, ABB manufactures locomotives. Manufacturing does not get much heavier than locomotives. In 1991, ABB restructured the entire $28.9 billion company and 215,000 employees into 5,000 profit centers, each owning its assets. As power was shifted to the profit centers, the 3,000-person central controlling office was reduced to 150 persons within a couple of months. ABB CEO Percy Barnevik said he would have incorporated each one of the 5,000 profit centers if it were not for the paperwork. The 5,000 profit centers make up 1,300 independently incorporated companies, averaging 200 persons per company. The average profit center of 50 persons has its own profit and loss statement, and each is broken into high-performance teams averaging ten persons per team and serving customers directly (Peters 1992).

We are seeing market forces pushing us away from centralized control of wealth creation to individual control of wealth creation. Through *natural selection*, society slowly shifts in this direction. With the trend toward localization of control of work in heavy industry, one of the next logical steps is the company as holding company. This is an arrangement whereby the company invests money in ventures on the basis of a prospectus or past record but with no say in how the day-to-day business operates. This is nothing new. Investors invest billions of dollars each day into organizations in which they have no say in day-to-day operations. The holding company is the ultimate flattening of the organization. Managers are squashed out of existence, leaving only value-adding work and workers as business owners. Let's look at ABB as a theoretical holding company in the year 2020.

ABB AS A HOLDING COMPANY IN THE YEAR 2020

Like the former Soviet bloc countries, ABB years ago offered employees a *privatization* plan. The 5,000 profit centers were broken into 21,000 profit centers, each team being a profit center. The 1,300 companies were divided into 8,500 independent businesses or business units. Each business unit comprises several self-directed teams (averaging three to four teams). Power Products is one of the businesses. As part of the *privatization* package ABB traded 60% of ownership of Power Products to the former employees, now partners. Employees are not merely being called partners or associates but *are* real partners. In return for the ownership, ABB2020 receives a percentage of the profit produced from each business in the form of a quarterly dividend payment based on a specified percentage of the profits produced.

As part of the *privatization* agreement ABB2020 and Power Products partners agreed that Power Products would accept and ABB2020 would provide "high directive" support until Power Products partners developed the expertise to operate as a high-performing team. Team theory states that one cannot go from being a passive employee to being an empowered owner without going through four stages of team development—forming, storming, norming, and performing. So that the ABB2020 partner businesses would not be thrown into a sink-or-swim situation, as are most upstart businesses that fail, there was a period in which the business contractually had to follow the directives of an ABB2020 representative. So that the representatives' interests were properly aligned, they were compensated on the basis of a percentage of Power Products profits.

ABB2020 has zero labor costs, zero management costs, zero overhead costs, no union headaches, zero benefits costs, zero utilities or facilities costs, and a lot less government regulation. There are no managers or employees. Power Products partners receive no standardized salaries, wages, or benefits. There is precedence for this in heavy industry. Lincoln Electric workers receive no salaries, wages, vacation days, or holiday pay because of their ownership-based compensation systems (Posner 1988). As partners making far more money than employees, Power Products partners no longer *depend* on entitlements from the bureaucracy. Through networks the partners leverage their purchasing power and purchase services customized for themselves directly from suppliers.

Power Products produces power transformers for the utility industry. Thirty-three people work in the Power Products business unit in three self-directed teams. Power Products has the option of leasing its production equipment and space from ABB2020 or from another supplier. When offered the *privatization* package, Power Products moved its production equipment and people out of the larger factory of 500 employees. It found a small building where the lease on floor space was 45% less than the quote from ABB2020. They did, however, lease the production equipment from ABB2020.

Power Products sells its transformers through an ABB-networked enterprise of sales representatives focused on the utility industry. Customers purchase products from Power Products and pay Power Products directly, not some corporate accounting department. Power Products in turn pays its suppliers. One of these suppliers is ABB2020, which receives a monthly payment for leased equipment.

The 33 Power Products partners perform most of the work of the organization, from building the product to customer service to much of the equipment maintenance to much of the product and process design. Some work is vendored out to former ABB2020 managers who work as external suppliers. The pyramid has truly been inverted, and management has become true suppliers. However, because it is a free market, Power Products partners have the option of using other suppliers. The former managers likewise consult with other mass privatization enterprises.

Power Products contracts with former engineers, accountants, and others as needed. No industrial engineers conduct formal time studies, divide work, dictate rigid work standards, or talk down to the people doing the work, as in the old days. No former managers dictate to Power Products partners or take disciplinary action against them. Managers and engineers who remain dictators, who cannot adapt to being customer-focused suppliers, are not profitable and quickly go out of business.

The 33 team members share the work of the business. There is little division of labor and no division between the front office and factory floor, because there is no front office. Customer calls go directly to the factory floor and are answered by the scheduling team leader. There are many other team leaders, including preventive maintenance, process consistency, materials, purchasing, and quality. These are people with more expertise or passion in given areas who lead facilitation efforts in these areas.

Of the three teams in the business unit, two are suppliers to the third team, the customer team. The customer team is the one that receives income from external customers and places orders with and pays the other two teams as suppliers. The ten members of the customer team split profit relatively equally. Adjustment is made on the basis of a peer evaluation conducted each month. In addition, a knowledge leveraging compensation system is used whereby 15% of the three teams' profits are pooled and split equally among the teams. In this system 10% of Power Products profits are pooled with those of all other ABB2020 business units; the pooled profits are divided equally and redistributed. This system provides incentive for interconnectedness, communication, and generosity in helping one another.

Why did ABB2020 trade away part of its ownership? Because ABB2020 could make far more money investing in partners than managing employees, it could profit more from human liberation than from human control. Passionate, engaged, learning owners are far more efficient and effective at meeting customer needs, adding value, and creating wealth than are representative employees who do not have ownership. Workers now receive far more income, and it comes from a win/win system whereby the more partners make, the more the holding company makes. ABB2020's profits have increased and ABB2020 is growing faster than before because of the privatization package. Customers are getting better quality, service, and more customized products faster. Everyone has won!

The example is intended only to show that mass privatization can exist today with the use of practical and proven concepts, systems, and technology. It is not intended to show all the details of mass privatization in heavy industry. There are too many variables to allow one to predict the details of mass privatization. In addition, these details are handled differently for each organization.

OTHER MASS PRIVATIZATION OPTIONS IN MANUFACTURING

There are many ways mass privatization will evolve in industry. In 1993, I ran across a virtual molding company. Envision an injection plastic molding company with 1,000 molding machines. Undoubtedly it would be the largest molding business in the world. But the surprise is that there is no factory. Each of the molding machines is owned and operated in individual partners' garages. In this networked organization private workers in their homes did the manufacturing work.

In addition to the privatization of manufacturing, we must consider the effect of automation on manufacturing. Over time we can expect to see automation turn *mass-produced* products into commodities with little human involvement in production. The precedent has been set since the Agricultural Age, when 70% of people worked in agriculture; less than 1% do so today. From 1960 to the early 1990s, the number of people working in manufacturing decreased by 32%. We can expect this trend to continue. In Ted's whole work, manufacturing is integrated seamlessly into the overall wealth-creation process as opposed to being an entity unto itself. The bottom line is that manufacturing will become a nonissue for workers, because few people will be working in the isolated fragment of the wealth-creation process known as manufacturing.

THE END OF BUREAUCRACY

The mass privatization system is slowly replacing the company and other controlled economies as the primary wealth-creation institution in society. The foundation and core building blocks for mass privatization are being developed all around us within controlled economies. We merely need to synthesize the various activities in business and society and extend the trends out a few years to clearly see where we are headed—toward win/win free market–based wealth-creation institutions with unlimited economic freedom for the individual.

6

Decentralized Wealth Creation

A World of Six Billion Freely Trading and Collaborating Individuals

Not since the days of Noah has there been the opportunity to recreate society as there is today.

—Thomas Payne, 1775

When we synthesize mass privatization (changes occurring in work, business, and wealth creation) with historical change, today's social stagnation and decay, and the changes occurring in government, education, and the family, we see an entirely new wealth-creation system emerging—decentralized wealth creation.

Whereas mass privatization is the organizing structure for individual organizations, decentralized wealth creation is the entire wealth-creation system produced by a society that is a mosaic of overlapping and intertwined mass privatization organizations— a society with citizens operating as suppliers, customers, and partners interdependent on one another. The organizations or communities are interconnected through the developing information superhighway. They are locally and globally interdependent, all working to help themselves by meeting others' needs. Mass privatization communities are without boundaries in the sense that one cannot determine where one community ends and another begins, because most individuals and teams participate in more than one organization.

THE AGE-WAVE HISTORICAL PERSPECTIVE

*Aside from the Third Wave concept there is no effective system
of analysis which makes sense of the frustrations and confusion
which characterizes politics and government virtually everywhere in the industrialized world.*

—Newt Gingrich

In Figure 6–1 I expand on Alvin Toffler's (1980) age-wave concept to
show some of the differences between civilizations based on localized wealth creation, the wealth-creation system for the Agricultural
Age, centralized wealth creation of the Industrial Age, and decentralized wealth creation of the Information Age.

With the localized wealth creation of the Agricultural Age, most
people worked in bondage as serfs or slaves. They worked on the
land in hierarchical fiefdoms and kingdoms. The power used to create wealth was physical force or violent power. It was the primary
fuel that propelled the entire civilization as serfs and slaves were
forced to work on the land. Serfs were compensated according to a
percentage of the wealth produced. The only activity that was seen
as creating wealth was direct agricultural production.

With the transition into the centralized wealth creation of the
Industrial Age, most people went from working as serfs to working
as employees. They went from working in hierarchy-based fiefdoms
on the land in bondage to working in bureaucracy-based, controlled
economies contained within single buildings. They worked as representatives of the owners and were compensated for their time with
standardized compensation—wages and salaries. The power used to
organize people shifted from brute force to dollar wealth. And the
view of wealth creation expanded from food production to include
the making, mining, and growing of things; the making of things
dominated wealth creation.

As we shift to the decentralized wealth creation of the Information Age, we are at the very beginning of a shift from people working
as employees in single buildings to people working as owning partners via the information superhighway. The shift is from people
working in controlled economy–based bureaucracies to people
working in free market–based networks of self-directed virtual
teams, or teamnets. People are shifting from working as representa-

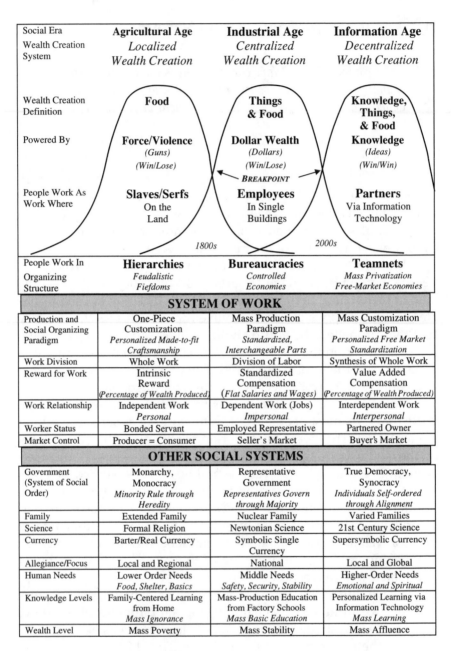

Social Era	**Agricultural Age**	**Industrial Age**	**Information Age**
Wealth Creation System	*Localized Wealth Creation*	*Centralized Wealth Creation*	*Decentralized Wealth Creation*
Wealth Creation Definition	**Food**	**Things & Food**	**Knowledge, Things, & Food**
Powered By	**Force/Violence** *(Guns)* *(Win/Lose)*	**Dollar Wealth** *(Dollars)* *(Win/Lose)* *BREAKPOINT*	**Knowledge** *(Ideas)* *(Win/Win)*
People Work As / Work Where	**Slaves/Serfs** On the Land	**Employees** In Single Buildings	**Partners** Via Information Technology
		1800s *2000s*	
People Work In / Organizing Structure	**Hierarchies** *Feudalistic Fiefdoms*	**Bureaucracies** *Controlled Economies*	**Teamnets** *Mass Privatization Free-Market Economies*

SYSTEM OF WORK			
Production and Social Organizing Paradigm	One-Piece Customization *Personalized Made-to-fit Craftsmanship*	Mass Production Paradigm *Standardized, Interchangeable Parts*	Mass Customization Paradigm *Personalized Free Market Standardization*
Work Division	Whole Work	Division of Labor	Synthesis of Whole Work
Reward for Work	Intrinsic Reward *(Percentage of Wealth Produced)*	Standardized Compensation *(Flat Salaries and Wages)*	Value Added Compensation *(Percentage of Wealth Produced)*
Work Relationship	Independent Work *Personal*	Dependent Work (Jobs) *Impersonal*	Interdependent Work *Interpersonal*
Worker Status	Bonded Servant	Employed Representative	Partnered Owner
Market Control	Producer = Consumer	Seller's Market	Buyer's Market

OTHER SOCIAL SYSTEMS			
Government (System of Social Order)	Monarchy, Monocracy *Minority Rule through Heredity*	Representative Government *Representatives Govern through Majority*	True Democracy, Synocracy *Individuals Self-ordered through Alignment*
Family	Extended Family	Nuclear Family	Varied Families
Science	Formal Religion	Newtonian Science	21st Century Science
Currency	Barter/Real Currency	Symbolic Single Currency	Supersymbolic Currency
Allegiance/Focus	Local and Regional	National	Local and Global
Human Needs	Lower Order Needs *Food, Shelter, Basics*	Middle Needs *Safety, Security, Stability*	Higher-Order Needs *Emotional and Spiritual*
Knowledge Levels	Family-Centered Learning from Home *Mass Ignorance*	Mass-Production Education from Factory Schools *Mass Basic Education*	Personalized Learning via Information Technology *Mass Learning*
Wealth Level	Mass Poverty	Mass Stability	Mass Affluence

FIGURE 6–1   Age-Wave Chart

tives of the owners and receiving standardized compensation to being owners compensated on the basis of the direct value they add for customers. The power driving society is shifting from finite dollar power to infinite knowledge power. Our view of wealth creation is expanding from the making, mining, and growing of things to include knowledge-based wealth creation. This list goes on to include shifts in other social systems, defined later.

For a more detailed age-wave chart and more detail on age-wave theory, see *Age-Wave Theory, Detailed Age-Wave Chart* at the WinWinWorld.net website at **http://www.winwinworld.net**

AS GOES WEALTH CREATION
SO GOES CIVILIZATION

Wealth creation is the driver of all human civilizations; it propels everything else. All civilizations are built on and rest on the wealth and wealth-creation paradigm and system of the period. The wealth-creation system is based on the current worldview, and the worldview is based on the latest science of the day. Built on this foundation are all of the social institutions of the period: work, family, spirituality, justice, government, education, commerce. These social institutions must be compatible with the wealth-creation paradigm and system of the era. As the wealth-creation system and paradigm change so too must all of the institutions.

The institutions of an era must be compatible with one another. Institutions from different eras cannot effectively be mixed and matched. The social institutions of the Agricultural Age did not work for the Industrial Age. Serfdom and slavery did not work with representative democracy. Likewise ownerless employment is not effective in a knowledge era in which workers by default own the knowledge-producing equipment, thus the means of production, in society. To change one piece, we must change it all. The different eras require institutions, thinking, science, and a worldview that synthesize and to some degree match one another to form a whole civilization. Because every part of every civilization rests on its own wealth-creation foundation, as goes wealth creation so goes civilization. The company is being replaced or transformed as well as all of our controlled economy–based institutions—nonprofit and charity organizations, public and private schools, government agencies, universities, hospitals, and more. All controlled economies, like companies, are in the business of meeting human needs.

THE SHIFT TO A FAMILY-CENTERED CIVILIZATION

We, in essence, live in a bureaucracy-centered society in which our family members look to various bureaucracies focused on specialized fragments of life to meet our various needs. It has been an era of the bureaucratization of the family. This was not so in the Agricultural Age, which was a more natural time in which most people had their needs met through the family. Children learned at home what they needed to live. They participated in the family business from a very young age, learning as they worked. Working on the land was not even considered a business; it was part of family life. Work, learning, and family life were one, undivided whole.

To give perspective to our Industrial Age world of work lets us look at a serf whose family is transported through time from the 1450s to 1958. He would likely be shocked at the lack of caring, family values, responsibility, and spirituality inherent to the social systems established to meet his family's needs. He would also be horrified at his lack of ability to directly control or change these things for his family. The aristocrats controlled him and it was brutal and a worse system than bureaucracy, but the control was more at a macro level. In addition, the daily details of his and his family's life were within his direct control and not in the direct control of careless bureaucrats.

Imagine the serf who was used to controlling the details of his daily life going off to work in a factory where he has to ask permission to get a drink of water, use the restroom, or take a break. In the controlled economy he does not do these things when the biological need hits, instead he must wait for a standardized break.

His work routine is laid out in specific detail, in "standardized work." It is defined down to which hand turns the screwdriver and how many turns to make. He is used to defining the details of his work. If he is ten seconds late getting to his work station his pay is docked and he is given a tardy on his attendance record, which will lead to the loss of his job after a certain number of tardies. He is used to working sun up to sun down plus or minus an hour or so.

The serf has been a hard worker all of his life and able to keep a percentage of the fruits of his labor. In the controlled economy, however, regardless of how hard he works or how much he produces his pay is the same as everyone else's. In fact some people doing little to nothing make more than he does. His wife goes off to a second controlled economy structured the same way.

He must send his five family members off to five separate bureaucracies to have their needs met. He does not get to see, talk, or interact with his family members for up to nine to eleven hours a day. Once sleep time is removed he is left with a few hours per day to interact with and raise his family. Since family members are on different wavelengths, spending their days living in different worlds, they find little to interact and talk about when they are together. They do separate things like homework, watching television, and reading, and only a few minutes are spent in group dialogue. The serf is a person used to spending all day with his family, on the same wavelength, interacting, teaching, and living while working with his family.

He is a person used to teaching his children what they need to know in order for them to survive in the world. Now he is told that he must send his children off to separate bureaucracies to be taught by other people. These people do not know him or his children, nor do they usually care deeply about the children's long-term well-being, however, it is mandated by law that he send his children to school. The children sit in a room with dozens of other children for six hours and listen to this "relative," noncaring person tell them how to survive in life. This relative, noncaring person is one who has never done any work in the environment that he or she is teaching the child to survive in.

Surely the serf sees this wealth-creation system as less brutal and more enlightened, but one that is not family centered. The family is not at the center and in control of its daily activities; those who control the bureaucracies are. The notion of giving up control of his family's lives to noncaring bureaucrats and employees and to rigid policy manuals and internal organizational politics would seem unnatural and insane.

On the other hand, if he were transported to the year 2020 he would see the civilization of mass-privatization communities as very much fitting with his values. Decentralized wealth creation replaces our entire bureaucracy-centered society with a family-centered society. It is a society where individual's needs—learning, work, trade, social order, emotional growth, recreation, rest, and spirituality—are met, controlled, and facilitated locally through the family. It is a return to a more natural system of organization similar to that of the

Agricultural Age and the Hunter-Gatherer Age. For all of human history, the family has been the institution through which we meet our needs. Only recently have we evolved to a system where each family member goes off to a different bureaucracy each day to have his or her unique needs met.

As historians 300 to 1,000 years into the future look back over all of human history they will likely see the Industrial Age as a period of abnormality, unlike anything before or after. It will likely be seen as an era where the natural family's role was vendored out to rigid, mechanistic organizations and shallow employees and bureaucrats who did not usually have the individual family member's complete best interest at heart. Perhaps it will be classified as period of irresponsibility with low "family values" since our bureaucratic structures do not *directly* support ownership, responsibility, or family values.

As we shift to decentralized wealth creation, we are shifting back to a family-centered civilization. Our family members' need for learning, work and trade, social order, emotional growth, recreation, connectedness, retirement, and spirituality are being integrated back into our daily lives within the family and back into one undivided whole. With decentralized wealth creation, the family is being put back into a position of direct responsibility for the needs of family members. The norm for an Information Age will be one of people working from home connected through the information superhighway to suppliers, partners, and customers. Children will do the bulk of their learning from home though the information superhighway. People will, therefore, be meeting their needs through the family as opposed to factory-style schools, companies, government agencies, and other bureaucracies. With the incoming family-centered civilization we begin to see the end of the fragmentation of the family.

Perhaps I see this new world evolving because as stated in Chapter 2, I come from a long line of private workers based upon agrarian values. My values are those of a bygone era and one not yet fully born. All of my life I have systematically rejected the artificial values of employment, fragmentation, bureaucracy, and representation.

FROM EDUCATION TO LEARNING

With decentralized wealth creation we can expect to see schools and the notion of education replaced with a new system based on the broader concept of knowledge creation and knowledge flow. Education is externally driven and done by one person to another. As in all controlled economies one person is in control. On the other hand, knowledge creation and knowledge flow are internally driven, self-directed, and fun. The concept of knowledge creation and knowledge flow is naturally interwoven into every aspect of every person's life every day, as opposed to education confined to the younger years of one's life.

With decentralized wealth creation and mass privatization, children acquire a large part of their learning at home through advanced information technology. Parents have full and direct control of and responsibility for their children's learning. Many people will work from home or a combination of home and office. Parents will be able to merge their children's learning with their own work, because much of children's learning comes through information technology that is very much aligned with the parents' work.

Socialization can take place daily through many diverse means, including small local and global learning communities, clubs, and organizations. Rather than mass production–based factory schools with hundreds and thousands of children in single buildings, local, privately owned, for-profit learning communities can meet in small buildings equipped with the latest in advanced information technology. Global learning organizations will meet through the virtual-reality information superhighway.

In regard to socialization we must ask ourselves, why do our children have to be socialized with hundreds and thousands of others in a single building? When and where in society do people have to interact in large numbers like this on a routine basis? This only occurs in factories. Factory-style schools may have been needed for the Industrial Age. Children were taught by rote; they were taught not to think and be creative but to follow the rules, obey authority, be on time, fragment through analysis, adapt to routine, tedious work, and conform, all the while maintaining low emotional and spiritual intelligence. These are the things that factory-style schools teach for people to work successfully in "controlled" and stable factories. However, today we need a new learning model that socializes our children to thrive in a new world of collaboration within small groups, to rely on self-direction, creativity, and synergistic relationships. Mass privatization provides this model.

With mass privatization, our children's learning comes from a variety of sources, unlike the standardized schools of the Industrial

Age. Some learning occurs in small, specialized learning communities, and other learning comes from children working with their parents in their businesses, helping to meet other persons' needs. A third source is children's play as they go on line and play learning games. A fourth source is children operating their own businesses trading their ideas, knowledge, goods, and services with other children and with adults.

In the new world, children will be traveling and exploring the world and universe on the infinite information superhighway. This all sounds a bit scary because this type of learning lacks the control-based standardization of our current Industrial Age school system. However, we must have confidence in the invisible hand of the free market, chaos theory, to provide order in a complex system. For example, in the personal computer industry, we see global standardization and order without authoritarian controlling standards.

As children become adults, there will no longer be tangible graduate degrees and cutoff points at which one obtains a certificate and learning stops. People will be working and learning all of their lives. With the advent of decentralized wealth creation in learning, we see the unification of learning, play, spirituality, and work into one, undivided whole.

THE SHIFT A HOLISTIC LIFE

As demonstrated throughout this book, one of the trademarks of the Industrial Age has been newtonian fragmentation. Life itself could not escape this fragmentation. For 200 years we have witnessed the bureaucratization of life into separate cubbyholes. Because of fragmentation we do not see work as a part of life but something we must do so that we can live in our time off—we, in effect, sell part of our lives. We do not see the need to learn after graduation from school, because that fragment of life is over once work starts. We do not see the need to practice our spiritual values in work and business because business and spirituality are two separate fragments that we assume simply operate on different principles. And last, we have a separate cubbyhole for retirement and relaxation. The reality, however, is that learning, work, business, spirituality, retirement, and relaxation are life. They should all operate on the same principles and should occur throughout life, not in separate compartments. All of life was one in the Agricultural Age and will again be one in the

Information Age. Life was not whole in the Industrial Age because of our fragmented view of life and separate, incoherent institutions. As we shift to decentralized wealth creation, we are shifting to a system whereby we learn, work, grow emotionally and spiritually, govern, recreate, create wealth, trade, retire, and live all of the time in virtually everything we do. To do one is to do them all. It is to live!

For more information on the end of the bureaucratization of life, see *The End of the Bureaucratization of Life*; for more information on decentralized wealth creation, see *From Charities to Helping Others, From Church to Spirituality, Back to the Natural Laws of the Farm, The End of Taxes* at the WinWinWorld.net website at **http://www.winwinworld.net**

A NATURAL SHIFT

Many people when they see the age-wave chart, comment "You mean, we're going back to systems of the farm days; barter, home and family-based education, owning one's work, income and reward based on what one creates and trades with others, home-based work, production based on individual customization? That's nuts!" However, when one steps back and looks at the big picture, it makes sense.

We see natural systems in an Agricultural Age and through all of human history. To move from the primitiveness and *separateness* of an Agricultural Age, to a civilization in which things worked on massive scales, mass production, mass communication, mass marketing, mass work, mass government, and so on, artificial, machine-based, command-and-control systems were needed to organize people and mass work. Today we are developing the information technology to connect people and create communities that enable mass work in more natural ways.

7

The Infinite Wealth Potential of Liberated Humans

Abundance via the Free Flow of Work and Knowledge

Tom Peters had the following to say about a camera he purchased in 1992, which had more brainpower than the Apple II computer he bought in 1982:

> I spent seven hundred bucks on that camera. What did I buy? I bought about three dollars worth of plastic. I bought about $15 worth of optical glass. I bought about $682 worth of software, computer power, and imagination. We are in an age in which brawn is not the driving force; human imagination is the driving force.

Alvin Toffler, in *PowerShift* (1990), identifies violence, wealth, and knowledge as the three primary forms of power in society. He shows violence to be the lowest quality of power, dollar wealth to be second, and knowledge to be the highest-quality power, because of its leverage potential, versatility, and limitlessness.

In the transition from the Agricultural Age to the Industrial Age, people went from working and creating wealth on the land, powered primarily by force or violence, to working on things, powered by dollar wealth as shown on the age-wave chart (see Figure 6–1 in Chapter 6). Today wealth creation is shifting from the making of things powered by dollar wealth to the creation of knowledge powered by information. Information technology is turning knowledge into the premier power in society.

In *PowerShift*, to explain the power of knowledge Toffler demonstrates that one idea can be used simultaneously by 50 or 500 or 500 million people. One gun (representing violence power) or one dollar (representing dollar power) can be used by only one person at a time. In the past, one therefore had strong motivation to hold on tightly to what power (dollars and guns) one had and not to share them with anyone.

Today and even more so tomorrow, sharing power (information and knowledge) directly with others under correctly aligned conditions can create *more* wealth for oneself. Sharing knowledge under the right conditions, such as mass privatization, is quickly becoming the best and fastest way for an individual to win. Mass privatization provides tremendous leverage to the individual who helps others. This change gives humanity the opportunity to shift from tens of thousands of years of win/lose norms to a win/win norm.

ERA OF INFINITE WEALTH

Because one idea can be shared by billions of people and they all win and because ideas and knowledge are infinite, wealth has become infinite. Paul Pilzer, in *Unlimited Wealth* (1990), shows how technology, which rests entirely on knowledge power, is the driver of a new alchemistic world with new rules of wealth creation. The dream of alchemists was to turn lead into gold. Today, using knowledge and ideas, we, for example, turn *sand* into something more valuable per pound than gold, *computer semiconductor chips*.

Infinite wealth goes against common sense and our experience. Infinite wealth is too good to be true. It is like creating something from nothing. This nothing, however, is actually something. It is ideas in people's heads that come from knowledge, which is created from information inside of billions of neurons and neural connections. Tangible wealth today is created from information.

Deepak Chopra in *Creating Affluence* (1993) approaches infinite wealth from a scientific and spiritual perspective. He shows that ideas, beliefs, and knowledge are the creators of physical and non-physical wealth and of the universe itself. Using quantum physics, Chopra shows that atoms, which make up everything in the universe, are made of information, knowledge, and intelligence, not solid material. Though the nature of quantum physics is explained in more detail later, the bottom line is:

Information, knowledge, and intelligence today are the primary forces driving wealth creation, and the human brain is the primary creator of knowledge. For the first time in history the masses of individuals own the means of production—their own minds and brains.

Wealth creation, therefore, can no longer be *controlled*; it must be *liberated* and based on individual freedom.

THE VISION OF A REAL FREE MARKET

Our thinking regarding free markets is incoherent and not fully developed. Like many other paradigms, it is limited. What we have seen for the past 200 years has not been a free market. Today most people equate a free market with companies, managers, stock markets, corporations, and win/lose competition for limited resources and customers. We think of hard and tough "businessmen" honed on the gridiron for fierce competition who are willing to do anything to win. Real free markets have little to do with any of this.

Real free markets are about win/win interactions and free exchange in all mediums. They are soft and based on collaboration, love, interconnection, and the free flow of wealth and knowledge between people. People collaborate to create more wealth from an infinite source instead of competing for scarce wealth. Free markets are about human liberation and the free exchange of ideas, knowledge, and work. They are about exploration, discovery, learning, creativity, and spirituality. Most of all they are about caring for others, helping each other, and love.

Yes, this is a radical departure from our traditional definition; the words *love* and *free market* in the same sentence sound odd. The broader and more accurate definition of a free market is a community in which humans are free to create, exchange, interact, and interconnect to meet each others' needs and create wealth for themselves, others, and society.

INFINITE POWER OF FREE HUMANS

Wealth is not something that is static, finite, or absolute. As is discussed in more detail later, wealth is created through the meeting of human needs. Because wealth is created when people trade work or interact with one another and meet human needs, wealth and wealth creation are infinite. Why?

The more people, the more needs there are. With more needs comes more work; the more work there is, the more income and wealth there are. Traditionally we have thought that the more people there are, the less wealth there is for each. This is not true. What we find is that the more people there are, the more wealth there is for everyone.

If we think about this deeply, we see that there is absolutely no reason why there is not plenty of work and wealth for everyone. By answering the following four questions, we must conclude that wealth is abundant:

1. *Is there a lack of desire to work?* No, most people want to work and receive handsome income from that work.
2. *Do people want the goods and services that the income from their work purchases?* Yes, virtually everyone wants the goods and services that income produces.
3. *Is there a void of human needs to be met?* No, there are hundreds of billions, trillions, and perhaps infinite human needs for people to meet and from which to receive income.
4. *Is there a shortage of people to perform this work?* No, there are plenty of people to produce and consume the products and services of this work.

What then is standing in the way of infinite wealth? Why are there poverty, unemployment, and people starving in the world? Let's take an even closer look at wealth creation to find out what is restraining it.

1. As people perform work, their ideas, knowledge, and work when traded meet human needs and thus create wealth.
2. With the compensation they receive for their work, people purchase products and services to meet their own needs.
3. This spending creates demand for more work and ideas, which generate compensation for other people.
4. This additional compensation produces more spending, which allows creation of more work, ideas, and wealth.

The cycle of work, which produces income, which produces spending, which creates more work, can be self-perpetual and infinite in a knowledge-based free-market economy. The catch is

that the flow and trade of work, ideas, and knowledge must be unhindered. The freer and more fluid the flow and trade of work, ideas, and knowledge, the wealthier we all become.

If wealth has the potential to be infinite we must ask what in our economy causes it to be finite? Controlled economies, representative government, and centralized wealth creation—the systems that have produced our current levels of wealth—also are the systems in society that prevent wealth from being infinite. "Our greatest strength is our greatest weakness" (Tuck 1994). Controlled economies today are constipating the wealth-creation process because of their inherent focus on controlling the wealth process instead of facilitating the unrestricted flow of wealth. Control produces scarcity, whereas free flow produces abundance.

The head financial officer in a controlled economy is called a *controller* for good reason. Within controlled economies performance is achieved through consistency and process control. Consistency is achieved with forced, rigid standardization based on average performance. Controlled economies are machines, and each part must be identical within a tolerance, just like parts of a machine. We should all walk alike, think alike, dress alike, and park in specific parking spaces, "a place for everything and everything in its place." Averages are everything to a mass production–based, controlled economy.

Companies, for example, have almost as hard a time with many of their top performers as with their bottom performers. This is because the top performers produce too much variability, making mass production systems difficult for bureaucrats to control. Controlled economies prefer average performers because of consistency. I have witnessed many cases in manufacturing plants where fast workers wreak havoc on slower-paced cultures, creating conflict and confusion. As a manager I have coached fast workers to slow down. Manufacturers use statistical process control to produce quality products. The statistical process control definition of being in control is to have a consistent amount of process variability; the thrust is continuously to reduce process variability. The obsession with averages and reducing variability forces a controlled economy to thrive on mediocrity. Like Antonio Salieri, Mozart's rival in the movie *Amadeus*, the controlled economy is the champion of mediocrity. Today, however, to be in control is to be out of control.

What is needed to unleash the infinite power of wealth creation in an Information Age is a system such as mass privatization, which allows people to freely trade their work output, information, and knowledge. This system must allow trade to occur easily and quickly without hindrance. The system should facilitate and encourage free flow of trade. The last thing our wealth-creation institutions should be doing is attempting to control the wealth-creation process.

Decentralized wealth creation and mass privatization operate on the basis of chaos theory, in which the norm is the more variation, the better. The weirder the ideas, the better, because in a mass customization era a wide variety of ideas are mandatory to meet customer needs. As documented in many books, success comes only through many tries and failures. Mass privatization achieves order from individuals' trying lots of wild ideas, usually failing, and having the freedom and incentive for thousands of individuals to calibrate from each other's best ideas and successes. This calibration occurs of the individual's own free choice.

For more information on finite and infinite wealth, see *Constipated Wealth Creation, Nonprofit Organizations Produce Gridlock* at the WinWinWorld.net website at **http://www.winwinworld.net**

PRIVATE CAPITAL AND THE FREE TRADE OF WORK

I spent two years living in rural Southside Virginia, near where I was born and raised. We lived on a large, beautiful lake—the largest and most secluded lake on the entire east coast. The surrounding community, however, was quite poor, or at least this was their perception. Southside Virginia had been a thriving hub of commerce in the Agricultural Age. With the decline of that era came the decline of this rural area. As work in agriculture decreased and manufacturing increased, industry was not attracted to this rural community.

Though there are tremendously talented people in Southside Virginia, they don't perceive it this way. Their egos have been bludgeoned by continuous decline since the end of the Agricultural Age. When my wife, Linda, told an acquaintance that we had recently relocated there from Southern California, her response was, "Oh, I'm sorry, things must really be going bad for you." She thought that surely no one in his or her right mind would move here from Southern California unless there was no other choice.

The people in this area of Virginia think of themselves as dumb and poor. They also don't perceive their time as valuable. After traveling the world and working with the best and brightest, I can honestly say that I knew people from Southside Virginia who were barely surviving but were as talented as any engineer, artist, or manager anywhere I'd been. They perceive themselves as dumb and poor because they have less dollar capital than people do in more industrialized areas. They have been trapped by the Industrial Age paradigm of dollar capital. Today they need only a shift in perception to see their abundance of tangible wealth.

Though people in Southside Virginia have little dollar capital, there is no shortage of capital. *Capital* is defined as a stock of accumulated goods. These people have an overwhelming stock of accumulated knowledge, talent, intelligence, creativity, and desire to work. Because wealth creation merely comprises people trading their work with one another and because there is plenty of capital, all that is missing is a **means to exchange work** with one another. The Industrial Age, with its controlled economies and public work, made dollar capital the sole means of exchanging work, and employment was the primary method. In Southside Virginia, where there is relatively little industry and with dollar capital in such short supply, the perception is *scarcity*.

Alvin Toffler, in *PowerShift*, shows that we are moving to a supersymbolic economy with supersymbolic capital. As shown in the agewave chart (Figure 6–1 in Chapter 6), in the Agricultural Age a dollar was represented by a piece of metal or something worth one dollar—a dollar's worth of bartered potatoes, chickens, or smoked bacon. The dollar piece, for example, was made of one dollar's worth of gold, silver, or another precious metal. As we shifted to the Industrial Age, a dollar came to be represented by a piece of paper. The paper dollar is perhaps worth less than a penny in real value. It symbolically *represents* a dollar's worth of work or value. It is "symbolic" money. In the Information Age today, the bulk of dollars that change hands are never touched. They are transferred from one person's bank account to another, as electronic symbols flow from one computer to another. These electronic symbols represent paper dollars, which represent a dollar's worth of value—hence *supersymbolic money.*

Money is merely a means to measure how much value has been added or wealth created by one's work. It is a way to measure how much work each person has performed. Money allows one person's work to easily be exchanged for another person's work. An electronic barter bank would allow jobless and moneyless individuals who want to trade their work, to do so, and thus increase individual and collective wealth.

With the advance of information technology, virtually anyone today can set up an electronic computer barter bank using a personal computer. There is therefore no reason why people in Southside Virginia should be restrained in trading their work simply because there is a shortage of controlled economy–based jobs and U.S. dollar capital. There is, after all, an abundance of human-knowledge capital, plenty of human needs to be met, abundant information technology, and plenty of people ready to work.

The limited availability of monopolistic dollar capital has twisted and blocked our perception of reality; it has tricked us into thinking that wealth is limited. It has slowed the trade of work and constipated the wealth-creation process—the meeting of human needs. Today, we are in an era of supersymbolic money in which a mere shortage of dollar capital is not a valid reason to keep people from working, trading their work, creating wealth, meeting human needs, and growing wealthy. We merely need a shift in perception.

When we combine an understanding of what money is with the following facts, it becomes self-evident that parallel sources of capital—private capital—will explode to break loose our present constriction in wealth creation:

1. Supersymbolic monies are merely electronic symbols in computers that track people's accumulated work or wealth.
2. Today the computers and people needed to set up and run supersymbolic electronic barter banks are abundant.
3. The infrastructure to connect thousands of private capital barter banks already exists with the Internet.
4. There is no shortage of human capital.
5. We are moving to a decentralized wealth-creation and mass privatization paradigm whereby work and people are a lot more flexible and the free trade of work is mandatory.

Toffler, in *PowerShift*, speaks of parallel forms of capital coming into being in the Information Age. One thing holding back Southside Virginia and many other communities nationally and globally is their perception of money, capital, and themselves. Barter banks are springing up already to fill the dollar-capital void. In Raleigh, North Carolina, a local barter bank has been started with hundreds of members. An article in *Mother Earth News*, October/November 1993, showed that private citizens in Ithaca, New York, and Myrtle Beach, South Carolina, have established parallel sources of capital. Roger Langrick in the book *Barter Systems* (1994) begins to define the shift to private capital in society. On the Internet there is E-Gold, which is a parallel source of capital.

Regarding the residents of southern Virginia and those elsewhere, a shift in perception toward the private electronic exchange of work through networked private capital will allow for a more free-flowing exchange of work. A shift in their perception of themselves as worthy human beings, as discussed later, is needed before they will acquire the wealth lying within them.

As shown in the age-wave chart (see Figure 6–1 in Chapter 6), we are making the transition from a system of trade based on one *monopolistic* currency, which today restricts the free trade of work, to a system of supersymbolic multiple currencies networked together to form a global system of fluid and freely trading work. As local electronic barter banks and Internet barter systems begin to connect with one another globally through the information superhighway, they are producing a network of seamless, global multiple currencies. These multiple currencies, which are an integral part of mass privatization and decentralized wealth creation, will further liberate the free and fluid flow and trade of work, ideas, and wealth.

PRIVATE CAPITAL BARTER BANKS EMPOWERED BY INFORMATION TECHNOLOGY

Envision a networked barter bank of 5,000 people. The idea is to set up a barter bank for a given region. People, though they have little dollar capital, can trade what they do have—the ability to do things, fix things, make things, or provide a service. A barter bank is in essence a trading house. Each member has an account. For example, Jane, a member, has 200 P-dollars (private dollars) in her account. Jane needs her car repaired but does not have any traditional dollar money to pay. Bob, also a member of the network, agrees to repair the car for 80 P-dollars. When the job is complete, Bob's account is credited 80 P-dollars from Jane's account. Bob, who has retired, has no traditional dollars to spend because his social security check for the month is all budgeted. He does, however, have 80 P-dollars. He searches the network database for items or services for sale.

Bob finds Anne who is unemployed but talented at refinishing furniture. Bob's granddaughter's third birthday is coming soon. Bob has Anne refinish an old child's chair that was his when he was a child. Sixty-five P-dollars are transferred from Bob's account to Anne's account. Anne, being unemployed, is on a tight budget and her house very badly needs some repairs. She contracts with James, a young man right out of school who hasn't yet found a job. James, eager for income, does the repairs and is credited 200 P-dollars.

John, a local clothing retailer who is being hard hit by a recession, decides to begin listing some of his merchandise on the network. He figures it cannot hurt. James trades 200 P-dollars for a new suit for job interviews. John begins to move merchandise at four times his normal rate through the network, even though he is selling this material at a relatively higher price than what is paid in his store with dollar capital. John has a problem. He has lots of P-dollars but no dollars to restock his store. His suppliers are hundreds of miles away and haven't even heard of a barter bank and have no interest in his P-dollars.

John decides to put some of his P-dollars up for sale on the network, in exchange for dollar capital. For the people in the network who have access to traditional dollar capital, this is a bargain. They buy John's P-dollars for 75% of their value with traditional dollars. The people who purchased John's P-dollars have plenty of dollar capital and see this as an opportunity to obtain products and services at a discounted price below the dollar capital rate.

John uses the cash to restock his store. Everybody wins. Even though John sold his P-dollars at a discount, the volume and lack of advertising and other overhead to sell the merchandise have made it quite a profitable deal.

John uses some of the additional P-dollars to have some remodeling done on his house by James and others in the network with carpentry and masonry skills. The bottom line is that the gross wealth of the community and standard of living of many people have been increased merely by injecting a parallel form of capital into the system and enabling work to be traded more freely. Parallel sources of capital in essence jump-start stalled parts of an economy. They empower people to pull themselves out of a hole by trading work that would not have been traded and meeting needs that would not have been met without an additional source of capital. Parallel sources of capital or electronic barter provide a system of self-regulation that eliminates restrictions in the wealth-creation process.

In the example, people are able to trade their work, receive income, and meet some additional needs only because there is a parallel source of capital. I know of talented people living in Mecklenburg County, Virginia, who sit idle each day receiving a government check, not working, not adding value for others, not receiving compensation. Many of their needs are unmet, partly because of gridlock created by having only one source of capital.

I know a man who can repair cars sitting idle while a women two miles away has needed her car repaired for months. This man needs furniture refinished and the woman, who has furniture refinishing skills, has nothing to do. Neither has money to pay the other. They fail to see the wealth they already own and do not trade their work because of their dollar-capital paradigm. They both live below the poverty line while receiving a government check. Both sit idle each day with little to do, with little money, and with many needs going unmet. Billions of people globally are hindered in trading their work for the same reason—the dollar capital paradigm. What a waste!

The new parallel forms of private capital may not replace dollar capital. Parallel forms of capital complement each other in the forming of a truer free market. They keep things in balance, break bottlenecks, and keep things flowing. These parallel forms of capital break the logjams dollar capital creates through a monopoly. They allow work to be traded more freely. Parallel forms of capital have begun to and will continue to spring up around the country and the world. There is too much pressure on dollar capital; people are dollar capital starved in a capital-rich world.

As the growth of information technology reaches critical mass, networked private capital will become a norm. It is also inevitable that information technology will turn local private capital into regional, national, and even global private capital. It will obliterate national boundaries. It will make billionaires of the individuals who pioneer electronic barter banks, enabling billions of other people to win. The freer we make the flow of information and the trade of work, the wealthier we all become. Parallel forms of private capital are an inherent part of mass privatization. They empower the individual to trade work, information, and knowledge quickly, easily, and without hindrance. Parallel forms of private capital support the paradigm of infinite wealth.

INFORMATION TECHNOLOGY, FREE TRADE, AND INFINITE WEALTH

In *The Virtual Corporation* William Davidow and Michael Malone (1992) show a correlation between major historical growth periods and the orders of magnitude of improvement in technology needed to create them. The authors state: "Historically, whenever important technological innovations have resulted in improvements equal to at least one order of magnitude, revolutionary changes have occurred in the way people live their lives and conduct their business" (p. 73).

Davidow and Malone show that from 1770 to 1851 the productivity of production workers jumped roughly 300%, or two orders of magnitude. This increase in productivity fueled the start of the industrial revolution. The authors go on to show the orders-of-magnitude change in information processing in recent decades.

> Although, strictly speaking, one cannot add all advances together because there would be double counting, it can be said that forty years of computing has experienced a combined improvement in five dimensions—mass storage, reliability, cost, power consumption and processing speed—of thirty orders of magnitude. Such a level of change is almost beyond human comprehension. It is equal to the jump from the diameter of a single atom to that of the Milky Way galaxy. As we noted above, it took a change of two orders of magnitude to spark the Industrial Revolution and one of only four orders of magnitude to end World War II and redirect human history (*with the creation of the atomic bomb*). (Davidow and Malone, p. 79, emphasis added)

I know about the change in information technology all too well. As an example of some of this improvement, in 1986, when I founded CheckMate, I purchased a 120-megabyte hard drive for my personal computer. It cost $2,800. People told me that I'd never need that much space. Most people had 20- to 30-megabyte drives. In 1991 when I replaced it, I paid $495. In 1993, the last time I priced a 120-megabyte drive, it was less than $200, and I was told that I'd be lucky to find one. By 1994, 120-megabyte drives were no longer available because they were too small. By 1998 I could get a 13,600-megabyte drive for $299. The price went from $23.30 per megabyte to 2 cents per megabyte or from $2,800 for 120 megbytes to $2.40 for 120 megabytes. That's improvement by a factor of 1,059 in 12 years. In the same time speed more than doubled, and power consumption and sheer weight dropped to a mere fraction of the original "boat anchor" I purchased in 1986.

Davidow and Malone show that consensus is building among many noted economists regarding the value computers have added to society from our system of centralized wealth creation. The data show that there has been little to no gain in productivity from the orders-of-magnitude increase in information-processing technology. Harvard economist Gary Loveman (1991) wrote:

> I'm here to tell you that after several years, my results have been poor and the results of many of my colleagues who have tried similar things are also poor. Poor in the sense that we simply can't find evidence that there has been any substantial productivity increase—and in some cases any productivity increase—from the substantial growth in information technology.

Davidow and Malone (1992) show that historical evidence shows a lag between huge advances in new technologies and the real results they deliver. A 30-order-of-magnitude change is equal to the jump from the size of an atom to that of the Milky Way galaxy (Dumaine 1991). With technology improvement of this size sitting idle, we must ask what is holding back its impact on society. The infinite wealth explosion is waiting for a system of wealth creation that at its core is based on the free flow of work, knowledge, and wealth—mass privatization and decentralized wealth creation. When we think about it, the free flow of work, knowledge, and wealth is exactly what information technology does best. The thing that is holding back the impact of information technology on society is the control of wealth creation that comes from controlled economies and centralized wealth creation. We have a wealth-creation system that is not aligned with and does not match the new technology—it can only tap a fraction of the potential power of the 30-orders-of-magnitude improvement. As long as information technology is used merely to pave Industrial Age cow paths, we shall realize little relative benefit from it. Like the water wheel and the steam engine, technologies and institutions from different eras cannot effectively be mixed.

Mass privatization, which at its core embraces the free flow of work, knowledge, and wealth, provides a system that fully utilizes advances in information technology. As a critical mass of mass privatization and the information superhighway are developed, we shall see an economic growth explosion unparalleled in history that will shift us all into an era of mass affluence.

For more information regarding the idle potential energy in Industrial Age society poised to fuel growth in the Information Age, see *The Propellant of a New Civilization* and *The Growth Explosion Ahead* at the WinWinWorld.net website at **http://www.winwin world.net**

GROWTH LIMITED ONLY BY OUR IMAGINATIONS

Mass privatization empowers individuals to create their own work and to find their own niches. This is opposed to an individual finding a job that a centralized government or company bureaucracy has created. We should remember that a free market is simply an environment that provides maximum freedoms and options for individuals. A true free market is about human freedom, the human spirit, compassion, and helping others. It is about humans collaborating to meet human needs and is therefore about creating wealth.

With mass privatization and decentralized wealth creation people will be liberated throughout the world to add value where they see fit. They will be liberated to search out human needs and meet them. They will be liberated to discover human needs that customers did not even know existed. They will be liberated to create human needs and meet them.

We are looking at a civilization in which six billion individuals work hard to figure out how to help each other and one in which the people who do this best create more wealth for themselves. WOW!

With six billion liberated humans there will be more gross wealth and it will be distributed into more people's hands. After my awakening to mass privatization, I looked deeper into the consequences of this new paradigm, synthesizing more and more pieces. It became clear to me that the concept was a stepping stone to something even bigger than I could have ever imagined. This shift in perception is jolting. It presents us with the opportunity for far more than merely a new type of wealth-creation enterprise to replace the company. It presents us with the opportunity for an entirely new wealth-creation paradigm—a new civilization unlike anything before it, a civilization of win/win, abundance, and infinite wealth.

This shift to win/win will unleash enormous positive powers. The pain humanity is experiencing is part of the greatest emancipation in the history of the world. It is the emancipation of the human spirit.

In the shift from the Agricultural Age to the Industrial Age, a simple change in wealth-creation power from violence to dollar wealth released tremendously powerful advances in human growth. With the shift from the Industrial Age to the Information Age, there is far more potential to increase standard of living, quality of life, productivity, and advancement than there was during the shift from Agricultural Age to Industrial Age. This is because of the enormous power delta between knowledge and wealth versus wealth and violence. This delta includes the win/win nature of knowledge, its leverage potential, and the infinite nature of knowledge. The magnitude of advances made in the Industrial Age will be dwarfed by the magnitude of advances to come as the infinitely powerful win/win knowledge fuel kicks in with decentralized wealth creation.

There is nothing in our imaginations today that can even come close to showing what is possible in ours, our children's, and our grandchildren's lifetimes. The shift from dollar wealth power to knowledge power as the fuel powering civilization, and the shift to mass privatization organizations as the engines are revolutionary changes. They lay the foundation to thrust us at the speed of light into a new dimension. In this dimension will occur the worldwide end of poverty, unemployment, racial strife, hatred, and war within a relatively short period. These shifts will produce tens of millions of millionaires and at the same time end government taxation and government itself. The shifts will dramatically increase everyone's standard of living and quality of life. And all this is likely to happen within a single lifetime.

The shift to mass privatization will enable the repayment of trillions of dollars of government debt. It will pay off billions in personal and business debt, repay third-world debt, and repay the debt all of industrialized nations. It will end our quality deficits, educational deficits, and environmental deficits. It will enable repayment of the national debt left from the Agricultural Age owed to Indians, descendants of slaves, and others. This will not come from the mass wealth redistribution and affirmative action programs mandatory to attempt balance in the Industrial Age. It will come through wealth-creation opportunity and economic freedom for the individual. It will end our crime, violence, education, and quality deficits and most of our other win/lose deficits. It will provide a foundation and means to end our abundance of fear, hatred, and self-hatred. It will do this by providing a strong motive for cooperative opportunity. It will do all of this with no taxes, no welfare, no giveaways, and no government.

What we are speaking of when we talk about a free-market economy in an Information Age is a self-perpetuating, supercharged engine that runs off of the highest-quality power there is, knowledge and wisdom. I am speaking about human freedom, choice, and options.

For more information on the potential for infinite wealth in an Information Age, see *Unlimited Economic Freedom for the Individual* at the WinWinWorld.net website at **http://www.winwin world.net**

PART IV

True Democracy
The Dream Realized

8

Unlimited Individual Power via Information Technology

The Mandate for Win/Win Wealth Creation

To have a stable society there must be a balance between social and economic freedoms. If people are wealthy but are severely limited in what they can do and how and when they can do it, there will be turmoil. This turmoil comes as people use their wealth and power to purchase social freedoms. They will bribe, buy influence from those in power, or pay for others to bend the laws.

On the other hand, if people are allowed to do whatever they want whenever they want and have little money or few avenues to obtain money, there will be turmoil. Many people will use their social freedoms to do whatever they want whenever they desire to obtain money or wealth. They will steal, commit violent crimes, sell drugs, and join gangs. There will be con artists and corruption. All of this occurs because people have broad social freedoms that prevent them from being penalized for their actions.

In an ordered society, social and economic freedoms *must* be balanced or there will be chaos.

ORDER AND THE GOOD OLD DAYS

Some people yearn for the good old days when things were simpler and people had respect for others. It was a time when there was order and people were responsible and were held accountable for their actions. It was a more peaceful time; it was safe to walk down the street and leave our doors unlocked at night. Our leaders were respected, and our justice system worked.

Unfortunately, because of analysis, we have selective memories. We remember the best fragments from the past. When we look at the *whole* picture, I do not believe the good old days can be classified as such. Taking the entire era into consideration, I don't believe there were the respect, responsibility, or accountability we remember. Yes, there was less chaotic crime and violence in society, but there was a very high cost for this order. This cost came in the form of severely limited social freedoms for the masses of individuals. People did not have a great deal of economic freedom, but they also had limited social freedom. Therefore there was a reasonable level of order.

As we look back over the Industrial Age, we see norms of oppression whereby one group limits another. Within the mainstream population individuals were stifled by conformity through standardized behavior, thinking, and speaking. The norms of the last 100 to 200 years include exploitative child labor practices, legalized lynching, castration, mutilation, legalized racism, sexism, hatred, limited worker rights, and mass poverty. Voting rights initially belonged only to white, male landowners. As workers tried to organize for improved working conditions, many were violently oppressed; some were even murdered. In the 1940s and 1950s people were jailed, blackballed, followed, harassed, searched, monitored, and in some cases tried and sentenced to death because of their political beliefs. All of these practices represent limitation of social and economic freedom.

The United States appears not to have been much better at upholding human rights during the peak of the Industrial Age, the 1940s and 1950s, than was South Africa in the 1980s. We look at a country like South Africa as it was in the 1980s and see oppression of blacks. To oppress blacks, however, an entire society must have limited options and freedoms. There must be a very tight code of narrow and rigid behavior for all. You cannot have individual white people standing up and fighting the system—it rocks the boat and creates disorder for all. Most whites in South Africa in the 1970s (or in the southern United States during the 1940s) who disagreed with segregationist policies did so quietly. After all, who wanted to be accused of being a "nigger lover" by neighbors, friends, business associates, and customers? Your business could be ruined or you could lose your job or become a social outcast. Whether in South Africa, the

Soviet Union, or China during the 1980s or the United States in the 1930s, 1940s, or 1950s, people did not step out of line because there simply was little social freedom for the vast majority of people.

EXPANDED SOCIAL FREEDOMS

In the past several decades, information technology and knowledge power have produced significant increases in social freedoms to the masses. To date, however, the increases in economic freedoms for people have not kept pace, creating instability throughout society. This imbalance lies at the heart of our crime, violence, terrorism, and gang problems. The only answer is significantly expanded economic freedom for all, and mass privatization offers this.

Since the 1950s, social freedoms in the United States have exploded. In the 1930s or 1940s in the southern United States a black man who was slightly out of line could be castrated, lynched, or severely beaten by any white person who decided to do so. That was truly an era of "zero tolerance." Today, however, many black men commit heinous crimes with relatively few or no ramifications. There is a good chance of not being caught, of getting off on a technicality, or of getting off because of lack of proof beyond a reasonable doubt or a plea of insanity or other loophole. There is also a good chance of becoming lost in red tape. In Seattle, for example, in the early 1990s 66% of persons who committed a crime with a gun never made it to court because of delays that took years, some eventually skipping bail.

Even if a guilty black man is convicted today, prisons are more humane than they were in the past; they provide educational opportunities, libraries, televisions, and fitness centers. In addition, full sentences rarely are served because of overcrowding and lenient parole laws. This example represents enormous gains in social freedoms for black men and is a measure of the expanded social freedom of all citizens. Though some may disagree that black men today enjoy great social freedom, arguing that black men are persecuted by police and the criminal justice system, the problem is relatively minor compared with the history of slavery, lynching, segregation, and violent oppression as the social norm.

Today people openly believe in the politics they desire, dress in any way they desire, use drugs, become pregnant out of wedlock, practice devil worship, and produce and listen to any kind of music (even that advocating violence against police and the government) they want to. This is all a reflection of an enormous increase in social freedom.

INFORMATION TECHNOLOGY AND INCREASED SOCIAL FREEDOMS

Information technology and the knowledge power of an Information Age are the primary drivers behind the expanded social freedoms of the past decades. They enabled the "do-your-own-thing" movement. It is no coincidence that the 1960s were a wild decade of hippies, sex, and drugs. Young people were empowered through information technology and rebelled against rigid limits on their social freedoms. People wanted to do what they wanted, when and how they wanted to do it. They rebelled against standardized thinking and conformity. People rebelled against the government and its war with Vietnam; they rebelled against racism and sexism. How did information technology trigger this chaotic nonconformity?

Information technology produced the first "living room war" in history. Disturbing pictures of death counts, body bags, protests, opposing views, corruption, and the general horrors of war were broadcast into everyone's living room each night. Before television, the realities and horrors of war simply were not real to people. Neither are the 35,000 or so people who die of starvation each day worldwide. Because we do not see these people, their situation simply is not real to us. In addition, before the Information Age, governments could more easily put positive spins on reality by presenting only fragments of the *whole* picture.

Although protest against the Vietnam War started slowly, more and more people joined the bandwagon. The result was enough internal political pressure for the United States to opt out. Today most people agree that we never should have been there. Information and knowledge empowered people to stop blindly following authoritarian leaders, who in the past had controlled limited information—it empowered people to think for themselves. It empowered people to produce synergy by letting them know that there were others with thoughts similar to their own.

As the documentary *The History of Rock and Roll* showed, the birth of rock and roll marked the beginning of the worldview of one humanity, a *global* worldview. It was the beginning of the coming together of all cultures of the world, which synthesized music of diverse cultures into harmonious tunes that touched the masses of people. Many of the artists in the documentary state that their intent was to do exactly that. The explosion of rock and roll was possible only because of information technology through radio, television, phonographs, compact discs, amplifying systems, electric instruments, computers, and more. It allowed humanity to begin to interconnect as one.

Most people would consider the civil rights movement to have had nothing to do with the Information Age, information technology, or knowledge power. Nothing could be further from the truth. The civil rights movement was successful **only** because of new information technology and knowledge power. Without television and information technology, there would likely be the same degree of segregation and injustice now as there was 75 years ago for blacks in the South. The primary tools in the shift in people's attitudes were the television set and television camera. These tools brought disturbing pictures of a new reality into every household in the nation. Viewers saw police with dogs and water cannons abusing nonviolent people. As long as people were not *directly* aware of what was occurring in the South and local officials controlled the information presented to the world, things would most likely have remained the same indefinitely.

Information was used to shift people's perception of reality. Perhaps Martin Luther King, Jr., understood knowledge power earlier than most. Perhaps he understood that information as a form of power was far stronger than the powers of violence or wealth. As Alvin Toffler (1990) has shown, violence and wealth were the two primary forms of power in civilization until the Information Age. The Information Age has made knowledge the primary power in civilization.

Martin Luther King, Jr., demonstrated this as he used knowledge power with a kind of martial arts strategy. He allowed his opponents to defeat themselves through their own violence and wealth power. He used the higher-quality power of awareness and knowledge, through television and information technology, to bring about shifts in the consciousness of the masses. We live in an era of new and strange power—power that operates with vastly different nonlinear rules than the wealth and violence power to which we have become accustomed.

We see the same liberating trend for individuals and restraining force on central authorities with the Rodney King incident and many other police brutality cases caught with personal video cameras. Corrupt policemen are hindered by this kind of scrutiny, because video cameras are in the hands of the masses everywhere. Legitimate police activity also is severely handicapped because of the red tape produced by expanding social freedoms. Many complain that the judicial system favors the accused far more than the victims of crime.

The eclipse of power is also apparent in governments. Politicians and leaders are no more corrupt than they have ever been. They are quite likely less corrupt than at any time in history. However, the horizontal connecting of individual minds enabled by information technology has increased our awareness and thus limits the power of those in authority. How many presidents have had extra marital sexual relationships and lied about it? Likely many, however, today we do not tolerate it. Information technology allows us to wake up to a reality that has existed for decades and centuries. We saw this connection of minds defeat Marcos in the Philippines; we saw it in Poland and in the collapse of the Soviet Union; we saw it in South Africa with the defeat of apartheid.

SOCIAL AND ECONOMIC FREEDOM IMBALANCE EQUALS EXPLOSION

The problem with the transition to a knowledge era is that we have an imbalance of freedoms. As the Information Age delivers more freedom to the individual, it initially brings a dramatically higher degree of social freedom than economic freedom. This is because we are still tied to the limits on economic freedom of the Industrial Age wealth-creation structures. Decades ago people had neither money nor tolerance from society to do a wide variety of things. Today, there is the tolerance but not the money. We therefore have chaos.

After centuries of control through serfdom, slavery, racism, sexism, and employment and a diet of pain, fear, torture, and oppression, much negative, distorted distress can be expected to emerge when social freedom is delivered. This is especially true if economic freedom does not arrive at the same time as social freedom.

The imbalance between social and economic freedom is nothing new. In the late 1980s the Tienanmen Square uprising in China and subsequent massacre came from an imbalance between social and economic freedom. People in China had begun to enjoy a level of affluence that led them to expect greater latitude of social freedom. The results were the Tienanmen Square slaughter. The government has temporarily denied this social freedom through violence power.

As the Soviet Union and Soviet bloc collapsed, they left in their oppressive wake tremendous social freedom but little economic freedom. This mismatch has produced drug and alcohol abuse, crime, violence, racism, war, ethnic cleansing, death camps, rape, child murder, disintegration of countries, and disorder.

There is a direct correlation between the two freedoms—when they are out of balance, all hell breaks loose. Our current problems with crime and violence will not be solved until there is a balance between social and economic freedoms. Today this imbalance threatens to destroy all of civilization if it is not restored.

THE EMPOWERMENT OF LOSERS

A knowledge era automatically decentralizes power to the individual. Today as the knowledge era delivers more social freedom to individuals each day, it is empowering individuals who have been on the losing side of the win/lose game for decades and centuries. Many people oppressed for the past few hundred years now have a "loser" paradigm. With expanded social freedoms many "losers" now have the social freedom to cause you, your family, and much of society to lose with them. This empowerment grows daily with expanding information technology.

Because the losers have nothing to lose and now have the power to force others to lose with them, many are choosing to exercise their new power. Win/lose is evolving to lose/lose directly before our eyes. This lose/lose reality surfaces today as terrorism, gangs, violence, riots, robbery, rape, crime, radical militias, and hate groups. Lose/lose is simply a reflection of our win/lose paradigm, as individuals become empowered in a knowledge society in which social freedoms precede economic freedoms.

In the 1990s lose/lose violence reached epidemic proportions. Tens of thousands of people were killed on our streets in violent acts such as drive-by shootings and gang warfare, tourist killings in Florida, mass suicide in Texas, and everyday murders. There were the bombings of the World Trade Center, the Oklahoma City federal building, and the Atlanta Olympics. There were airplane bombings, mass public shootings, freeway shootings, routine post office killings, hijacking of passenger planes, burning of hundreds of houses in arson forest fires in California, carjackings, and the hijacking of a cruise liner.

Already we have more people dying each day, over 65 in many recent years, from violence as died each day the Vietnam War (U.S. Dept. of Justice, April 1994). We all know of famous people, such as Bill Cosby and Michael Jordan, who lost family members because of the current power shift. However, tens of thousands of nameless and faceless people face the same pain each year.

LOSE/LOSE PLUS EMPOWERED INDIVIDUALS EQUALS THE BIG BANG

Though our present level of lose/lose violence is at epidemic proportions, nuclear weapons in the hands of people with lose/lose paradigms put a whole new light on the issue. In a knowledge era, it becomes more and more difficult to protect, control, or contain knowledge. Today any individual can learn to make a nuclear bomb from books in public libraries. This was demonstrated and proved in the 1970s. Bomb-making instructions are readily available on the Internet, and nuclear-grade plutonium is for sale in the Russian black market. Even the most sensitive knowledge will eventually leak in a knowledge era. More important in the knowledge era is that a wide variety of people will be able to create the desired knowledge for highly destructive weapons.

No explanation is required for what could happen as a few people with lose/lose paradigms explode a few nuclear weapons in a few of the largest cities of the United States or the world. Today there is no shortage of internal or external lose/lose terrorists from whom this type of activity could come, and this list will only grow longer as win/lose continues to shift to lose/lose.

Nuclear weapons are not the only means by which small groups of individuals can bring an Information Age society to a halt. Chemical or biologic weapons such as anthrax bacteria can easily be delivered to New York, Los Angeles, or Chicago with crop duster airplanes at night. One person can kill hundreds of thousands. A small team of individuals hitting several cities at once can kill millions and throw our society and economy into chaos. In 1994, *60 Minutes* presented a segment on an invisible and odorless poisonous gas that can be delivered to a city like Boston by someone driving a boat through the harbor. A pound of gas delivered today can cause hundreds of thousands of people to begin dropping dead tomorrow.

Our Information-Age society and economy rest on fragile technological pillars. As the information superhighway becomes the infrastructure for civilization, the pillars of society become relatively easy to sabotage. As we advance into the Information Age, protecting these pillars from persons who have lose/lose paradigms becomes harder and harder and eventually will be impossible.

Alvin and Heidi Toffler in *War and Anti-War* (1993) spoke to a senior intelligence official who said, "Give me $1 million and 20 people and I'll shut America down." In an Information Age, power is greatly decentralized to the individual. Fifty years ago a million dollars and 20 people didn't stand a chance of shutting down America. In the next five years the shut-down-America figure will be far lower, perhaps $500,000 and ten people. In ten years it may be $100,000 and five people. In fifteen years it maybe one person and $10,000. This, however, is only the tip of the iceberg. The longer term holds almost certain devastation unless we shift to win/win. A knowledge era will provide individuals with enormous power. We are sure to develop the knowledge for far more powerful weapons and destructive ability. Individuals and small groups in a knowledge era will eventually be able to produce new, more powerful weapons. We will not be able to regulate these individuals into not having or using these weapons.

Within the coming decades every individual on the planet will have unlimited power to destroy or create; each will have the power to blow up the planet and end civilization. We are moving to a state of *mass autocracy*, in which each individual has unlimited power.

> *And another reason that I'm happy to live in this period is that we have been forced to a point where we are going to have to grapple with the problems that men have been trying to grapple with through history, but the demands didn't force them to do it. Survival now demands that we grapple with them. Men, for years, have been talking about war and peace. But now, no longer can they just talk about it. It is no longer a choice between violence and nonviolence in the world; it's violence and nonexistence.*
> —Martin Luther King, Jr., *I've Been to the Mountain Top*

Our destructive power is simply far too great to continue our win/lose paradigm. This is because it reaches a point where one loser can set us all back a thousand years. The systemic effects of our win/lose worldview are catching up with us not only through intentional violence but also through other means such as the destruction and neglect of the environment. When we measure profit on the basis of the fragmented piece of product cost for which one today can be held accountable while ignoring the part that others in the future pay for, we are practicing win/lose-based wealth creation. I win by making a profit today producing electricity from nuclear power, but people in the future may lose by having to pay to clean up my waste.

When we do not pay the full cost for what we get, we practice win/lose wealth creation. When we try to get people to work for as little as possible while getting them to produce as much as possible, we practice win/lose wealth creation. We have a name for people who do not believe in paying the full cost for what they receive—welfare recipients. Though some may refer to it as good business, good bargaining, or good negotiating, paying an engineer $36,000 simply because she is naïve when you believe she is adding at least $50,000 in value is welfare, and you are a welfare recipient.

Although reports are presented and denied regarding the state of the environment and the effects of our actions, the bottom line is that there are limits to the amount of destruction we can cause to the environment before we reach the point of no return. Other areas such as genetics and human cloning have equally devastating potential if approached with a win/lose worldview. These technologies cannot and will not be contained or controlled.

Today it is truly "win/win or no deal" (Covey 1989). The evidence shows that a knowledge society must evolve out of its win/lose heritage or perish. Win/lose simply will not cut it any longer. It is not compatible with the power brought to the individual in an era of mass autocracy. We are in a knowledge era that has only just begun to provide social freedoms. As information technology grows, it will continue to expand social freedoms faster and faster. The longer we delay in getting economic freedom up to par, the more we shall all lose.

In the next several decades we shall likely see information technology expand social freedoms and individual power beyond the breakpoint of human regulation—the point at which individual humans cannot be controlled through laws and microrules. Each individual at some point in the future will have the ability to destroy all of civilization. At the human-regulation breakpoint and beyond, humanity must have systems in place to operate a civilization with win/win-based norms and not win/lose-based regulation. "When mores are strong enough, laws are not needed, and when mores are not strong enough, laws are irrelevant" (Covey 1992).

The alternative to a win/win civilization is bleak. It includes a likely road warrior era, as depicted in the *Mad Max* films (1979, 1981, 1985), a second dark ages, as human knowledge and technology for the second time in history outpace human maturity. We cannot grow in technology and knowledge without relatively equal growth in wisdom and maturity. Nature will keep these two in balance even if it means going back a thousand years to align technology with maturity.

Balance between social and economic freedoms is critical for peace and prosperity. It is the link to our maturity and the survival of our planet. We are not going back to the limited social freedoms of a pre-Information Age, unless information technology regresses 50 years or civilization crashes. The present cautious wait-and-see, go-slow, reactive, analytical, and continuous-improvement approach must be discarded. We must move rapidly toward as much economic freedom as possible for individuals in order to match the social freedoms being automatically granted through knowledge power. The only practical system with the power to expand economic freedom fast enough is mass privatization and decentralized wealth creation whereby individuals are free to control their own destinies and are motivated to heal themselves.

For more detail on the importance of social and economic freedom, see *The Balance Between Social and Economic Freedoms, Win/Lose and Competition the Norm of Civilization, The Evolution of Win/Lose to Lose/Lose, Lose/Lose and Empowered Individuals Equals the Big Bang, Hell and the Fall Backwards: The Second Dark Ages* at the WinWinWorld.net website at **http://www.winwin world.net**

9

Breakpoint to the New Civilization

The Rapid Shift and Why You Must Act Now

> *The science of natural change and growth shows that at critical*
> *points in the development of anything the rules shift. . . . At*
> *Breakpoint the rule change is so sharp that continuing to use*
> *the old rules not only doesn't work, it erects great, sometimes*
> *insurmountable, barriers to success.*
> —George Land and Beth Jarman, *Breakpoint and Beyond*

At the dawn of the Information Age, there are serious questions to be asked. How and when do we make it past breakpoint? Can this occur without catastrophic violence, death, and turmoil? Is there the likelihood that we will not make it into the new era? Can the transition occur with only slow, continuous improvement, or is it an all-or-none proposition? Throughout the rest of this book, these questions are answered. In short, slow, continuous change alone is a doomed strategy. The science of breakpoint and precedence indicates that the change will be abrupt and quick.

BREAKPOINT: SUDDEN, ABRUPT, AND RADICAL TRANSITION

We will remain on the Industrial Age foundation of centralized wealth creation until we hit what George Land and Beth Jarman in *Breakpoint and Beyond* (1992) call *breakpoint*. It is a climax through which we must pass to make the transition from an Industrial Age to an Information Age and from the Win/Lose Era to the Win/Win Era. Breakpoints are natural phenomena in the development of any evolving system in which the rules suddenly and sharply shift. The old rules no longer apply and even become counterproductive. In explaining the science of breakpoint, Land and Jarman write, "The science of natural change and growth shows that at critical points in the development of anything the rules shift." After breakpoint, many things operate opposite of pre-breakpoint. Using science and social change, Land and Jarman build a compelling case to show how breakpoints work, as follows:

- As breakpoint is approached, actions that were once very productive begin to have diminishing returns; systems become ineffective and inefficient. For example, today it is commonly understood that the management of people is quite an ineffective means of running a business, though we have productively done it for 200 years. Books such as *Managing People Is Like Herding Cats* and *The Unnatural Act of Management* document this trend. A second example can be seen with the focus on material wealth creation versus nonmaterial wealth as described in Chapter 1 in the example of IBM and Microsoft.

- Once breakpoint is reached, the old systems simply do not work and even become counterproductive. For example, serfdom and aristocracy after the French Revolution simply were not possible. Agricultural wealth creation after the start of the industrial revolution produced millions of failing family farms as people were herded into factories. Likewise we will likely see the rapid decline of employment after breakpoint to mass privatization.

- Many things that produced nothing and were liabilities before breakpoint become the new producers after breakpoint. For example, workers in controlled economies are liabilities. This is from the financial perspective of win/lose, standardized compensation that exists with employment. Workers are a cost. Workers, however, become the primary asset in the win/win, value-added compensation system of mass privatization. When you look at the new on-line mass privatization communities evolving on the Internet, a primary focus is to get more people in the communities. The same is true of Network Marketing as well as the Amazon.com associates program.

Perhaps the most compelling trait of breakpoints is that they are all-or-none and all-at-once propositions. We cannot safely and effectively "continuously improve" our way past breakpoint, because the Information Age is not a mere linear extension of the Industrial Age.

On the basis of precedence and current trends, we are near the breakpoint of a completely new wealth-creation paradigm and civilization. Because of the level of advancement of our society, this promises to be the sharpest and largest change in all of human history in the shortest time span. On the basis of precedence, we can expect a dramatic, sharp, and abrupt shift whereby controlled economies, employment, representative government, and all other Industrial Age institutions are replaced **as the norms and power systems in society** over the span of a few years.

THREE HISTORICAL BREAKPOINTS: LINEAR THINKING FROM THE PAST

People who live in a civilization that has lasted for hundreds or thousands of years or even just a few decades tend to believe that the current institutions are all that is possible. Their thinking becomes straightlined and linear. The future is simply more of the past. Things will continue the same way indefinitely. The precedent also shows that these abrupt, directional changes result in massive chaos and upheaval, because people are usually caught off guard, thinking that things are destined to continue in a straight line (see Figure 9–1). These people therefore ignore or resist the change, producing pain for themselves. They literally miss the turnoff to the future.

As we look back in history we see people in preindustrial societies who clashed with those from the Industrial Age. In the United States 9.6 million out of 10 million Native Americans died because of the clash. We see the same trend in Mexico by the Spanish, in Africa, and in many other countries as they were colonized by emerging industrial powers. In all that would become the industrialized world the agrarian wealth-creation system of serfdom, slavery, and monarchy was systematically replaced. In the French Revolution, those who resisted the new paradigm had their heads chopped off; Russia experienced the Bolshevik Revolution; in the United States a first breakpoint came with the American Revolution. However, the southern United States committed to sticking to an agrarian civilization, which necessitated a second breakpoint with the Civil War.

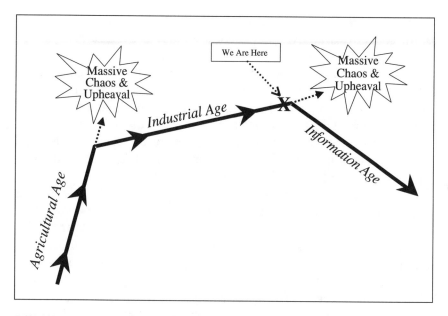

FIGURE 9–1 Historical Change Is Nonlinear

Southern plantation owners ignored and then resisted the steamroller forces of the coming and unstoppable industrial revolution; many people lost fortunes, lives, and family. Many lost all that they had built because of their out-of-date wealth-creation paradigm. Plantation owners had to be taken hostage and forced into the industrial revolution with the Civil War. Their ignorance and unwillingness to shift paradigms and see the future cost 600,000 lives and the destruction of much of what they had created.

Throughout the world those who resisted or ignored the incoming industrial revolution caused mass destruction, a fate we can avoid by aligning ourselves with today's shift. The precedent clearly shows that the true risk at breakpoint lies in (1) linear thinking, (2) not breaking away from old-world views, and (3) not aligning with the collective change. As Peter Drucker wrote, "every organization has to be prepared for the abandonment of every thing it does" (1992).

THE COLLAPSE HAS BEGUN

As we look at the United States, the most advanced of the industrialized nations and the leader into the Information Age, we see a society nearing breakpoint. A society that fits the first rule of the breakpoint concept—that systems become ineffective and inefficient. In our schools we have dropped to the bottom of the rankings of all industrialized nations. Wasteful and declining bureaucracies are not effectively meeting customer needs, government is gridlocked, and taxes are increasing. Gangs, drugs, corrupt leaders, high crime and violence, terrorism, and homelessness are prevalent. There is talk of secession by counties, states, and regions in the United States and other industrialized nations. Traditions and infrastructure are collapsing, and families are declining.

Already tens of thousands die each year in the United States as a result of the shift. Think of the magnitude of the disillusionment of southern plantation owners immediately after the Civil War. This is the pain we face without more alignment with an Information Age. What must we do to avoid this pain? We must abandon our present civilization and create a new one.

We should learn from the plantation owners' mistakes. We need to protect our years of investment by embracing the information revolution and its new social institutions. We need to abandon the old institutions while creating the new ones in parallel. This is the only way in which we can protect our years of investment.

For more detail on the decline of Industrial Age society, see *The Collapse Has Begun* at the WinWinWorld.net website at **http:// www.winwinworld.net**

LESSONS FOR THE PLANTATION OWNERS

Because breakpoints are rapid and violent, we need consciously to begin creating the new systems with all deliberate speed. Continuous improvement of present systems alone will actually create more problems than it solves. When he heard the previous sentence, a friend of mine replied, "Bunk!" He said up until the Civil War, plantations were still creating wealth. He was implying that we should follow our present course of slow, continuous improvement within centralized wealth creation. He said, "If you're making good money, stay with it and ride the system down until it falls apart and let others worry about the consequences." I commented that *we'd* be the ones who would have to worry about the consequences.

If we look back to the plantation owners, there was an illusion of wealth being created in the South immediately before the Civil

War. Five years before the war, the plantation owners were setting the stage for the destruction of much of what they had created. Though each year the individual plantations and bank accounts may have registered a profit, they were in reality building huge deficits. These deficits were rapidly paid within a few years after the start of the Civil War with the draining of plantation owners' bank accounts to fund the war. The plantation owners paid with their blood and lives and those of their sons, the brutal destruction of their plantations, cities, infrastructure, and civilization, and the rapes of their wives and daughters.

Are we doing the same today? Are we as companies and individuals showing illusionary profits that we will have to repay in a few years? Are we setting the stage for millions of deaths and the destruction of much of what we have built? Are you setting the stage for the deaths of your loved ones because you refuse to open your eyes, begin synthesizing information, and taking action? Because of the enormous power bestowed on individuals with a win/lose paradigm in the knowledge era, we probably are repeating the sins of our ancestors.

The barbarians are at the gate as millions of empowered, losing individuals want what you have and are gaining the power to take it by any means necessary. Either you begin win/win wealth creation today and begin truly caring about others, or you and your family stand to lose it all.

The plantation owners chose to improve the plantation—they chose to "care less" about the losers in pain and bondage. As winners they had years and decades invested in the old system. Their vision was a linear one—an aristocratic society that would last a thousand years. Because they saw opportunity as a threat to this investment and vision, plantation owners chose to protect their investment by staying within the old system. There was only one way for the plantation owners to protect their years of investment; that was by abandoning their civilization and creating and embracing the new one.

What if the plantation owners had had a powerful vision of the coming industrial revolution and had passionately embraced it? What if they had accepted Industrial Age social institutions five years before the Civil War—a strong central government, companies, employment, factories, farms, mechanized farming, the nuclear family? What if they had voluntarily abandoned plantations, slavery, and broad states' rights for these new institutions? They may have been able to make profitably the transition to factories and farms, their plantations could have supported them until the new investments became profitable. Perhaps they could have recovered their slave investments by selling each slave his or her own freedom. They could have hired slaves out, allowing them to keep a portion of the income to purchase their own freedom. They could have recouped much of their investment and had a relatively smooth transition into an Industrial Age. But all of this would have taken a powerful vision of what was occurring.

Today we have the same opportunity as the plantation owners, but we are following in the plantation owners' footsteps. We lack a powerful enough vision of what is going on. We cling to the old system without understanding that a completely new system is required. We protect our investment and illusionary personal profits by staying with the old paradigm. We accept the illusion that our present social institutions are all that is or ever will be possible—education in schools, working in companies, governing by representation. As Toffler (1990) stated, we are literally going to have to reinvent civilization. We must abandon the old civilization and create a new one. We must begin win/win wealth creation with all deliberate speed.

10

The Rise of True Democracy through Synergy

An Era of Real Individual Liberty and Full Participation

You are living in a period of time that will produce more change for humanity than any previous era in history. It is a time of extraordinary importance that will fundamentally reshape almost every aspect of your life during the next two decades. Wholesale change is taking place in almost every segment of your reality and the pace will only increase in the coming years.
—John Peterson, *The Road to 2015*

For those desiring more freedom from government control, it is critical to understand that the institutions for an era all fit together. The government limits personal liberty because this is required for a system of centralized wealth creation built upon controlled economies. To obtain considerably more personal liberty from government, we must have a substantially different way of organizing work, business, and all of our institutions. If you are a business owner railing against the governmental infringements on your personal freedoms, consider the limits of creative freedom and ownership that your system of organizing work in your company places on your employees.

I could spend several chapters defining the problems with mass representative democracy and why it cannot work in an Information Age. (See *The Death of Representative Government* at the WinWin-World.net website at **http://www.winwinworld.net**) However, we all deep down *intuitively* know that something is gravely wrong with the system of politicians, taxes, representation, and elections. We know that it is so deep it will not be fixed simply by electing a new president or even a whole new Congress. However, we simply cannot imagine anything beyond traditional democracy or what would replace it. More than 200 years ago Thomas Jefferson, a founding father of mass representative democracy, warned us of the limits of the system, as follows:

> I am not an advocate for frequent changes in laws and constitutions. But laws and institutions must go hand in hand with the progress of the human mind. As that becomes more developed, more enlightened, and as new discoveries are made, new truths discovered and manners and opinions change, with that change of circumstances, institutions must advance also to keep pace with the times. We might as well require a man to wear the coat which fitted him as a boy, as civilized society to remain ever under the regimen of their barbarous ancestors. (Jefferson Memorial, Washington, DC)

By today's standards even Jefferson would have to admit that he was "barbarous" being that he was a slave owner. With his own words Jefferson himself sowed the seeds for replacement of the representative system of government and civilization that he helped to establish. We continuously look back to see what our forefathers intended. Above all they intended for humanity never to be stuck in outmoded institutions.

The monarchy overthrown by Thomas Jefferson and his associates 200 years ago was part of a system of wealth creation for an agrarian society that was outgrown and replaced with a system for an industrial society. A new and fresh foundation was needed, one that inherently supplied the levels of liberty, ownership, and freedom to harness the power and growth of the coming industrial revolution.

There seems to be a trend in which humanity requires more liberty and freedom as it grows and evolves to continue growth and development. As humanity has grown, developed, and become more mature over the past decades and centuries, we have reached the limits of liberty, ownership, and freedom of our present system of representation. We need a new system that will provide individuals with even more inherent individual liberty, ownership, and freedom. Having outgrown the Industrial Age wealth-creation system, we must take Jefferson's advice and do what he and his clan did—cast aside the old system and help usher in the new system of social order.

THE QUEST FOR TRUE DEMOCRACY:
OUR INTUITIVE IDEAL

When we synthesize decentralized wealth creation with expanded social and economic freedoms from information technology, we see a new system of true democracy arising to replace representation. Most people intuitively know what true democracy is. However, this idealistic view does not fit the representative government that we have had for the past 200 years.

Most people intuitively understand democracy as a system of individual liberty, one free of authoritarian controls and restraints on our individual liberty, one with opportunity for all. We envision a system based on synergy whereby individuals come together through free-market interactions to create more than they could separately. These free interactions include thoughts, ideals, culture, products, values, and more. We envision a system whereby social order is largely a by-product of our free-market interactions and therefore requires little authoritarian control. We envision a system with family values at the core that is based on responsibility and ownership, a system with spirituality interwoven into the very fabric of the system and our daily lives.

Unfortunately, because of technical and other limitations, this has been a mere dream. We have not experienced true democracy over the past 200 years. At this point in our history we must make a distinction between the "beginner's democracy" of the Industrial Age and the true democracy of the Information Age into which we are moving. For this reason I refer to the beginner's democracy of the past 200 years as one form of representative government (see Figure 6–1 in Chapter 6). Representative government covers everything from beginner's democracy to communism to dictatorships—all of which use representatives, elected or imposed, to makes decisions for the masses.

Beginner's democracy is a good system relative to the primitiveness and control of monarchy and serfdom. It offered significantly more liberty for our ancestors' transitioning from an Agricultural Age. Today, however, it simply does not offer the liberty, interconnectedness, and opportunity for all that is required to propel an information society. When we analyze exactly what beginner's democracy means and compare the definition with how it operates, we are shocked that our form of government is not exactly what we thought we had. Merriam-Webster's Collegiate Dictionary, 10th edition, defines *democracy* as follows:

1 a: government by the people; esp: rule of the majority **b:** a government in which the supreme power is vested in the people and exercised by them directly or indirectly through a system of representation usu. involving periodically held free elections. . . . **5:** the absence of hereditary or arbitrary class distinctions or privileges.

Beginner's democracy is a system of government based on *rule* by the majority of people through elected representative politicians who through laws attempt to deliver social equality to all.

When we analyze the definition we find even more surprises. The dictionary defines *government* as "the act or process of governing; authoritative direction or control." *Govern* is defined as "to control, direct," "to rule," "to restrain." To *rule* is defined as "to exert control, direction, or influence on," "to exercise control over, esp. by curbing or restraining," "to exercise authority or power over often harshly or arbitrarily."

One can logically define beginner's democracy as a system of social organization based on providing *individuals* with a relatively small *degree* of liberty whereby the majority selects the people who will dominate, restrain, rule over, or control society with the ideal of treating everyone equally.

On a relative scale, traditional democracy is an *authoritarian* system in which the majority merely gets to elect who will be in *authority*. Some may see this as a specious argument based on formal dictionary definitions. Many in this group may feel that the answer to the problems of representative democracy can be found with a simple shift from federal to local governmental control.

THE FAILURE OF LOCAL REPRESENTATIVE GOVERNMENT

The thinking of the local government movement is that local government will get control back into the hands of the people. This is the same logic that managers in companies are using as they attempt to fix their problems by converting to smaller, baby bureaucracies within larger bureaucracies (for example, profit centers, business units, teams, and horizontal organizations). Though both local government and corporate decentralization show the direction of change, neither is the answer nor is our final destination in an Information Age.

From 1992 to 1996 I worked closely with the public school system in Greene County, North Carolina. The school superintendent, Dr. Paul Browning, was extremely progressive. He brought a new level of customer service, openness, democracy, and learning to the school system and county. He led the effort to bring two of the county's four schools to exemplary status. Refusing to play the political game, Browning accomplished things in the best interest of the children and county but offended some well-connected people. Eventually Browning was forced to resign and was paid $125,000 for the buyout of his contract. Citizens were outraged about losing this excellent leader.

In a county where citizens rarely speak out because of apathy and fear of reprisal, hundreds showed up at board of education meetings. In meeting after meeting citizens demanded answers regarding what had happened. Newspapers led with editorial headlines reading, "Tell the People Why!" Board of education meetings were broadcast on the local news. In one meeting that filled a school auditorium, citizens repeatedly asked why the action had been taken. The board members sat silently and did not answer a single question as the questions flew for a couple of hours. The board of education lawyer instead responded to all of the questions. In a nutshell the board's position was as follows:

It does not matter what you people want, think, or believe. You have elected these politicians to represent you and they have the legal *authority* to take the action they have taken and to run the school system as they please. This is our system of government. Good or bad, the system, education included, is based on *politics*. If you don't like the decisions these people have made, then don't vote for them in the next election. However, they do not owe you any answers for their actions and will not answer any of your questions.

The lawyer made it clear that *they*, the authorities, not *we the people* control the school system and the education of our children. In future meetings the citizens were treated as serfs. We were constantly reminded that the meetings were not for us, that we the citizens were external to the government, and that *they* were in charge. In many cases we could not hear the discussions. Board members would whisper to one another. We never received handouts of information being presented to the board for consideration and thus could not follow the issues being reviewed. The room was designed so that people who brought proposals to the board for review sat with their backs to the citizens, symbolically and literally leaving the citizens out of the meeting.

Overhead projectors and other tools that most organizations use to communicate to groups were hardly ever used. In one case a presenter did use a transparency projector. The screen hung in the back of the room where the citizens sat. When it was pulled down from the ceiling it came down directly in front of people in the back row. Not only could they not see the presentation but also the back of the screen was inches from their faces, pinning them against the back wall of the room. The balance of citizens had to turn their necks at a very bad angle to see or could not see at all. At the end of the meeting I asked why were they not using standard seating arrangements and communication tools that organizations use as a matter of course when they want to communicate. Needless to say, I received no answer.

As of this writing all of the board members who voted for the buyout lost their bid for reelection. The leader of the coup, the chairman of the board, finished next to last out of a field of more than six. The board members' losses proved that the majority of citizens did not agree with the board's action. One could say that beginner's democracy prevailed because the citizens had the last word. However, the citizens did not get what they wanted. The customers' needs were not met. Browning was gone forever, and my four children and other children in the county will get a poorer education because of this. Local mass representative democracy had failed to meet its prime mission, majority rule, and was and is light years away from individual liberty. Ironically, part of the defense used by board members was that they knew best what was right because they were local and not state or federal politicians. Though local representation is closer to the people, why were they not willing to follow their logic to its natural conclusion and go all of the way and trust "we the people." We see this same "Boss Hog"–type corruption in companies with fad decentralization programs. These programs in many cases create minikingdoms with one dictating ruler systematically crushing the entire organization's intelligence so that his will can be expressed.

Just as corporate decentralization is not the answer to our problems, neither is local mass representative democracy. One may say that the example is an exception; however, local papers nationwide each week have many similar problems. Within two years Greene County had a repeat of a similar issue with the board of county commissioners regarding a regional landfill. Again citizens were treated as lowly serfs, and the landfill was pushed through against strong citizen opposition.

We have the liberty to choose our dictators, and this is largely where our liberty ends. Though people may say *dictator* is too harsh a word, I refer to the Greene County citizen who told me, "I cannot say anything regarding my opposition. All it takes is one phone call to the state board of —————, and I am out of business." I met many citizens who made similar statements. Even today I leave out the name of the state board because of fear of reprisal for the individual.

The best we can hope for with mass representative democracy is an *enlightened dictatorship*. Even with this, as much as 49% of the population may not be getting what they desire because mass representative democracy is based on rule by the majority. Even when one's candidate does win, **none** of the individuals voting for that candidate gets all of the things they believe in. Customers' needs therefore go unmet. This is because mass representative democracy is a mass-production system whereby regardless of individual needs, the focus is on the average.

Today people ranging from radical militias to conservatives to libertarians to liberals to minorities to many upstart organizations are almost in rebellion against what they perceive as the tyranny of beginner's democracy. Most believe that the true ideals of representative democracy have been subverted. However, these ideals have not been subverted, because beginner's democracy at its core governs, rules, controls, and restrains the individual in society through laws, taxes, and microrules. Beginner's democracy is more democratic than ever because our politicians are more intelligent, honest, law-abiding, and ethical than ever. The problem is that our expectations have been raised, primarily through information technology, because we better connect and yearn for levels of liberty and maturity beyond what beginner's democracy can deliver.

We must remember that beginner's democracy is an archaic, mass-production system whereby everyone receives the same equal and "average" treatment as determined by representatives of the majority regardless of the individual's specific needs. The rage people feel against beginner's democracy is the yearning for more liberty, therefore more customization, from a more mature form of democracy for a more mature humanity. We are six-year-olds demanding that our training wheels be removed, and they are being removed.

Beginner's democracy is a system of social organization in which order comes from a source external to and separate from the individuals in society—elected representatives in governing bodies. It is a primitive system of liberty that provides basic freedoms in which there is very little direct participation by individuals.

Even when beginner's democracy is directly participatory, individuals directly voting for or against something, it is still about narrow win/lose choices. It is rigid, lifeless, and mostly void of synergy; there are two or sometimes three *opposing* win/lose viewpoints, whereas the world contains infinite viewpoints. Beginner's democracy is about debating, pointing out the weaknesses and negatives in others' views, and furthering one's own point of view at the expense of others. It is mostly void of synergy because it is about analyzing and fragmenting reality and focusing only on one's own perspective as opposed to integrating and building on many perspectives. Rather than pulling humans together to become interconnected, beginner's democracy is about maintaining our separateness and divisions. Beginner's democracy is mechanistic, newtonian, analytical, reactionary, linear, and slow. True democracy replaces beginner's democracy with a new, more liberating, and enlightened system. It also replaces the very notion of government with the broader notion of *social order*.

A NEW PARADIGM OF DEMOCRACY FROM ITS ROOTS

The common belief of most people is that democracy has its roots in European culture. Jack Weatherford shows in his book *Indian Givers: How the Indians of the Americas Transformed the World* that the roots of democracy lie in the Indian cultures of the Americas. It is commonly understood that American democracy was an outgrowth of the political thought of seventeenth century enlightenment. Weatherford outlines how reports on the political systems and way of life of the American Indians inspired those seventeenth century thinkers.

Europe in the seventeenth century was an intensely authoritarian, class-bound society. The word *freedom* itself was not defined as "personal liberty" in European languages before the discovery of the Americas but generally referred to a nation's independence or a slave's release from bondage. Once they began to observe native cultures, New World explorers experienced "amazement at the Indians' personal liberty, in particular their freedom from rulers and social classes based on ownership of property. For the first time the French and the British became aware of the possibility of living in social harmony and prosperity without the rule of a king" (Weatherford 1988, p. 123). These ideas provoked a good deal of thinking and writing in the early sixteenth century. By the seventeenth century many more reports had found an interested audience, particularly in France. A very popular writer, Baron de Lahontan, published a number of works based on his observations of the Huron. He reported on the statement of one Huron to him, "We are born free and united brothers, each as much a great lord as the other, while you are the slaves of one sole man. I am the master of my body, I dispose of myself, I do what I wish, I am the first and the last of my Nation . . . subject only to the Great Spirit" (Brandon 1986, p. 90).

De Lahontan's ideas were adapted into a "hit" play, *Arlequin Sauvage*, by Delisle de la Drevetiere. In true French romantic fashion, the play was about an American Indian who travels to Paris. A young Frenchwoman named Violette falls in love with him and travels back with him to the New World so that she might live in liberty. This play made a great impression on young Jean-Jacques Rousseau, who subsequently wrote *Discourse on the Origins of Inequality* (1754). His name is always mentioned in the list of European thinkers who influenced the American founding fathers.

Another important name on that list is Thomas Paine. At the age of 37, Paine visited Benjamin Franklin in Pennsylvania and became interested in the Iroquois. During the American Revolution Paine was employed as secretary to the commissioner sent to negotiate with the Iroquois. He learned their language and in the rest of his writings, including *Common Sense, The Rights of Man*, and *The Age of Reason*, used the Indians as models of how a free society might be organized. Following the pattern of the Iroquois League of Nations, Paine coined the name "United States of America."

The first person in recorded history to suggest a union of the colonies was the Iroquois chief Canassatego in 1744. He complained that the separate colonies, each with its own policies, were difficult to communicate and deal with and that life would be easier for everyone involved if the colonies could unite and speak with one voice, as the Iroquois League did.

Benjamin Franklin also studied the Iroquois extensively. As early as 1754 at the Albany Congress Franklin called for the colonies to unite into a league similar to that of the Iroquois. Decades later, as the U.S. government was being framed, Franklin continued to promote many of the details of Iroquois government to the founding fathers, many of which were adopted.

Charles Thomson also studied the Iroquois extensively and at Thomas Jefferson's request wrote a lengthy report that was included in Jefferson's *Notes on the State of Virginia*. The concept of a united federation of states was described, as were many other details of government that were later adopted into the U.S. Constitution. Thomson described political leadership won by election, not heredity. He proposed separation of military leadership from civil leadership, the concept of impeachment, and the concept of ratification of new states as equal members. The European model was one of colonization—a new land that was to forever remain a vassal to the colonizing nation. But in our country new lands became territories, which were nurtured from the outset to become *equal partners*.

Another uncanny similarity between Iroquois culture and U.S. government is in the concept of an electoral college. There was also a tradition of changing the name of a new leader, which anticipates the practice in the Senate of addressing a senator by his senate title, not his personal name, which is never mentioned on the Senate floor.

Franklin wanted to use the Iroquois word for "grand council" rather than the Latin-based *congress*. Franklin proposed, in imitation of the Iroquois, that U.S. officials not be paid for their work. This proposal was not adopted, but the principle apparently was noted, because the founding fathers did arrange for officeholders' salaries to be minimal, just enough to pay for living expenses. Franklin was also very excited about the Iroquois custom of election of military leaders by the men they led. He even formed a militia organized this way. Our government did not adopt this practice, but they did abandon the European custom of purchase of military posts by the wealthy. The government also allowed a great deal of movement through the ranks and avoided domination by the wealthy aristocracy or oligarchy.

Another likely imitation of Iroquois government is the custom of allowing only one person to speak at a time. (European parliament traditionally has allowed the shouting down of any speaker who displeases noisy members.) "The purpose of debate in Indian councils was to persuade and educate, not to confront. Unlike European parliaments, in which opposing factions battle an issue in the public arena, the council of the Indians sought to reach an agreement through compromise" (Weatherford 1988, p. 141).

One aspect of Iroquois social order that never was adopted but is very intriguing is that the councils adopted policies only when concurrence was *unanimous*. This is the destiny to which democracy must return. If we are to have a win/win world based on synergy and synthesis, it must come through collaborative dialogue that can produce unanimous concurrence. It is the kind of communication that can occur in mass privatization but will never work in controlled economies, representative government, or bureaucracies.

Later research into the workings of Indian systems of social order throughout the Americas has shown that this democratic organization was common. Throughout the western hemisphere, a chief never possessed the kind of power to which Europeans were accustomed. Even in the highly complex Aztec culture, the Spaniards found that Moctezuma was the supreme *speaker* of the nation, not its emperor.

DEMOCRACY: THE DREAM REALIZED AT LAST

It is important to understand the history of democracy. However, this is not just about the history of beginner's democracy of the Industrial Age. The Indians have also given us a model to follow for true democracy of the Information Age. There are significant differences between beginner's democracy and the system of social order of Indian democracy. Weatherford illustrates the difference in his description of a recent powwow in Fargo, North Dakota. Weatherford (1988, p. 117) states:

> To an outsider . . . powwows often appear chaotic. Even though posted signs promise that the dances will begin at four o'clock, there is still no dancing at five-thirty. Drummers scheduled to play never arrive, and some groups drum without being on the program. Impromptu family ceremonies intertwine with the official scheduled events, and the microphone passes among scores of announcers during the evening. No one is in control. This seems to be typical of Indian community events: no one is in control. No master of ceremony tells everyone what to do and no one orders dances to appear. The announcer acts as herald or possibly as facilitator of ceremonies, but no chief rises to demand anything of anyone.

Having attended a recent Iroquois powwow in Washington, North Carolina, I find that Weatherford seems to be describing the very powwow I attended. Beginner's democracy is authority based, whereas Indian democracy is more egalitarian. In beginner's democracy someone must be in control—in authority. According to Weatherford's description, Indian democracy was more natural and free flowing, artistic and spiritual, synergistic and synthesizing. At the same time it was practical and supported their system of wealth creation and social order. Indian democracy worked because people lived and worked in small communities connected to other small communities.

As we move into an Information Age in which information technology is used to create a global village of interconnected, diverse, small mass privatization communities, a more natural and liberating form of democracy is mandatory. Alvin Toffler (1990) refers to the new government for an Information Age as a mosaic democracy—a society of overlapping organizations with direct participation. Peter Drucker (1992) calls it a society of organizations. An Information Age must have a system of social order that moves toward a more natural democracy. Perhaps we can provide a new and concise definition of true democracy: social order and abundance through people's free interactions, interdependence, and interconnectedness. To be even more concise, the definition could be as follows: social order and abundance through synergy and synthesis—hence *synocracy* or *mass synocracy.*

> **mass:** *adj.* (1773) **1a:** of or relating to the mass of people
> **synergy:** [from Greek *synergos,* working together] (1660): interaction of discrete agencies . . . , agents, or conditions such that the total effect is greater than the sum of the individual effects.
> **synthesis:** [Greek from *syntithenai,* to put together] (1589): **1c:** the combining of often diverse conceptions into a coherent whole **2b:** the dialectic combination of thesis and antithesis into a higher stage of truth
> **-cracy:** [from Greek *-kratia* from *kratos,* strength, power] **3:** theory of social organization <technocracy>
>
> (*Merriam-Webster's Collegiate Dictionary,* 1993)

True democracy or mass synocracy moves us away from governing, ruling, or dictating even when it is self-induced governing, ruling, or dictating. Synocracy is about engaging each individual and each viewpoint in society—the more the merrier. Whereas beginner's democracy chokes on diversity in seeking a homogeneous melting pot, synocracy thrives on seeking a diverse mosaic. Synocracy is alive with people's ideas freely flowing and building on one another through dialogue, seeking first to understand, brainstorming, connecting, and communicating.

True democracy, or synocracy, is a synthesizing and synergistic process of creativity, artistic flow, and continuous evolution to higher abundant and spiritual states. It is a system of connecting and integrating that reveals underlying quantum wholeness to the universe. Synocracy at its core is a highly liberating, participatory, and customizing form of social organization whereby self-determination and each individual's needs and liberty are of highest priority. Through this highest priority the greatest group collaboration is produced.

With mass synocracy, social order is self-generating from within the system. With each individual creating wealth and working, he or she automatically participates in producing an ordered society based on norms, not laws or microrules. Beginner's democracy supports a fragmented newtonian worldview by separating social order from wealth creation (government should stay out of business). Mass synocracy synthesizes social order into the wealth-creation process itself.

Beginner's democracy also separates social order from spirituality. It must do this or risk abuse of power and oppression of people's religious beliefs, hence the long-standing newtonian separation of church and state. With mass synocracy there is no division between spirituality, wealth creation, and social order. These three and more have been synthesized into one, undivided natural whole called *life*.

Mass synocracy is the system of true democracy that results when a society operates with mass privatization, decentralized wealth creation, and mass autocracy. Thousands of global mass privatization communities have the common mission of meeting other people's needs and the shared vision of a win/win world. As these communities deeply interconnect, overlap, and interact, social order and abundance in society are naturally produced. Social order comes through norms, principles, and a shared vision of the interdependent whole of which we are a part. Each individual is connected and has some relationship with every other individual globally, either directly or indirectly. It is a system whereby all boats rise together. An individual's wealth increases directly as the

wealth of other individuals and the whole group increases; thus win/win and collaboration are the primary norm.

For more detail on a society based on mass synocracy, see *Increased Quality to the Individual, Core Demands of the New Wealth Creation* at the WinWinWorld.net website at **http://www. winwinworld.net**

> *I am reminded of the teachings I received from one of my elders on speaking in council. He used to state quite frequently that when we come to discuss a particular problem or concern, we are to speak only from our own experience. In that way we are not guessing. What we speak has to be the truth as much as we know it to be. When we speak we are also to refrain from attacking others. We are only to speak with the understanding we have been given. When we take part in a discussion about an issue we should put forward only those of our thoughts and beliefs that will help lead to a solution. We are to speak recognizing that when we bring our own individual truth to the truth put forward by others we will all arrive at a greater truth and understanding. We are not to speak against another person's beliefs or ideals but to only speak for ourselves as we are given insight and wisdom. Nowadays that is a hard thing to do, especially when we are taught the arts of adversarialism in all branches of education, whether they be educational, political, social, or religious.*
>
> —Terry Widrick, Iroquois

PART V

The Awakening to a Win/Win World

11

The Metamorphosis of Wealth Creation

The Shift to Knowledge Power and Emotional Intelligence

Today we are witnessing a change in the very definition of wealth creation from the self-centered making, mining, and growing of things to the others-centered meeting of human needs. It is a power shift that sets the stage for a win/win world.

WEALTH CREATION MOVES BEYOND SELF-INTEREST

In defining the invisible hand of the Industrial Age free market in *The Wealth of Nations*, Adam Smith drove home the point that civilization advances and creates wealth when each individual looks out for his or her own self-interest. By each individual looking out for his or her own interests, the invisible hand of the free market ensures that civilization also advances. We have order from chaos.

Smith was absolutely correct that Industrial Age wealth creation is driven by self-interest. However, as with all paradigms, a larger paradigm encompasses the smaller one. Self-interest as the driver of wealth creation is not wrong. It is just incomplete and incoherent. Individuals can attain some levels and dimensions of wealth by only looking out for themselves, but deeper levels, broader dimensions, and greater amounts of wealth are attained by looking out for others while helping oneself—win/win.

The rallying cry for organizations in the 1990s was "growth by meeting customers' needs." This cry is being expanded to include all

189

stakeholders—customers, suppliers, partners, and others. The frantic change in the last 20 years has been about a shift to win/win wealth creation—the customer and quality movements, teams and collaboration, empowerment, incentive pay, and far more. Today one must do far more than be interested in self-gain if one is to thrive financially.

As society has advanced, developed, and reached breakpoint, Smith's Industrial Age paradigm has simply run out of steam. It is an immature newtonian worldview based on fragmentation—we are separate from one another and the universe, and we can help ourselves while hurting or not caring about others or the environment. What we are discovering through experience is that there is only so far that self-interest alone can propel a civilization. Looking out for oneself and dickering, haggling, and negotiating to have one's way, to see only from one's narrow perspective, does add value in a relatively primitive civilization and a relatively immature humanity. Civilizations after all advanced and created wealth through slavery; however, far more wealth has been created though the less win/lose system of employment.

As we again shift civilizations we must make another leap toward greater win/win in wealth creation to continue advancing. Today we must look out not only for ourselves but also for customers and all stakeholders, all of humanity, and our environment. This change moves us to a new level of maturity and the opportunity to tap infinite wealth through collaboration. Smith's view of self-interest driving wealth creation is win/lose, a sales paradigm—making the sale and meeting my needs regardless of whether the product meets your needs. The sales paradigm was the core of wealth creation during the Industrial Age. It is no longer valid.

THE SHIFT FROM A SALES TO A SERVICE PARADIGM

When I'm ready to purchase a computer, I call Ted at Applied Computer. He is a partner whom I can trust to look out for my needs. Virtually every company has written a mission statement in the last few years. Most are mere plaques on the wall, because controlled economies, which operate on the laws of the school, have little real desire or capacity to follow through. However, most mission statements say something to the effect of "growth by meeting customer needs." Another way to put this is, "winning by helping other people to win."

In the 1970s General Motors stated that its mission was "making money." It was not long after this that things started going very badly for General Motors. In 1992, Revlon's senior management published a similar mission stating that its primary objective was profit. Within months most of the senior management team was replaced. What we are seeing is a shift from a sales to a service paradigm whereby people with a "me first" sales paradigm produce less wealth for themselves.

A sales paradigm focuses on meeting one's own needs regardless of other people's needs. A service paradigm focuses on meeting one's needs through meeting other people's needs. The sales paradigm is win/lose—"I do not care if you win or lose as long as I win." It does not have to be a paradigm of hatred, merely lack of caring (Williamson 1986). In the new era, organizations like Revlon and General Motors, as well as individuals who are focused merely on their own personal needs, will find that meeting their own needs will become more and more difficult unless other people's needs are met first.

As shown in Chapter 1, thriving organizations such as Wal-Mart, Nordstrom, Rosenbluth Travel, Amway, Nucor Steel, Lincoln Electric, Johnsonville Foods, Mary Kay Cosmetics, and many others are shifting away from the sales paradigm to the service paradigm. This includes service to internal and external customers as well as other stakeholders. Whereas the golden rule used to be to treat others as *you* would like to be treated, the new mass customization–based golden rule for the empathic era is to treat others as *they* would like to be treated.

For more detail on the shift to a win/win world, see *A Civilization of Abundance, Win/Win and Interconnectedness* at the WinWinWorld.net website at **http://www.winwinworld.net**

WEALTH CREATION MOVES BEYOND MATERIAL WEALTH

Abraham Maslow (Newstrom and Davis 1993) showed that a hierarchy of needs motivates people. In general, people are motivated to satisfy the needs at the base of the pyramid before they satisfy higher-order needs. A person who has no air is not likely to search for shelter. A person with no shelter is not likely to seek personal growth, and so on.

Overlaying Maslow's needs hierarchy on Alvin Toffler's (1980) age-wave theory, as in the age-wave chart (see Figure 6–1 in Chapter 6), leads to a striking observation. The Agricultural Age can be classified as a basic needs–building period in which people spent most of their time on the most basic needs: food and shelter. In an Industrial Age, people spent most of their time on middle needs: safety, security, and stability with jobs, schools, stable incomes, and the like. As we move into an Information Age and the Wisdom Age, which is discussed later, we spend more time on the higher-order needs—knowledge, self-esteem, self-actualization, and *true* spiritual needs.

It appears that the definition or view of wealth creation has changed through the ages depending on what people spent most of their time doing to meet their needs. In the Agricultural Age, most human work time was spent on basic needs, mostly food production and other physiological needs from the land. Prior to the 1600s as much as 90% of the population worked on the land. By 1840 the number had decreased to 70%, by 1960 10% worked the land (Quinn 1992, p. 4). Today less than 1% work the land. While writing this book I sit in my home office near Snow Hill, North Carolina, watching a two-person mobile mass-production factory harvest a 100-acre field of cotton in a matter of hours. Two hundred years ago this job would have taken many slaves weeks. Because in an early Agricultural Age, most of humanity's time was spent on the land, the definition of wealth creation was likely limited to physiological needs, primarily food production.

Adam Smith, in *The Wealth of Nations*, speaks of a group of French economists, from the 1700s, called *physiocrats*. They believed that agriculture was the only form of productive labor and that land was the source of all wealth. They referred to manufacturing and commerce as sterile. The physiocrats in essence believed that meeting physiological needs was the only way to create wealth. This was likely a mainstream view in early agrarian civilization. As the Agricultural Age matured and the Industrial Age began climbing the age-wave curve, the physiocrat's view was becoming dated, a remnant of the early agrarian civilization. By 1776, when Smith wrote *The Wealth of Nations*, he was making fun of the obsolete notion held by the physiocrats.

Manufacture of goods in an early Agricultural Age likely took up such a small portion of time as to hardly be considered wealth creation. A manufactured tool may have been something with which one attained or protected wealth but likely was not considered wealth itself. A plow was a thing used to produce food. However, because it did not directly stop the hunger pains in one's stomach or meet some other lower-order need, the plow likely was not considered wealth. An early herdsman's wealth was measured by how many goats or cows he had.

As the Agricultural Age matured, manufactured "things" became a larger part of wealth creation. As we began up the slope to the Industrial Age, even prebreakpoint, the paradigm or definition of wealth creation expanded to be more inclusive of manufactured things. Eventually the paradigm came to be dominated by the manufactured things needed to meet needs higher in the hierarchy.

The classic Industrial Age definition of wealth creation is the making, mining, or growing of something hard and tangible—manufactured items, raw materials, or food. This is where people have spent most of their time working in the past 200 years. We have become the physiocrats of the Information Age as we consider wealth to be created only through the making, mining, and growing of things. In an Industrial Age, knowledge was seen as something one used to attain wealth but not as wealth itself. As knowledge work rapidly increases, knowledge is beginning to be seen as wealth, not just a tool for creating wealth.

The increase in knowledge work is occurring from many perspectives. First, more and more people are knowledge workers. They perform strictly knowledge work; they do not build a physical product in their daily work routines. They are engineers, writers, therapists, fitness trainers, programmers, network marketers, accountants, salespeople, health-care workers, buyers, technicians, mechanics, and more.

Second, among the people directly making, mining, or growing things, the knowledge content of their work is dramatically increasing. For example, many people in hands-on manufacturing are beginning to perform knowledge work as they make the transition to self-directed teams and empowerment. The team members are required to perform work previously performed by specialized knowledge workers, such as engineers, planners, supervisors, and even customer service representatives. In agriculture, the two-person cotton-harvesting factory described earlier had one fellow in an air-conditioned harvester with his stereo playing. He arrived at the cotton field in his four-wheel drive sports utility vehicle wearing a golf shift and slacks. The inside of the harvester looked a little like the cockpit of a jet. Though the driver did not have a laptop computer with him, it would not have surprised me if he did.

Third, the manufacturing or tangible part of work is being enfolded into the entire work process as we shift to the synthesis of whole work. Those like Ted at Applied Computer build "tangible" computers as one small part of an entire business process. Most of Ted's time is spent on the knowledge work of his entire business: billing, ordering parts, accounting, shipping, sales, marketing, engineering, receiving, customer service, programming, and more. The actual time Ted spends building computers is very small, perhaps 2% to 5%.

Fourth, at home we are all spending more time on knowledge-based work or activity, such as working with computers, programming VCRs and televisions, exchanging knowledge on the Internet, shopping through home-shopping channels or the Internet, reading, watching news or educational channels on television, and budgeting with computers and on line.

The knowledge content of work, of industrialized nations, is rising at a dramatic rate as more and more of all of our time is spent doing knowledge work. As the percentage of time we spend performing knowledge work increases, knowledge itself becomes wealth. This is because we define wealth creation on the basis of where people spend most of their time working.

Knowledge, however, has always been wealth, as have manufactured items. However, as the physiocrats considered manufactured goods, we never recognized knowledge as wealth. In fact we have made fun of geeks, nerds, and brainy people. However, brainy Bill Gates has become one of the wealthiest people in the world. I believe we are in the midst of a paradigm shift.

Beyond Toffler's third wave (1980) is the fourth wave, as described by Herman Maynard and Susan Mehrtens in *The Fourth Wave: Business in the 21st Century* (1993). In the third wave we learn that we are connected and must cooperate. The fourth wave is the age of wisdom, in which we come to understand, as quantum physics tells us, that we are one and choose to cocreate. Whereas the Information Age is driven primarily by knowledge power, the Wisdom Age is driven primarily by emotional and spiritual intelligence.

Our definition of wealth creation is today being expanded to include emotional and spiritual intelligence. This happens as people spend more and more time on these higher-order needs as an integrated part of their daily work and lives. People are spending more time on emotional and spiritual intelligence, because with the mass privatization trend people meet their own needs by connecting with others and meeting others' needs. Thus in the new wealth-creation system people are inherently developing emotional and spiritual intelligence as they work.

Emotional and spiritual intelligence includes such things as relationship intelligence, personal health (body, mind, and soul), happiness, wisdom, and environmental health. At the top of Maslow's needs hierarchy are self-esteem, self-actualization, and spiritual awareness—emotional and spiritual intelligence.

Emotional and spiritual intelligence is about actualizing our infinite potential and deeply understanding ourselves and our relations to others and the larger universe. It is about taking responsibility for ourselves, our situations, and our lives. It is about the ability to effectively interact, collaborate, and produce synergy with others. Emotional and spiritual intelligence includes the ability to shift paradigms to see from many different perspectives, to synthesize and see larger wholes, to live fully in and appreciate the present, and to be deeply connected with all things and the universe.

A very large part of emotional and spiritual intelligence is moving beyond oneself. It is about helping others, connecting with others, and meeting other people's needs. It is about the ability to transcend current realities by shifting our perception. Finally it is about seeing the universal reality of love, win/win, and abundance that has always existed.

Suppose we were to discover that we are all one being who has infinite potential as we synthesize our various wholes into a larger whole. Emotional and spiritual intelligence, as defined earlier, would make sense as the ultimate driver of wealth creation. Win/win wealth creation would be critical to infinite wealth. If, however, as newtonian thinking leads us to believe, we are all separate and can gain as individuals by taking from others, win/lose wealth creation makes more sense. As this chapter shows, science is proving that we are all whole parts of a larger whole being.

Today the definition of wealth creation has expanded to include all material and nonmaterial wealth. Each day that we move further into the Win/Win Era, intangible wealth is easier and easier to convert directly into tangible wealth, dollars, goods, or power.

As shown in the book *How to Build a Network of Power Relationships* by Harvey Mackay (1993), the more relationships and connections one has with other people, the more dollars one has the potential to generate. Like neurons in the brain, whose connections determine intelligence, our connections to other people determine our potential for dollar and other forms of wealth. Mackay even shows that a couple of United States presidents have networked their way into the White House.

People who are mentally or physically healthy or happy are able to convert their happiness into dollars with books, "how to" videos, television exercise shows, audiotapes, and more. The explosion in the mental and physical health industries attests to the increasing ease with which personal health is converted into dollars. Organizations that help the environment are able to convert this service into dollars from increased sales to the growing number of environmentally awakened consumers, as documented in a host of business ecology books, such as *The Bottom Line of Green is Black* by Tedd Saunders (1993).

The dollars produced from intangible wealth can be converted back to relationships, environmental health, personal health, and happiness. People with dollars can have a relatively easier time establishing relationships (given that they have good interpersonal skills) because others desire knowing those with money and power. Organizations with more dollars have more to spend protecting the environment. Individuals with money can hire personal trainers or therapists or purchase sophisticated exercise equipment to improve mental and physical health. In general, those with dollars have more time to focus on higher-order needs.

As we near the top of the needs hierarchy, wealth has the capability to flow from being material to nonmaterial wealth and back again. It can flow from one form to another with relative ease, and the more easily it flows, the wealthier we all become. The more fluid wealth flows in all capacities, the wealthier we all become.

The shift to emotional and spiritual intelligence has everything to do with the shift in organizations' missions today from making profits to meeting people's needs. In the past, we considered an organization's mission to be merely making profit because, like people, organizations also have a hierarchy of needs. Near the bottom of the organizational needs hierarchy is profit. If a person does not have air, he or she will not be around very long; likewise, an organization without profit will not be around very long. On the other hand, a person's mission in life is not simply to breathe air.

As humanity collectively matures and moves up the hierarchy of needs to focus on higher-order needs, so too must organizational types as their focus broadens from mere personal profits. The simple shift in organizations' missions toward meeting human needs represents a significant change in our view of wealth creation. In an Information Age, the mere act of increasing one's emotional and spiritual intelligence, completely void of any material object, is in and of itself creating wealth.

For more detail on the shift in wealth creation or how we are shifting to win/win-based wealth creation, see *The Metamorphosis of Wealth Creation* at the WinWinWorld.net website at **http:// www.winwinworld.net**

AS GOES WEALTH CREATION, SO GOES HUMAN NATURE

Though attaining nonmaterial wealth sounds great, most people today are still more concerned with material wealth. After all, we must eat and have shelter, cars, clothes, computers, and other material items that cost money. The shift to the broader definition of wealth creation, the meeting of human needs, means that higher emotional and spiritual intelligence is a requirement for attaining greater material wealth as well as nonmaterial wealth.

At a practical level, emotional and spiritual wealth is far more important than material wealth, because in the Win/Win Era, the higher one's emotional and spiritual intelligence, the more material and nonmaterial wealth one is able to create.

This is a radical departure from the Win/Lose Era. Control and victimization of the masses fueled the wealth-creation systems of the Win/Lose Era—employment, serfdom, and slavery. Hence they were eras of mass victimization. One problem with mass victimization is that it limits and lowers the levels of emotional and spiritual intelligence. This includes both the people being controlled and those doing the controlling.

Mass victimization was done in the name of satisfying one's own practical, immediate needs. You held a slave in bondage, control, and pain to serve your own needs. Because wealth creation was more about attaining something at someone else's expense, one's emotional and spiritual intelligence, as defined earlier, would have to be somewhat low to do this. One would have to be willing to gain by causing someone else to lose—one would have to see oneself as separate from the other—and this by definition is low spiritual intelligence. We do not usually see those who participate in illegal win/lose activity (criminals) as having high emotional and spiritual intelligence. Likewise we who participate in legal win/lose activities also have relatively low emotional and spiritual intelligence. This is true on a relative scale whether the competition is in sports, business, war, or for fun.

We must remember that the line between legal and illegal win/ lose activity is arbitrary. Slavery is illegal today but was a "respectable trade" 200 years ago. Guerrilla warfare, during war time, is legal today but was not 300 years ago in Europe. We will eventually come to understand that legal and illegal win/lose activity hurts us all as individuals and as a whole and that legality versus illegality is irrelevant. Perhaps one day employment will be illegal! After all, from a liberty perspective, the only real difference between slavery and employment is that employees have the freedom to change plantations. However, most employees must stay on someone's plantation. As one manager once said, "I want to hire people who are deep in debt because they are easier to control." They are more "bonded" to the boss and his or her will.

Most people see spiritual intelligence and wealth creation as opposites. The Bible says that it is more difficult for a rich man to get into heaven than it is for a camel to fit through the eye of a needle. This reflects the misalignment between wealth creation and spirituality throughout human history. A customer-driven empathic era will force empathy and increased emotional and spiritual intelligence of the individual. This is because a customer-driven buyer's market demands that people see from other people's perspectives in order to tend to these people's needs. Suppliers who are good at understanding and attending to others' diverse needs prosper and grow. Suppliers who do this poorly or are mediocre either go out of business or increase their emotional and spiritual intelligence. For the first time in human history, wealth creation is becoming aligned with higher-order human needs to reveal a more coherent whole reality.

Great spiritual leaders like Jesus and Buddha thousands of years ago spoke of a win/win and abundant reality. However, without aligned structures, we have not accepted this reality. Without direct alignment, which shows how the effects of our benevolent actions help us, we have had too little motivation to see the systemic win/win reality of the universe. We, therefore, talk a good game on Sunday and other holy days, but our actions for the other six days of the week when it comes to meeting our practical needs run counter to what we preach.

The customer-driven movement is extremely powerful because of the new alignment between wealth creation and emotional and spiritual intelligence. Within the new paradigm, there is no difference between growing emotionally and spiritually, helping others, and wealth creation. They have all been synthesized into one undivided whole.

Box 11–1 shows the drivers of wealth creation in the Win/Lose and Win/Win Eras. It illustrates that the two eras are driven by almost completely opposite forces. The shift to the Win/Win era represents a complete reversal from all of human history. This is consistent with the science of breakpoint, which shows that systems operate as complete opposites before and after breakpoint (Land and Jarman 1992).

The shift to win/win now is practical because of humanity's level of advancement in maturity, knowledge, technology, and spirituality. Eventually, however, we shall see and come to understand that win/win and abundance have always been available to humanity, just as the great spiritual leaders throughout history have claimed. We, however, were not mature enough to see it. We humans have always been on a journey. It has been a journey of maturation. We have confused an immature humanity with an unchangeable human nature. We are about to reach a new level of maturity and with it comes more liberty.

For more detail on how and why wealth creation in the past has been fueled by mass victimization and why win/lose competition is the source of our low emotional and spiritual intelligence and therefore our problems, see *Win/Lose and Competition, The Norm of Civilization* at the WinWinWorld.net website at **http://www.win winworld.net**

EMOTIONAL AND SPIRITUAL INTELLIGENCE, WEALTH CREATION, AND LOVE

Stephen Covey's book *The Seven Habits of Highly Effective People* (1989) has maintained itself on the business books bestseller list and

BOX 11–1   Human Activities That Drive Wealth Creation

WEALTH PARADIGM

WIN/LOSE ERA	WIN/WIN ERA
Scarcity Paradigm	Abundance Paradigm
Finite Wealth	Infinite Wealth
Win/Lose	Win/Win
Fear-driven Competition	Love-driven Collaboration

WORK PARADIGM

WIN/LOSE ERA	WIN/WIN ERA
Work Is Unpleasant	Work Is Fun
Work Is Done in Order to Live	Working Is Living

HUMAN WORK RELATIONSHIPS

WIN/LOSE ERA	WIN/WIN ERA
Adversarial/Subordinate	Partnered
Controlled/Authoritarian	Chaotic/Synocratic
Sales (Meet My Needs)	Service (Meet Your Needs)
Self-centered	Empathic
Self-interested	Considerate
Selfish	Generous
Separate	Interconnected
Independent/Dependent	Interdependent
Fear-based	Love-based
Embraces Homogeneity	Embraces Diversity
Controlling Others Produces Wealth	Helping Others Produces Wealth
Debate/Discussion (Get Your Point Across)	Dialogue (Understand Others)

INDIVIDUAL WORK OUTLOOK

WIN/LOSE ERA	WIN/WIN ERA
Victims (Powerless to Effect Change)	Self-empowered
Mass Passivity (Masses Follow)	Mass Activism (Everyone Leads)
Competition for Limited Resources	Collaboration to Tap Infinite Wealth
Judgment	Imagination/Creativity/Intuition
Strength from Fear	Strength from Love
Impersonal Work Relationships	Interpersonal Work Relationships
Self-protecting, Defensive, Tough	Open, Secure, Confident, Soft
Advances Vertically	Advances through Connections

on most trade bestseller lists for nearly a decade. This is unprecedented among business books. These seven habits are about increasing one's emotional and spiritual intelligence to produce more wealth for oneself and others. It is no accident that this book has appeared today and not 25, 50, or 100 years ago.

These habits are more about effectiveness in the Win/Win Era than the Win/Lose Era. For example, thinking win/win, habit number four, would not be very practical in the competitive Win/Lose Era. How could you think win/win about the opposing team in the middle of a football game while the opponent is intently focused on defeating you? If we were to compile a list of the most "effective" people in history and looked at their most common traits, most of the seven habits would not be on the list (*effective* by most people's definition of success: money, wealth, power, high standard of living, and quality of life). The seven habits are as follows: (1) be proactive, (2) begin with the end in mind, (3) put first things first, (4) think win/win, (5) seek first to understand, (6) participate in synergy, (7) sharpen the saw. As we shift to the Win/Win Era, companies and other controlled economies are attempting to implement Covey's seven habits.

Just as organizations today with higher collective IQs, creativity, intuition, and multiple intelligences are more capable than lower-IQ organizations, organizations with higher emotional and spiritual intelligence are more capable than companies with lower emotional and spiritual intelligence. There is even a new booming industry in which consultants help organizations increase their emotional and spiritual intelligence. Jan Nickerson, founder of The Prosperity Collaborative, shares her emotional and spiritual intelligence with organizations. She helps expand organizations' emotional and spiritual intelligence so that the organizations can better collaborate, meet human needs, and reap bigger profits.

Today's workers in self-directed teams must have high levels of emotional intelligence for the teams to function effectively. As the world is now shifting toward win/win and we attempt to mature and throw off the shackles of supervision, regulation, and control, we run headlong into our low emotional and spiritual intelligence.

When a regulating supervisor is removed while implementing self-directed teams, all hell breaks lose. This behavior is a direct result of individuals' low levels of emotional intelligence, which result from a history of win/lose human relations. This low emotional and spiritual intelligence includes low tolerance levels, quickness to judge, blame and find fault, obsession with being heard, inability to listen, a lack of empathy, and an inability to transcend paradigms to see from other perspectives. By far the most prevalent problem among newly formed self-directed teams is the perception by most individuals that they are victims being picked on by others. An obsession with being a victim can be expected after thousands of years of mass victimization.

I counseled a self-directed team that reported to me regarding an incident in which one person incorrectly perceived an attack by another. I asked the first person not to be so defensive and judgmental with others, to give people the benefit of the doubt and he'd feel less need to be offensively aggressive. Toward the end of the conservation he said something quite profound, "With the way things used to work, before teams, if I didn't look out for myself, nobody else would." This simple statement is the key to wealth creation in an Information Age and this entire book. A partner-based customer-driven empathic age is about people looking out for the needs of others.

According to Don Carew, coauthor of *The One-Minute Manager Builds High Performance Teams* (1995), teams that have broken through to become super high performing all have one thing in common. They all have a very high degree of *caring* for one another. They focus on each other's needs; they are interconnected; there is love. A high degree of caring for others is a key trait of individuals with high emotional and spiritual intelligence. To be a highly functioning team, members cannot themselves be dysfunctional.

The team, which is the heart of mass privatization, has at its core the need to move beyond self. It needs to focus on other people's needs to contribute to others and to society. I refer to this as interconnectedness or spirituality. Some, however, simply call it love.

12

The Synthesis of a Win/Win World

Wealth Creation and the Wholeness of Quantum Physics

The failure to strive for completeness is probably the most common failing in the thinking of all individuals. We focus our eyes on one small truth so hypnotically that we neglect all other truths.

—Sam Keen

When we synthesize mass privatization and decentralized wealth creation with the metamorphosis of wealth creation and the shift to true democracy, the age-wave historical precedence, and the changes occurring in spirituality, religion, psychology, human maturity, and science, we see the rise of a new win/win world. It is a world of infinite wealth potential and abundance. It is a world of creativity and infinite possibilities. It is a world in which the more we help others, the more wealth we produce for ourselves.

EMPATHY, WHOLENESS, AND WIN/WIN

In the Win/Lose Era it was imperative that one focus intently on one's own needs. A hunter in the Hunter-Gatherer Age could not afford to empathize with the opponent, because a split-second distraction could mean his own death. Today in sports or business you

203

surely would not hesitate and wait for competitors to act while empathizing and considering the pain of their loss, because it could cause you to lose. The result is a world filled with people seeking to win at other people's expense; we talk but have little ability to listen. It is a world filled with people feeling like victims when they lose but unable to see the opponent as a victim when the opponent is losing. We see from narrow, limited, fragmented perspectives and do not care about and are unable to see from other people's perspectives.

A world of competition is one based on good guys and bad guys. "I" and "we" are the good guys and "he" and "they" are the bad guys. A win/win knowledge civilization cannot exist when people's primary focus is on perceiving only from their own limited fragment of reality—when empathy is not the core of our actions. Win/win cannot exist when people are focused on finding the "bad guy" in other people in order to see themselves as "good guys"; it cannot exist when we see ourselves as victims who are owed something.

The ability to see win/win realities boils down to not merely seeing from other people's perspectives but from embracing many other people's perspectives. The late David Bohm, quantum physicist and author of *The Undivided Universe* (1993) says that all of existence is one undivided, interconnected whole. We, however, see ourselves as separate individuals. In reality, we are all part of one whole, but we see from different perspectives with different paradigms and different realities from within that whole.

We debate our various views, trying to convince others that what we see is correct. However, we are all merely seeing incoherent fragments, of which none are completely correct. Only by synthesizing all of our various, fragmented perspectives together do we stand a chance of understanding the synthesized whole. In *Thought as a System* (1994) Bohm wrote, "Our thoughts are incoherent, and the resulting counter-productiveness lies at the root of the world's problems." Bohm asserted that communication must come through win/win-based dialogue and understanding as opposed to win/lose-based debate or discussion.

Stephen Covey's (1989) habit number five is, "seek first to understand and then be understood." The ability to see win/win is about tolerance and the assumption that other people perceive correctly though differently. Win/win is a reality void of judgment and blame because we realize that others are merely seeing with different paradigms. Joel Barker, in *Paradigms* (1992), writes that when he disagrees with someone he searches to determine the paradigm from which the other person is seeing in order to find the source of disagreement.

Within our win/lose paradigm, individuals are not willing to understand others because there is little in it for them. A mass victimization world based on win/lose competition always produces more losers than winners. Even the people who are winning feel like victims because of fear-based socialization. In the win/lose world one thrives on getting one's own point across and not on empathizing or listening to others. We live in a world filled with people starved to be heard and understood. Being an insecure victim leaves one's own need to be heard unfulfilled. We therefore continually step on others as we compete to be heard and understood.

HEALING OUR SEPARATION THROUGH CONNECTING

As we prepare for the Win/Win Era, tremendous healing work is going on in recovery programs, support groups, and self-directed work teams through psychotherapy and the like. These groups and methods are preparing us for an era of win/win wealth creation. Programs such as reevaluation counseling are based on the concept that people already have the solutions to their own problems; they merely need to be heard and understood in order to be healed. The support group or cocounselor empathetically listens to individuals and supports them as they find their own solutions. The cocounselor asks questions to help the individual "discharge," heal, or remap false neural connections or low-intelligence habits. This usually occurs as the individual discharges the pain by crying, throwing a temper tantrum, screaming, punching a pillow, and laughing or through some other emotional outlet. The key is having someone listen to one's pain.

People on the television show *Rescue 911* almost always cry when they describe a painful event: a daughter being hit by a car, a son falling into an icy lake, a husband shot. It is very difficult not to cry and discharge the pain with so many people watching and empathetically listening to your situation. Most of these people likely never expected themselves to cry on national television. We are discovering that the simple act of listening to others, empathizing, and truly connecting with one another has the power to heal and increase emotional and spiritual intelligence. The underlying reason for this is that we are all part of one whole. By connecting with one another we begin to become whole and healed.

The mass victimization norm of the Win/Lose Era thrived on not listening and not empathizing, focusing on one's own condition while ignoring others, and seeing only from one's own perspectives. It would make sense that listening to others heals the reality created from not listening to others. To listen empathetically is to connect with another. It is to interconnect, to synthesize, to become one. Interconnectedness, synthesis, and wholeness are the very essence of true spirituality as well as the science of quantum physics (Zukav 1979). Interconnectedness and synthesis are also the very essence of mass privatization and mass synocracy.

QUANTUM PHYSICS AND THE UNDIVIDED WHOLE

Eastern religions are built on the notion that humans, the universe, and God are all part of one undivided, seamless, inseparable whole—one collective consciousness. Quantum physics today is pointing to this notion as reality. Physicist Walter Heitler, author of a standard textbook on light-matter interaction, says that in spite of its obvious partitions and boundaries, the world actually is a seamless and inseparable whole (Herbert 1985, p. 18). Fritjof Capra in *The Tao of Physics* (1991) and Deepak Chopra in *Creating Affluence* (1993) add to this concept. David Bohm, author of *The Undivided Universe* (1993), says, "one is led to a new notion of unbroken wholeness which denies the classical analyzability of the world into separate and independent parts. . . . The inseparable quantum interconnectedness of the whole universe is the fundamental reality." Irwin Schroedinger, the quantum physicist who developed the wave equation in quantum physics, says, "If we could just measure the sum total of the minds in the universe there would be just one." Albert Einstein said (Herbert 1985, p. 250),

> A human being is part of the whole, called by us "Universe"; a part limited in time and space. He experiences himself, his thoughts and feelings as something separated from the rest—a kind of optical delusion of his consciousness. This delusion is a kind of prison for us, restricting us to our personal desires and to affection for a few persons nearest us. Our task must be to free ourselves from this prison by widening our circle of compassion to

embrace all living creatures and the whole of nature in its beauty. Nobody is able to achieve this completely but the striving for such achievement is, in itself, a part of the liberation and a foundation for inner security.

Information technology and the drive for interconnectedness from mass privatization–based wealth creation today are putting humanity on a course for massive chaotic interconnectedness at a tangible level. If on the basis of quantum physics we are all interconnected at some deep level, then information technology is allowing us to interconnect in a basic and primitive but perhaps necessary way—building toward a more substantive spiritual interconnectedness. Information technology is so powerful today because it is allowing us to interconnect, to synthesize, better understand, and become the one global economy and the one *whole* that we are. Perhaps information technology is a spiritual maturation bridge necessary for those like ourselves obsessed with the need for empirical evidence of something before we will believe it. Or perhaps it is merely our training wheels.

QUANTUM PHYSICS AND THE WHOLENESS OF WEALTH CREATION

The definition of wealth creation is expanding because we are beginning to take a more holistic view of wealth creation. When a company makes a profit by not paying the full cost of producing their product or service today, then perhaps no profit has been made and no wealth created. In fact, that company is living on welfare, expecting someone to pay its costs. It is win/lose wealth creation and welfare when a company pollutes the environment, requiring future generations to pay the cost. If a manager intentionally negotiates a salary with a naïve employee for $20,000 less that the fair-market value, the company is on welfare. The manager is expecting something for nothing—a handout that has not been earned. The manager wants the employee to work for free part of the time. Though we say we hate welfare for able-bodied people, it turns out that welfare it is the heart of competition and win/lose wealth creation.

Our present view of profit and loss comes from a fragmented worldview based on analysis in which profit takes into account only a narrow sliver of the whole—"my sliver." If we lived in a newtonian, fragmented universe made of independent pieces, this win/lose approach would be valid. Quantum physics is showing that perhaps no wealth is created in many win/lose situations. This is because there can be a loss to the entire system when one person wins at another's expense.

REINFORCING FEEDBACK LOOPS AND NEW REALITIES

When management thinks of employees as dumb, employees respond by reinforcing management's expectations. Violence in television, movies, and music reflects and reinforces our reality and produces more violence. In some schools, classes are segregated according to perceived intelligence. Students perceived to be of lower intelligence are continuously given the message that they are less intelligent, and they perform accordingly. This is known as the Pygmalion Effect.

Reinforcing feedback loops cause us to produce more of what we see in a snowballing effect (Senge 1990). They lock us into the *status quo*. Here is what Peter Senge in *The Fifth Discipline* says about feedback loops:

> If you are in a reinforcing feedback system you may be blind to how small actions can grow into large consequences—for better or worse. . . . In reinforcing processes, a small change builds on itself. Whatever movement occurs is amplified, producing more movement in the same direction. A small action snowballs, with more and more and still more of the same, resembling compounding interest.

We see the win/lose reinforcing loops so clearly throughout society and the world that win/lose is thought by most people to be a law of nature. Competition is everywhere and permeates everything. We see this reality, we expect it and adapt to it, thereby perpetuating it. Because we expect competition, we get more. The more we see, the more we are convinced that this is the only reality. Reinforcing feedback loops are, however, what will deliver us into the new win/win reality. Though we are overwhelmed with a win/lose reality, the win/win reinforcing feedback loops increase daily and at some point will reach breakpoint.

Reinforcing feedback loops are why mass privatization is so critical to the transition to a win/win world. Mass privatization allows us to tangibly, directly, and immediately see that we win by helping others win. Without aligned structures, the win/win paradigm will likely be difficult, if not impossible, for most people today to accept, just as it has been for thousands of years.

THE WIN/WIN REINFORCING FEEDBACK LOOPS

The customer and quality movements of the last 20 years are part of a slowly building, win/win, reinforcing feedback loop. The shift to a buyer's market, a customer-driven society, and mass customization reflect small reinforcing loops growing larger. With the worker shift from subservient employee to empowered private worker, we also see win/win feedback loops grow larger. Wal-Mart increases quality and service. Other suppliers, unable to meet customer needs, such as Brendle's, K-Mart, and Rose's, struggle, restructure, close stores, or file for bankruptcy. Win/win reinforcing feedback loops like this cannot be ignored. They slowly increase the size of the win/win snowball.

We also see win/win reinforcing feedback loops operating in the area of emotional and spiritual intelligence. This is in the personal and spiritual growth movements. There are networks of individuals, support groups, recovery groups, healing groups, self-knowledge groups, observing consciousness groups, and many others. There are many people writing, studying, and communicating worldwide. People are coming together as never before to heal the pain of the past that causes us to see with our fear paradigm. They are working to increase emotional and spiritual intelligence to become more effective.

Information technology is the primary power behind the growing win/win feedback loops (see *Growing Win/Win Feedback Loops* at the WinWinWorld.net website at **http://www.winwinworld.net**)

INFORMATION TECHNOLOGY AND THE BREAKPOINT TO THE WIN/WIN ERA

Information technology connects and empowers individuals and customers in society. It is providing tangible, visible, and touchable evidence of the new and growing win/win civilization. As Deepak Chopra, Alvin Toffler, Peter Drucker, and Tom Peters all have shown, knowledge is the driver of wealth creation today. Knowledge is infinite and can be win/win power.

What is information technology but the basic raw tools of information processing, knowledge production, and knowledge flow? These tools have become tangible creators of infinite wealth for all to see. With interconnectedness as the essence of spirituality, we are witnessing the rise of the most powerful spiritual growth tool in history—information technology. Information technology is bringing humanity together; it is enabling synthesis, synergy, and wholeness.

It is critical that we see information technology for what it is, because we practical humans need tangible and touchable evidence of something before we will believe and act on it. Win/win, infinite wealth, and spiritual growth–producing tools are growing at the speed of light before our eyes. In reference to the growth of information technology, John Naisbitt writes in *Global Paradox* (1994), "If we had similar progress in automotive technology, today you could buy a Lexus for about $2. It would travel at the speed of sound, and go about 600 miles on a thimble of gas." We see the win/win characteristics of knowledge power when we see that one third of Microsoft's employees are millionaires.

Knowledge power within a mass privatization enterprise has enabled organizations like Amway to produce more millionaires than any other organization in history. In the past several decades, information technology has increased social freedom enormously for everyone. It has likely avoided many wars, because it brings the horrors of war directly into our living rooms through television and raises our consciousness. Information technology has reduced corruption worldwide because it increases our awareness regarding the true nature of centralized power. Information technology has reduced pollution, because we have become aware of the harm we are doing to the environment.

Information technology has increased awareness regarding police departments; a single video, the Rodney King tape, gave us all more understanding. A single video, shot by one person, showed dolphins being killed in fishing nets and raised our consciousness. We stopped buying tuna, and the industry changed; thousands of dolphins' lives have been saved as a result. Information technology has toppled dictatorships, replacing them with Industrial Age democracies. Mass privatization enterprises will interconnect people globally via the information superhighway. It will not be as easy to wage war against those whom we consider friends, partners, suppliers, and customers—those whom we have come to know, love and depend on.

Information technology has begun to reflect to us a new win/win reality that will allow us to continue creating that reality. We need to make a conscious effort to see information technology and the interconnectedness it offers as the key link in the transition from our win/lose past of scarcity to a win/win future of abundance. It is not just a hard, cold technology. It is a system that connects our minds, hearts, and souls into the coherent whole of which we are a part. Information technology is a relatively primitive, "hard-wired" forerunner of the much deeper "soft-wired" spiritual connections to come. Information technologies are our spiritual training wheels, and mass privatization is our first bicycle.

As illustrated earlier in this book, the information superhighway is being built from a host of various information technologies—virtual reality, Internet, hologram, and others. Mass privatization partners at some point in essence will have real person-to-person communication almost as if they have been physically transported to the same location.

As a critical mass of information technology synthesizes, mass privatization will begin to blossom. The information superhighway and mass privatization are providing the motive and means to chaotically interconnect humanity on a massive scale. This interconnection is moving us to a breakpoint in human maturity—a breakpoint to a world based on love. To love someone is to come to care for, to understand, to know, and to desire helping that person. Mass privatization partners, suppliers, and customers must interconnect and become interdependent on one another in meeting each other's unique, fickle, and customized needs. They must collaborate and come to know one another, they must empathize and synergize with one another; they must care about one another—they must act from love. Information technology and the shift to mass privatization are providing the most powerful *motive* and *means* in history for individuals to love one another. It is empowering humanity to produce synergy on a global scale, to mature, to come to know itself—to become one.

Today humanity is like a large brain of six billion neurons with very few neural connections. With our sparse neural connections, we are like the brain of a newborn baby. We have had dreams and nightmares while in the womb maturing. Information technology is just now allowing humanity to be born. We are about to

allow the six billion neurons to connect through massive, chaotic, and powerful neural networks that operate on chaos theory. "Each neuron is sprouting new dendrites, enhancing synaptic firings and creating new connections resulting in increased synergy and wealth for us all" (North 1999). These massive neural connections will multiply all of humanity's intelligences by many orders of magnitude, including emotional, spiritual, creative, intuitive, and intellectual intelligences.

OUR EXPECTATIONS ARE OUR PATH OUT OF HELL

Using the mass privatization concept, we have come on a very long trip to show the shift to a win/win world. Our journey started thousands of years ago. It is ironic that neither mass privatization nor the trip was ever necessary. Just as great spiritual leaders have told us, we have always had access to a win/win world. Today science supports this notion. Science now tells us that we create our reality out of our expectations, beliefs, and observations.

Wealth creation in the Win/Lose Era was more about attaining wealth at another's expense using low emotional and spiritual intelligence than about creating anything. The people doing the losing are victims. Victims are people whose control and power have been taken away. Victims attempt to win by taking power and control away from someone else. Both winners and losers in the Win/Lose Era come from a fear-based victim paradigm.

Real wealth is created when people are empowered and can actualize dormant potential, thus creating wealth. Empowerment is about creating a desired future and transcending current realities. Real wealth creation is about creating and cocreating. Empowerment and true wealth creation are the opposite of the helpless victim paradigm.

Suppose through some strange new science we come to understand that we create our own reality. This would mean that there is no such thing as a victim. If we create our own reality, we have always been in full control of our destiny and under the control of no one else. It would mean that we have always been fully empowered but perhaps too immature to realize it. Science is proving that we do create our own reality—the science of quantum physics.

Neils Bohr, the Danish physicist, and physicists such as Albert Einstein earlier in this century pioneered much of quantum theory. Perhaps no one has had more impact on the interpretations of the new physics than Bohr. The Copenhagen interpretation developed at Bohr's Copenhagen Institute states that (1) there is no deep reality and (2) we create our reality out of our observations (Herbert 1985). The Copenhagen interpretation is not a minority view. Most physicists at least partly accept the Copenhagen interpretation.

As we enter a knowledge era, perhaps the greatest discovery of our times is that expectations, beliefs, and observations create reality. There is no deep, objective reality to observe or to which to adapt. Reality depends on our perspective and on what we perceive. This is our path out of win/lose hell.

For all of human history we have viewed ourselves as helpless victims at the whim of a harsh universe and of those in power. We are now discovering that our negative expectations, which come from low emotional and spiritual intelligence, create our harsh win/lose reality. Win/lose competition and scarcity are not natural laws to which we must adapt. They are a reality created out of our immature beliefs. This means that by increasing our emotional and spiritual intelligence and changing our belief systems, we can create the reality and future we desire.

Figure 12–1 shows that virtually every segment of society has proven concepts that support the notion that we create our reality from our beliefs, expectations, and observations. We see it with the Pygmalion Effect in psychology, the Hawthorne Effect in business, paradigms in science, stereotyping in sociology, visualization in sports, the placebo effect in medicine, and far more.

For more explanation on these concepts see *Expectations Create Reality* at the WinWinWorld.net website at **http://www.win winworld.net**

As a college student, and for many years after, I was a strong proponent of facing reality directly and head on. Being competitive and driven, I believed that one should face reality directly no matter how painful because this was the way to adapt and best survive. I practiced enduring pain and thrived on it. I didn't take aspirin for headaches. I didn't have an air conditioner in my car. I'd yearly pick the coldest days in winter to take five-day solo canoe trips down the Stanton River in Virginia.

For hundreds of years we have thought that we can objectively observe the universe to determine reality and adapt to it for our benefit. With the victim paradigm we saw the things around us as happening *to* us, and we reacted to them. We saw ourselves as mere by-

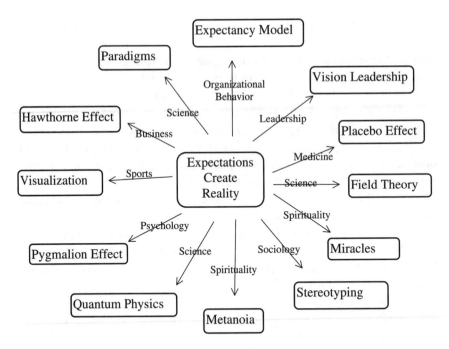

FIGURE 12–1   Expectations Create Reality

standers, separate from events as they happened to us. Therefore careful observation and analysis is what the science of the last few hundred years has been about. By observing and understanding, we could adapt to the environment, not knowing that we were merely adapting to a mirror image of our beliefs, expectations, and observations.

Within the win/lose paradigm, I was correct in attempting to face reality no matter how painful. The world is hard and tough, so I had to be hard and tough. Within the larger win/win paradigm, I was incorrect. Today the evidence shows that facing a painful and harsh reality directly and head on and adapting to it is not the most practical method of thriving.

Facing reality or being practical merely keeps us trapped in a limited "practical" paradigm; today that paradigm is a practical win/lose hell. The more win/lose we see, the more convinced we become that it is the only reality. We then feel compelled to adapt to the win/lose reality in order to survive.

The captain of the slave ship that brought Kunta Kinte to America in *Roots* opposed what he was doing but did it in the name of being practical. After all, he had to feed his family. Other workers on the ship never questioned what they were doing. Many at some point in their lives had adapted and learned to like holding others in pain. Whether they liked it or acted in disdain, their actions were performed in the name of being practical. Many Nazis in World War II did what they did out of being practical. They were merely following orders.

We are no different. We as prostituted employees perform work that we do not believe in, dislike, or even oppose just to fill our bellies for another day. We will come to understand that "being practical" has been the curse that has kept humanity trapped in hell for thousands of years. We have not been able to see the forest for the practicality of trees directly before us. What quantum physics tells us is that the captain, the Nazis, and we can step out of our practical hell any time we truly desire to.

As we synthesize quantum physics with changes in wealth, spirituality, and psychology, we find the key to the new Win/Win Era and to the Win/Lose Era. We have always created our own reality; however, in the Win/Lose Era, the reality we created came from a fear-based, victim paradigm of scarcity—low emotional and spiritual intelligence. Being practical and creating wealth within this paradigm kept us trapped in this paradigm.

We are finding that the higher one's emotional and spiritual intelligence, the more capable one is of creating the reality he or she desires, of transcending current realities. Someone working at the base of the hierarchy of needs is not likely to have very high emotional and spiritual intelligence and is likely to have limited ability to actualize his or her potential. This person will likely perceive what is directly before him or her as all of reality. Because it is *all*, it must be finite, and we must compete through fear of the finite *all*. When individuals see themselves as victims, they are driven to meet their own needs first or create wealth out of fear.

Humanity today is maturing, and its social systems, technology, and knowledge are reaching critical mass. As this happens, all humanity's emotional and spiritual intelligence is pushed to new highs. Our higher emotional and spiritual intelligence will move us into a new worldview of personal responsibility and self-empowerment. It will force us out of our victim paradigm so that we can see that we are truly empowered and in charge of creating our own environment and destiny.

What is the moral of this quantum physics story? We see what we believe or want to see. As the concept of paradigms shows, evidence that does not fit our paradigm is invisible. We cannot see it even if we look directly at it. If after reading this book you still are not seeing the shift to a win/win world, it does not matter. All that is necessary is that you believe it. When you believe it you will see it. What you see in the world is merely a reflection of your beliefs about yourself and the world—a reflection of your self-esteem, maturity, and self-actualization. You must ask yourself, Am I worthy of abundance, wealth, and happiness? Are my children worthy of a life of abundance, wealth, and happiness? If you see only a win/lose world, it is because you have been hurt, you have shut down, and you have closed your mind to certain possibilities in an effort to avoid being hurt again. You have toughened, hardened, become competitive, and adapted to a hard world—you have become a rock. But what is a rock? It is hard and tough, but it is dead, not sensing very much.

The challenge of our time is to transcend what we see as current reality. We, however, do not have to do this alone. The shift to mass privatization is providing growing visible and tangible evidence of the incoming win/win world. Perhaps the win/win feedback loops to the new world can help you jump-start new win/win wealth-creation habits even if these habits initially are formed from self-interest.

For more detail on how our expectations can lead to a win/win breakpoint, see *Our Expectations Are Our Path Out of Hell* at the WinWinWorld.net website at **http://www.winwinworld.net**

BREAKPOINT TO LOSE/LOSE HELL

There is, however, a downside to the shift from win/lose. When we turn on the news each night, what are our expectations—death, violence, corruption, murder, terrorism, and layoffs? We have an epidemic of win/lose expectations. Much of what we see is out-of-control win/lose. Expanded social freedoms are in the process of being thrust on six billion relatively immature individuals through information technology. At the same time, these individuals have little macroscopic vision of what is occurring. If our expectations remain win/lose, we are headed for the greatest chaotic hell that humanity has ever experienced. Unless we shift our expectations, we shall create this reality on a massive scale as win/lose devolves into mass lose/lose. As we near breakpoint, an expectation of win/lose as the norm is incompatible with human survival. How is it possible to change this expectation? The answer lies in our expectations and attitudes.

For more detail on the possible shift to a lose/lose hell, see *Hell and the Fall Backwards: The Second Dark Ages* at the WinWin-World.net website at **http://www.winwinworld.net**

Today, according to the concepts of quantum physics, it is win/win or no deal. We must learn to see from many different perspectives to see win/win. We must visualize today the win/win and abundance before us. If we are to survive, we must visualize win/win and make it the expectation. Though the reinforcing loops for win/win are tiny, they are growing, and we must look to find them.

Visualizing win/win based upon knowledge power and seeing the growing win/win feedback loops are the premiere challenges of our lifetime. We must have a powerful enough vision of a desired future to change our win/lose expectations. We must understand the concepts of quantum physics—the reality we see is merely a reflection of our thinking, not some independent, absolute reality. We cannot stay in our win/lose civilization. On the other hand, we cannot move to a win/win civilization without an intelligent vision. Because we humans crave the practical based on empirical, observable evidence, we must see and use mass privatization and information technology as the stepping stones of human maturity to a win/win world.

For more detail on the human journey of human maturation, see *The Human Journey: Human Liberation Is Human Maturity* at the WinWinWorld.net website at **http://www.winwinworld.net**

13

Intelligent Vision
For a Successful Transition

Breakpoint change abruptly and powerfully breaks the critical links with the past. What we are experiencing today is absolutely unprecedented in all of humanity's recorded history. We have run into change so different from anything preceding it that it totally demolishes normal standards. It has swept us into a massive transformation that will completely reorder all we know about living in this world. It demands totally new rules for success.
—George Land and Beth Jarman, *Breakpoint and Beyond*

Because we still operate with second-wave Industrial Age systems, is there hope for us entering the Wisdom Age—the fourth wave in our lifetimes? Yes, as Figure 6–1 (Chapter 6) shows, the waves start slowly and overlap. Though we are still operating on Industrial Age systems, and are probably years from breakpoint to the Information Age, we have already begun the ascent up the age-wave curve to the Wisdom Age. The waves also have accelerated their pace. The Hunter-Gatherer Age lasted tens of thousands of years. The Agricultural Age lasted about ten thousand years. The Industrial Age lasted only a couple hundred years. Today we see the Information Age and the Wisdom Age moving at us at the same time, starting only a couple of decades apart. In this book I make little distinction between the third and fourth waves, because they both shift us from the Win/Lose Era to the Win/Win Era. Both are driven by intangible wealth.

THE NEED FOR VISION

The single most important requirement for a successful transition to an Information Age is a powerful vision of what is occurring and where we are going. If we do not have vision, a successful transition will be difficult and painful. What happens when you turn off the lights at night in your house? With no vision you stumble in the dark, bump into things, and hurt yourself. In the transition from the Win/Lose Era, the stumbles, bumps, and pain come in the form of lost wealth, bankruptcy, death, destruction, terrorism, crime, corruption, social collapse, and perhaps even a second dark ages. This is something that you and your family must avoid.

Our vision must be one of win/win and abundance enjoyed by an interconnected humanity. It must be a vision of knowledge-based wealth creation seen by responsible individuals who own and are responsible for the wealth they create. It must be a vision of a Wisdom Age fueled with emotional and spiritual intelligence. It must be a vision of a new civilization that rests on a foundation of information technology, family, intelligence, individual freedom, personal responsibility, and caring for others. We are headed toward a global system of social order based on what the individual Huron told Baron de Lahontan and toward a win/win world far beyond this.

Our vision must be one where all are born free and united brothers and sisters, each as much as a great lord as the other, each the first and the last of his or her nation. Mass synocracy is a system of social order for the sovereign but interdependent individual. Mass privatization is a system that connects and thus empowers all individuals to come together and cocreate with one another, the universe, and God.

Because society will only begin to work well when the critical mass of the new system is in place, we must all, as individuals, work on our contribution. No longer can we blame politicians, welfare recipients, bureaucrats, managers, employees, oppressors, foreign competitors, or cheap foreign labor. Today everyone is a leader. If we are not leading toward the new civilization, then we are pulling against it. The absence of positive contribution to the new civilization is active resistance against it. There is no neutral ground. When there is no passion, there is no love, and the absence of love is fear.

Today if we are not actively, passionately, and lovingly working to build a win/win knowledge-based civilization, we are fiercely and automatically opposing it. The wait and see, go slow approach is a recipe for disaster. There are no objective observers and no middle ground. The following is a list of things you can begin doing to create the win/win world and win big for yourself:

- If you are an employee begin making tangible plans to shift from prostitution of your talents toward mass privatization and begin tapping your infinite potential to create the wealth you deserve. As the great Martin Luther King, Jr., said, "a man can't ride your back unless it is bent," (King 1963, p. 31). You are worthy of more than being a cog in an Industrial Age machine. You are pure creativity, able to create anything you desire, and worthy of all of the material and nonmaterial wealth of the universe (Chopra 1993). Try network marketing, get associated with one or more of the many on-line communities of thousands of people working to create a new civilization, start your own mass privatization enterprise, start your own business. Help lead the greatest peaceful revolution is history. Remember that "a true leader is not the one with the most followers but one who creates the most leaders" (Walsch 1997). Mass privatization is about turning everyone into a leader creating *businesses without bosses*. Become *the sovereign individual*.

- If you get the mass privatization message, pass it along. "A true teacher is not the one with the most knowledge but the one who causes the most others to have knowledge" (Walsch 1997). "When information flows cash flows," (Toffler 1990) and mass privatization is a knowledge flow system that produces the *intelligent enterprise*.

- If you are already self-employed, connect with others on the Internet and form a networked organization of teamnets for leverage, synergy, and increased wealth through *the teamnet factor*.

- If you are a small business owner, restructure your baby bureaucracy into a mass privatization enterprise for leverage, synergy, creativity, customization, speed, growth, and increased wealth. Produce *the end of bureaucracy and the rise of the intelligent organization*.

- Understand and perpetuate the role of information technology in liberating humanity and *building a win/win world*.

- Learn computers, use the Internet, and begin networking to produce *the death of distance*.

- Support progressive programs within organizations to create a *higher standard of leadership*. Work to integrate and synthesize these programs toward mass privatization to create *visionary business* as opposed to using the fad-of-the-month approach.

- As a customer, demand quality, service, customization, and speed from your suppliers to create *the accelerating organization*. Help push suppliers beyond the capabilities of their control-based systems. Sometimes we change only through crisis.

- Develop your creative and intuitive abilities *the artist's way*. Start by reading books on these subjects (see the reading list at the WinWinWorld.net website at **http://www.winwinworld.net**).

- Expand your vision and thus your wisdom—make it *2020 vision* for *conscious evolution*. Learn to synthesize and think systemically. Start by reading books on these subjects (see the reading list at the WinWinWorld.net website at **http://www.winwinworld.net**).

- Increase your emotional and spiritual intelligence through books, support groups, teams, and networks. Begin with *Putting Emotional Intelligence to Work* by David Ryback (1998). Practice Stephen Covey's (1989) seven habits of highly effective people and move on to deeper material such as Thomas Riskas's *Working Beneath the Surface* (1997) or Marianne Williamson's *Return to Love* (1992) (see the reading list at the WinWinWorld.net website at **http://www. winwinworld.net**).

- Begin working where your passion is. *Do what you love and the money will follow.*

- Embrace diversity and understand how and why it is needed for mass customization, your growth, and your wealth. Join *the web of inclusion*.

- Improve your ability to empathize and see from the perspectives of others. Understand that empathy is the key to *mass customization* and meeting others' needs and your wealth.

- Become a lifelong learner. Read, read, read! Listen to audiotapes while you drive. Remember that knowledge today is wealth and directly convertible to dollars. As you begin working in mass privatization communities, the more knowledge you have from which to draw, the more wealth you have and can create in *the knowledge economy* (see the reading list at the WinWinWorld.net website at **http://www.winwinworld.net**).

- Support expanded social and economic freedoms at every opportunity through *liberation management*.

If you decide voluntarily to accept the challenge of leading the creation of a new win/win civilization, beware.

> *There is nothing more difficult to take in hand, more perilous to*
> *conduct, or more uncertain in its success than to take the lead*
> *in the introduction of a new order of things.*
> —Niccolo Machiavelli, *The Prince*

For more detail on the practical things you can do to thrive in and help create the Information Age, see *Intelligent Vision* at the WinWinWorld.net website at **http://www.winwinworld.net**

CONCLUSION

Our social institutions are dying. The pain we feel is the pain of death and birth simultaneously, the death of one civilization and the birth of a new one. We have entered a period in which the conservative person who does not take risks and needs stability has become the risk taker, the radical, and the gambler. It is a period in which the one who refuses to change will surely be the one who will lose the most in the coming years. There is no going back to the way things used to be. Back to the basics is a failed policy. The future has already begun, and the trend is clear.

Starting today you must have a completely new outlook on life. You must be responsible. You can no longer depend on employers, unions, or governments to look out for your economic well-being, to provide you with a job, retirement, social security, health care, or a safety net.

From this day forward you and your global network of partners are responsible for creating work and wealth for yourselves. If you have no network you have no security. All of the rules have changed. The guarantees and promises made to you by Industrial Age society are null and void and will be breached.

The government and controlled economies have no choice. The power bestowed on them in the Industrial Age is slipping away—to you the individual supplier and customer. You the individual supplier and customer have no choice about accepting this responsibility. Mass victimization is no longer an option.

Because most companies and employees are not seriously preparing, the number of companies that fail to make the transition could be extremely high. And there likely will be no unemployment benefits, no welfare, and no Social Security safety nets to catch those who fall. Your network is your security. As we stand poised on the edge of the greatest advancement and growth boom in history, we may stumble. Many may lose life, fortune, and standard of living and suffer tremendous hardship.

We the individuals are the only ones who can make the change. Our corporate and political leaders do not have the power, vision, or intelligence to address the root causes. We the people must wake up from the Industrial Age sleep into which our factory-style schools, jobs, and governing system have lulled us. We must come out of our defined compartments and take responsibility. Our leaders cannot do what has to be done to correct our problems; this responsibility does not lie in their bureaus of specialty. It is not in their job descriptions.

History has shown that real change usually comes only through crisis. The evidence shows that the crisis has begun. Tens of thousands are dead from the transition. We can possibly lessen or prevent the crisis if we align ourselves with the change. Today we have the technology, knowledge, power, ability, intelligence, and willingness to move faster toward win/win wealth creation.

We must use intelligence to recognize what is occurring and move with the natural flow of things and with all deliberate speed. Either way, we have to make the transition. Meandering along simply means that we will pay a higher price in life, death, suffering, standard of living, and debt for our children. Meandering also risks complete collapse and possibly a dark millennium.

The universe does not guarantee our standard of living or our survival. Perhaps our ancestors had to meander during periods of social transition because there was little or no precedent and little knowledge to use the precedents there were. We are fortunate because we can learn from their mistakes. As the late Carl Sagan said, "we see further because we stand on their shoulders" (1980).

Becoming aligned with the coming change will allow us to avoid pain and to prosper. Let's get on with it. Let's stop the bleeding and start the fun, passion, and living! This will be the most fun and exciting time of our lives!

Glossary

Centralized wealth creation. The wealth-creation system of the Industrial Age whereby the control of wealth creation is centralized under the authority of *relatively* few people. This relative central control comes through a system of controlled economies.

Controlled economy. An organization or entire society in which the wealth-creation process of trade between individuals and groups is controlled, and individuals within the society are mostly void of ownership of the specific work they perform and of liberty.

Decentralized wealth creation. The wealth-creation system resulting from a society of overlapping and chaotically interconnected mass privatization organizations.

Knowledge-leveraging compensation. A system in which small portions of the partners' incomes are pooled and equally divided among the partners, aligning and highly motivating partners to collaborate and communicate successes and failures to other partners.

Mass autocracy. An inherent and unstoppable condition of the knowledge era whereby each individual has access to unlimited knowledge and therefore unlimited power.

Mass customization. Production in volume that gives individual customers different things according to each customer's unique needs. The opposite of mass production, whereby everyone receives the same thing regardless of individual needs.

Mass privatization. An organization in which individual workers or small teams of workers own the *specific* work they perform. These private owners work in partnership with other private owners through teams and networks.

Mass synocracy. A system of social organization whereby order occurs in a society made up of mass privatization enterprises and social order is an inherent by-product of people's daily work.

Public work. A system of work whereby the workers do not own the specific work they perform. The work of many people is owned collectively from a single, centralized point.

Synthesis of whole work. A way of organizing work whereby each individual owns an entire business, oversees the entire business process, and is connected to other individual business owners to form larger entire businesses.

Teamnet. A network of teams.

References

Ackoff, Russell. *The Democratic Corporation: A Radical Prescription for Recreating Corporate America and Rediscovering Success.* New York: Oxford University Press, 1994.

Ash, Mary Kay. *Mary Kay, You Can Have It All.* Rocklin, CA: Prima, 1995.

Ball, Edward. *Slaves in the Family.* New York: Ballantine, 1999.

Barker, Joel. *Paradigms: The Business of Discovering the Future.* New York: HarperCollins, 1992.

Bell, Chip. *Customers as Partners: Building Relationships That Last.* San Francisco: Berrett-Koehler, 1994, p. 5.

Bohm, David. *The Undivided Universe.* New York: Routledge, 1993.

Bohm, David. *Thought as a System.* New York: Routledge, 1994.

Brandon, William. *New Worlds for Old: Reports from the New World and Their Effect on the Development of Social Thought in Europe.* Athens, OH: Ohio University Press, 1986, p. 90.

Capra, Fritjof. *The Tao of Physics,* 3rd ed. Boston: Shambhala, 1991.

Carew, Don. Personal communication, 1995.

Chopra, Deepak. *Creating Affluence: Wealth Consciousness in the Field of All Possibilities.* San Rafael, CA: New World Library, 1993.

Covey, Stephen R. *The Seven Habits of Highly Effective People.* New York: Simon and Schuster, 1989.

Covey, Stephen R. *Principle Centered Leadership.* New York: Fireside, 1992.

Davidow, William, and Michael Malone. *The Virtual Corporation: Structuring and Revitalizing the Corporation for the 21st Century.* New York: HarperBusiness, 1992.

Davis, Stanley M. *Future Perfect.* Reading, MA: Addison-Wesley Publishing, 1987.

Drucker, Peter. *Harvard Business Review*, 1992.

Dumaine, Brian. "The Bureaucracy Busters," *Fortune* (17 June 1991): 46.

Gardner, Howard. *Multiple Intelligence: The Theory in Practice.* New York: Basic Books, 1993.

Henderson, Hazel. *Building a Win-Win World: Life Beyond Global Economic Warfare.* San Francisco: Berrett-Koehler, 1996.

Herbert, Nick. *Quantum Reality: Beyond the New Physics.* New York: Anchor Books, 1985.

Kelly, Kevin. *New Rules for the New Economy: Ten Radical Strategies for a Connected World.* New York: Viking Penguin, 1998.

King, Martin Luther, Jr. *I've Been to the Mountaintop.* San Francisco: HarperSanFrancisco, 1963, p. 31.

Land, George, and Beth Jarman. *Breakpoint and Beyond: Mastering the Future Today.* New York: HarperBusiness, 1992.

Langrick, Roger. *Barter Systems: A Business Guide for Trade and Exchanges.* Stamford, CT: Longmeadow Press, 1994.

Lipnack, Jessica, and Jeffrey Stamps. *The TeamNet Factor.* Essex Junction, VT: Oliver Wight Publications, 1993.

Lovemen, Gary. "Why Personal Computers Have Not Improved Productivity," Minutes of Stewart Alsop, 1991 computer conference, p. 39.

Mackay, Harvey. *How to Build a Network of Power Relationships.* Niles, IL: Nightingale-Conant, 1993.

Maynard, Herman, and Susan Mehrtens. *The Fourth Wave: Business in the 21st Century.* San Francisco: Berrett-Koehler, 1993.

McCarthy, Michael. *Mastering the Information Age: A Course in Power Thinking.* Niles, IL: Nightingale-Conant Corp., 1992.

McDermid, James. Personal communication, 1995.

Melohn, Tom. *The New Partnership: Profit by Bringing Out the Best in People, Customers and Yourself.* Essex Junction, VT: Oliver Wight Publications, 1994, backflap.

Mother Earth News (Oct./Nov. 1993).

Naisbitt, John. *Global Paradox: The Bigger the World Economy, the More Powerful Its Smaller Players.* New York: William Morrow and Company, 1994.

Naisbitt, John, and Patricia Aburdene. *Reinventing the Corporation: Transforming Your Job and Your Company for the New Information Society.* New York: Warner Books, 1985.

Newstrom, John and Keith Davis. *Organizational Behavior: Human Behavior at Work,* 9th ed. New York: McGraw Hill, 1993.

North, James. Uni-v.e.r.s.e. Network: http://www.Uni-verse.net.

Peppers, Don, and Martha Rogers. *Enterprise One to One: Tools for Competing in the Interactive Age.* New York: Currency/Doubleday, 1997.

Peters, Tom. *Liberation Management: Necessary Disorganization for the Nanosecond Nineties.* New York: Knopf, 1992, p. 657.

Peters, Tom. *The New Manager and the New Organization.* Boulder, CO: CareerTrack Publications, 1992.

Pilzer, Paul Zane. *Unlimited Wealth: The Theory and Practice of Economic Alchemy.* New York: Crown, 1990.

Pine, Joseph. *Mass Customization: The New Frontier in Business Competition.* Boston: Harvard Business School Press, 1993.

Posner, Bruce. "Right from the Start." *Inc.* (1988).

Quinn, James Brian. *Intelligent Enterprise: A New Paradigm for a New Era.* New York: Free Press, 1992.

Riskas, Thomas. *Working Beneath the Surface: Attending to the Soul's "Hidden Agenda" for Wholeness, Fulfillment, and Deep Spiritual Healing.* Provo, UT: Executive Excellence Publishing, 1997.

Robbins, Anthony. *Awaken the Giant Within: How to Take Control of Your Mental, Emotional, Physical and Financial Destiny.* New York: Summit Books, 1991, p. 120.

Roddick, Anita. *Body and Soul: Profits with Principles*. New York: Crown, 1991.

Rosenbluth, Hal, and Diane McFerrin Peters. *The Customer Comes Second: And Other Secrets of Exceptional Service*. New York: William Morrow and Company, 1992.

Ryback, David. *Putting Emotional Intelligence to Work: Successful Leadership Is More Than IQ*. Boston: Butterworth–Heinemann, 1998.

Sagan, Carl. *Cosmos*. New York: Random House, 1980.

Saunders, Tedd. *The Bottom Line of Green Is Black*. New York: HarperCollins, 1993.

Semler, Ricardo. *Maverick: The Success Story Behind the World's Most Unusual Workplace*. New York: Warner Books, 1993.

Senge, Peter M. *The Fifth Discipline: The Art and Practice of the Learning Organization*. New York: Doubleday-Currency, 1990.

Shelton, Charlotte. *Quantum Leaps: 7 Skills for Workplace ReCreation*. Boston: Butterworth–Heinemann, 1990.

Smith, Adam. *An Inquiry into the Nature and Causes of the Wealth of Nations*. New York: The Modern Library, 1994.

Snider, Jim, and Terra Ziporyn. *Future Shop: How Future Technologies Will Change the Way We Shop and What We Buy*. New York: Saint Martin's Press, 1992, p. 6.

Spector, Robert, and Patrick McCarthy. *The Nordstrom Way: The Inside Story of America's #1 Customer Service Company*. New York: John Wiley and Sons, 1995.

Stack, Jack. *The Great Game of Business: The Only Sensible Way to Run a Business*. New York: Doubleday-Currency, 1992.

Toffler, Alvin. *The Third Wave*. New York: William Morrow and Company, 1980.

Toffler, Alvin. *PowerShift: Knowledge, Wealth and Violence at the Edge of the 21st Century*. New York: Bantam, 1990.

Toffler, Alvin, and Heidi Toffler. *War and Anti-War: Survival at the Edge of the 21st Century*. Boston: Little, Brown, 1993.

Tuck, William. Personal communication, 1994.

U.S. Department of Justice, Bureau of Justice Statistics, NCJ-147486, April 1994. http://www.ojp.usdoj.gov:80/bjs/pub/pdf/viocrm.pdf.

Walsch, Neale Donald. *Conversations with God: An Uncommon Dialogue.* Book 2. Charlottesville, VA: Hampton Roads Publishing, 1997.

Weatherford, Jack. *Indian Givers: How the Indians of the Americas Transformed the World.* New York: Fawcett Columbine, 1988, p. 123.

Wheatley, Margaret J. *Leadership and the New Science: Learning about Organizations from an Orderly Universe.* San Francisco: Berrett-Koehler, 1992.

Williamson, Marianne. Personal communication, 1986.

Williamson, Marianne. *A Return to Love: Reflections on the Principles of a Course in Miracles.* New York: HarperCollins, 1992.

WinWinWorld.net website URL: http://www.winwinworld.net.

Womack, James P., and Daniel T. Jones. *Lean Thinking: Banish Waste and Create Wealth in Your Corporation.* New York: Simon and Schuster, 1996.

Zukav, Gary. *The Dancing Wu Li Masters: An Overview of the New Physics.* New York: Quill William Morrow, 1979.

Index

Butterworth–Heinemann Business Books... for Transforming Business

5th Generation Management, Co-creating Through Virtual Enterprising, Dynamic Teaming, and Knowledge Networking, Revised Edition,
Charles M. Savage, 0-7506-9701-6

Beyond Strategic Vision: Effective Corporate Action with Hoshin Planning,
Michael Cowley and Ellen Domb, 0-7506-9843-8

Beyond Time Management: Business with Purpose,
Robert A. Wright, 0-7506-9799-7

The Breakdown of Hierarchy: Communicating in the Evolving Workplace,
Eugene Marlow and Patricia O'Connor Wilson, 0-7056-9746-6

Business and the Feminine Principle: The Untapped Resource,
Carol R. Frenier, 0-7506-9829-2

Cultivating Common Ground: Releasing the Power of Relationships at Work,
Daniel S. Hanson, 0-7506-9832-2

Flight of the Phoenix: Soaring to Success in the 21st Century,
John Whiteside and Sandra Egli, 0-7506-9798-9

Getting a Grip on Tomorrow: Your Guide to Survival and Success in the Changed World of Work,
Mike Johnson, 0-7506-9758-X

Innovation Strategy for the Knowledge Economy: The Ken Awakening,
Debra M. Amidon, 0-7506-9841-1

The Intelligence Advantage: Organizing for Complexity,
Michael D. McMaster, 0-7506-9792-X

The Knowledge Evolution: Expanding Organizational Intelligence,
Verna Allee, 0-7506-9842-X

Leadership in a Challenging World: A Sacred Journey,
Barbara Shipka, 0-7506-9750-4

Leading from the Heart: Choosing Courage over Fear in the Workplace,
Kay Gilley, 0-7506-9835-7

Learning to Read the Signs: Reclaiming Pragmatism in Business,
F. Byron Nahser, 0-7506-9901-9

Marketing Plans that Work: Targeting Growth and Profitability,
    Malcolm H.B. McDonald and Warren J. Keegan, 0-7506-9828-4

A Place to Shine: Emerging from the Shadows at Work,
    Daniel S. Hanson, 0-7506-9738-5

Power Partnering: A Strategy for Business Excellence in the 21st Century
    Sean Gadman, 0-7506-9809-8

Resources for the Knowledge-Based Economy Series

  Knowledge Management and Organizational Design,
      Paul S. Myers, 0-7506-9749-0
  Knowledge Management Tools,
      Rudy L. Ruggles, III, 0-7506-9849-7
  Knowledge in Organizations,
      Laurence Prusak, 0-7506-9718-0
  The Strategic Management of Intellectual Capital,
      David A. Klein, 0-7506-9850-0

Setting the PACE® in Product Development: A Guide to Product
And Cycle-time Excellence,
    Michael E. McGrath, 0-7506-9789-X

Time to Take Control: The Impact of Change on Corporate Computer Systems,
    Tony Johnson, 0-7506-9863-2

The Transformation of Management,
    Mike Davidson, 0-7506-9814-4

Who We Could Be at Work, Revised Edition,
    Margaret A. Lulic, 0-7506-9739-3

To purchase a copy of any Butterworth–Heinemann Business title, please visit your
local bookstore or call 1-800-366-2665.

Barry Carter has spent the past 20 years working as change agent, on the front lines of organizations of various sizes, as employee, manager, engineer, consultant, and business owner. His career has been focused on the details of work, at the grassroots level, implementing change within organizations while learning about the state of work, human organization, and business firsthand. He has worked with many of the progressive management programs of the past 20 years as a hands-on frontline manager or implementer. He has been employed with a major computer manufacturer, a defense contractor, an industrial equipment manufacturer, and other medium to small companies. He has also worked as an improvement consultant to Revlon and Price Club and interfaced with various regulatory agencies.

Barry Carter has worked extensively with many suppliers and customers, again at the grassroots level, including IBM, HP, 3M, Wang, Tokyo Electronics Corporation, Data Products, Martin-Marietta, Kentek (Japan Radio Corporation), and dozens of other small, medium, and large companies. He also founded and ran his own information-processing business in California for five years. Prior to college graduation, he worked for ten years as a construction worker in his father's construction business, as a repair technician, and as a farmhand learning of the problems in and state of work and wealth creation firsthand.

Barry Carter synthesized the mass privatization trend—an evolving virtual networked organizing system—for the knowledge era, based upon ownership of specific work by the individual performing it. He is the founding partner of Win/WinWorld.net, a global mass privatization community of interconnected owning partners and organizations with the mission of expanding the mass privatization paradigm, thus helping introduce win/win wealth creation and usher in the Win/Win Era.

Website URL: http://www.winwinworld.net
E-mail: barryc@winwinworld.net